THE AUTOBIOGRAPHY OF
Michel de Montaigne

Voicy du grand Montaigne une entiere figure
Le Peinctre a peinct le corps, et luy son bel esprit ;
Le premier par son art égale la Naturé
Mais l'autre la surpasse en tout ce qu'il escrit.

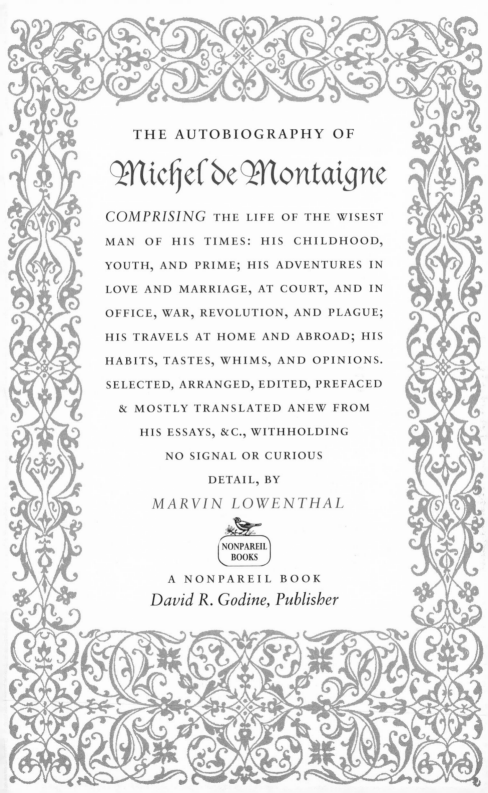

THE AUTOBIOGRAPHY OF

Michel de Montaigne

COMPRISING THE LIFE OF THE WISEST
MAN OF HIS TIMES: HIS CHILDHOOD,
YOUTH, AND PRIME; HIS ADVENTURES IN
LOVE AND MARRIAGE, AT COURT, AND IN
OFFICE, WAR, REVOLUTION, AND PLAGUE;
HIS TRAVELS AT HOME AND ABROAD; HIS
HABITS, TASTES, WHIMS, AND OPINIONS.
SELECTED, ARRANGED, EDITED, PREFACED
& MOSTLY TRANSLATED ANEW FROM
HIS ESSAYS, &C., WITHHOLDING
NO SIGNAL OR CURIOUS
DETAIL, BY

MARVIN LOWENTHAL

NONPAREIL
BOOKS

A NONPAREIL BOOK
David R. Godine, Publisher

This is a Nonpareil Book
first published in 1999 by
David R. Godine, Publisher, Inc.
Box 450
Jaffrey, New Hampshire 03452

Library of Congress Cataloging in Publication Data

Montaigne, Michel de, 1533–1592
[Selections. English. 1999]
The autobiography of Michel de Montaigne / selected, edited, and
translated by Marvin Lowenthal.
p.   cm.
1. Montaigne, Michel de, 1533–1592—Translations into English.
I. Lowenthal, Marvin, 1890–1969. II. Title.
PQ1642.E5L6825 1999
844'.3—dc21   98-36153   CIP

ISBN: 1–56792–098–5 (pbk.: alk. paper)

First Nonpareil printing, 1999

This book was printed on acid-free paper
in the United States of America

Contents

Montaigne: The Man and His World

ELIEVING that Michel de Montaigne has as much to say to the world today as anyone above or below ground, I have long been tempted to give an account of his life, thought, and times. But as I drew nearer the project I realized it would be folly and impertinence to write the life of a man who had spent his genius writing it himself, and who did it incomparably well.

No one before Freud — and possibly since — has better understood the springs and pattern of human behavior. No autobiographer or retailer of 'confessions' has, to my knowledge, more closely distinguished 'the skin from the shirt.' And, obviously, neither I nor anyone but Montaigne himself has lived for a moment under his shirt, to say nothing of his skin. I was quite willing to yield to his claim when he said, 'In what I have undertaken to write about'—which was himself—'I am the most learned man alive.'

So I decided to invite him to collaborate with me. Aided by scissors, paste, and patience, I have let him retell his life story.

The peculiar merit of the *Essays* and much of their spell lie, after all, in what their author reveals of himself. Unfortunately, many who have tried to read them in our hurried times have been baffled or deterred by their jungle of digressions, quotations, and literary allusions, as well as by the rank confusion and variety of the material. Unless the reader persisted, he never discovered that between the interminable paragraphs were a self-portrait and a 'confessions' that would make Cellini blush for modesty and Rousseau pale in shame for his own shuffling evasions.

The game of piecing together a continuous narrative from the helter-skelter of the *Essays,* from the *Journey, Letters,* and other sources, was much like solving a jigsaw puzzle, containing literally hundreds of fragments. The result: a portrait of the wisest and perhaps the most lovable man of our modern age. And somewhere among the strokes of folly and wisdom, every reader will discern the outline of his own face.

This is no accident. Montaigne was, in part, moved to paint himself because he sensed that, in doing so, he was painting others—because he knew that 'every man carries within himself the whole condition of humanity.' He was right in believing that what proved useful to himself 'may serve someone else.' Emerson is not the only reader who has felt, after he laid down the *Essays* of Montaigne, that he had written the book himself, so sincerely it spoke to his thought and experience. For most of us, the portrait is a mirror.

And through the hazards of history, Montaigne may serve us in another, and what for the present we like to think is a more pertinent, way. He lived in an age somewhat resembling our own. He too saw the wreck of a world: he too was faced with 'the notable spectacle of our public death.'

He brought to the crisis of his civilization a solution we may reject as either ineffectual or irrelevant today—though whether it is or not will lie with history and not with us to determine. It took Montaigne's world some two centuries, with breathing spells, to catch up to his common sense. We are told that the world moves quicker nowadays.

But apart from his immediate notions and persuasions, no one can read (or reread) Montaigne without, perhaps uneasily, appreciating in him an attitude we cannot dismiss or ignore. The atmosphere he creates is in our troubled times as much a lure, a challenge, and, to some people, a puzzling annoyance, as it was four hundred years ago.

A conservative of the twentieth century will dislike his bold opinions and mistrust his frank assault on injustice and treachery: a radical will despise his passivity, tolerance, and skepticism. But both, I suspect, will feel in his book something of the charm the man exerted in his life; and it is just possible that like Montaigne's friends of the sixteenth century, like a Henri of Navarre, they may be seduced momentarily—and we live but a moment—into decency.

Knowing the strength of this charm, I regret that Montaigne told neither the whole narrative of his life nor, as a friend once proposed he should do, the history of his times. For the reader who is mostly curious about the man, I am therefore obliged to furnish a few of the necessary touches which the portraitist omitted.

He had curious notions about that portrait of himself. To the dismay of gossips and historians, he believed that the true life of a man is not to be found in his deeds—'which,' he says, 'speak more of themselves than of us'—but in his thoughts. On the other hand, to the delight of Peeping Toms and psychologists, he had another strange notion that, although a man's deeds counted for little, his habits and whims meant a great deal. So I am compelled to tell something of Montaigne's negotiations between princes, whereas he himself will tell what he eats for dinner and how he likes to scratch his ear

Again, Montaigne was a soldier; but, except for a bare reference to the siege of La Fère, he neglects to state the time, place, or nature of his exploits—imagine Cellini gliding over a military campaign! Yet in what posture did Cellini prefer to beget posterity? On that point Montaigne is explicit. It is a matter of values. 'Our duty,' he says ironically, 'is to blush while we are creating life, but it is a glory to know how to destroy what we have created.'

Partly because of these notions and partly, too, because he never undertook to write the complete story—'there is nothing so contrary to my style as continuous narrative: I am always cutting myself short for lack of breath'—years pass without mention. Yet in the passage of the daily routine, the man strips to the skin. We know less today what goes on in our neighbor's house than in that sixteenth-century château on the knoll of Montaigne. Unlike most subjects of biography, it is Montaigne himself who supplies the local color, human interest, and racy detail; and it is the biographer who must furnish the mere events and dates.

A knowledge of some of these events is almost indispensable to those of us who have forgotten or never knew Renaissance France. Without it, the full intent and force of Montaigne's thought are lost. Indeed many of the conflicting judgments on the man arise from the failure to relive with him his hard century and far from easy life.

Generations of casual readers, who judge a writer by what others say of him rather than by what he reveals of himself, have looked on Montaigne as an indolent, skeptical, and selfish old gentleman who lived in an ivory tower lined with books, and preached a life fit only for men with the purse of a Crœsus and the disposition of a hermit. Seventeenth-century readers of this stamp thought him good-humored, garrulous, and quaint. The French Revolution clapped a liberty cap on his head, and the Bourbon Restoration which followed it hung from his neck a crucifix. Extracts from his *Essays* have been compiled under such diverse titles as 'Montaigne the Christian,' 'Montaigne the Epicurean,' and 'Montaigne the Scientist.'

Our contemporary legend pictures him much as he appeared in the reaction of a hundred years ago: a dyed-in-the-wool conservative, a Stoic, and a devout Catholic, whose tortuous and confused mind tossed up almost by chance an occasional liberal idea—the excretion of a dilettante. And conscientious scholars and critics, troubled by these diverse views, have come to agree that the man who took such extraordinary pains to explain himself is an altogether baffling figure.

Yet if we read his life as he saw and knew it, not dispersed among the volume of his writings but gathered—as I have tried to gather it—into a flowing whole, and if we recapture the world in which it was lived, the legend, the enigma, and most of the perplexities will vanish. We shall find that the difficulties lie not in Montaigne, but in ourselves.

His own method for understanding men was to try to understand himself—'I describe others in reporting one single ill-made individual.' As near as he could get to the bottom of Michel, so near he felt he was getting to the bottom of everyone else. But even as he plumbed himself, the depths grew profounder; and the bottom was never reached. Thus he has left the unusual spectacle of a man seeking to present his mind and character in their entirety, and, in the effort, exposing the most startling diversities of opinion and desire. 'Other authors reveal themselves by extrinsic traits; I, the first of them, by my whole being—as Michel de Montaigne, not as poet, lawyer, or grammarian.'

At least the variety is startling and the spectacle unusual to readers unaccustomed to examine the whole of their own being, with all its quirks and foibles. And literary critics and scholars, the men who spin the legends of Montaigne, are apt to be of this type. It is a critic's business—a genuine creative critic such as Sainte-Beuve—to make of his criticism a rounded work of art. It is the scholar's trade to treat his subject as an object, as something to be handled with a prophylactic pen, carefully guarded from any intrusion of his own personality. To both such men a contradiction or an obscurity is anathema: the critic, in order to better his case, will ignore it; and the scholar can justify his existence only by explaining it away. Nothing in the mental habits of either will lead them to use Montaigne's method for judging others in their judgment of Montaigne himself.

Yet to gauge and judge him aright, we have only to gauge and judge ourselves. We may not in this way resolve all his contradictions, but we will have no trouble in matching them with our own. The obscurity and elusiveness of the man will be found common to us all. If Montaigne remains an enigma, so do we. 'I complain,' he says, 'that the world does not so much as think of itself.' Once it does, it will not be so ready to complain of him.

Often, however, his elusiveness is deliberate. He had, he explains, reasons for speaking confusedly and by halves. His words—so he warns us—sometimes carry undertones meant only for ears that can catch his tune. These reasons will become apparent to anyone who glances at the world he inhabited and the circumstances and perils of his life. Once we learn them, we will have a secure basis for estimating his 'conservatism.' For a modern parallel, we might imagine that a volume of essays appeared in contemporary Germany, in which the author makes himself out to be a conforming Nazi; yet he drops a hundred phrases hinting his complete disapproval of Nazi policies, and, to leave no doubt, bids us read between his lines. Should we judge the author by the bulk of the volume or by the hundred phrases?

II

MONTAIGNE WAS BORN in 1533—the year Rabelais published *Pantagruel* and three years before Erasmus died. Europe was still flushed with hope at the discovery of America, rediscovery of antiquity, happy inventions in art, science, and industry, and fresh attempts at reforming religion. The smoke of a wool-carder burned alive at Meaux (1525)—the first victim of the Reformation in France—hardly obscured the new dawn.

Pierre Eyquem, the father of Montaigne, caught the fire of the

Renaissance, brought daring ideas on education back from Italy, entertained the latest lights of learning in his home, and almost symbolic of the joy in the air had his baby Michel awakened to the strain of music—a strain which echoes in the Abbey of Theleme. Yet the same mornings Michel leaped to music in his cradle, some forty Frenchmen marched to the pyre (1534–35).

Montaigne's account of his forbears is pure Renaissance—a boast and a fib. In an offhand manner he gives us to believe that the château of Montaigne was the place where the 'greater part' of his ancestors were born, and that his father, when buried there, was laid away in the 'ancestral' vault. As a matter of fact, his father was the first of the line to be born and the only one to be buried in the 'ancestral' home.

'My people,' writes Montaigne, 'were formerly called Eyquem.' Formerly? He himself bore the name more than half his life, abandoning it only after the death of his father. With dry humor he even takes occasion in the *Essays* to mock at people who call themselves after the title of their estate, and at upstarts who buy a family crest. Yet not sixty years before he was born, his great-grandfather, a plain bourgeois, purchased from another bourgeois the little fief, the title, and presumably the coat-of-arms of Montaigne (1477).

Who were these Eyquems whom Montaigne mentions, keeps mementoes of, knows about—he is entirely accurate in giving the date of his great-grandfather's birth—and omits to describe? Joseph Scaliger, a learned scholar and gossip of the day, thought he was spreading scandal when he said that the Eyquems were herring dealers. So they were. And—we may as well repeat the old quip—Montaigne has nothing to lose by it, and the herring dealers much to gain.

Raymon Eyquem, the great-grandfather born in 1402, was a wealthy Bordeaux dealer in herring, pastels, and wine. He and his family were married into the top of the Bordeaux bourgeoisie. What lay behind them is uncertain: possible parentage with an English branch (England ruled Guienne until 1453); possible descent from the former noble proprietors of the Château Eyquem, still noble in its vintage; or a possible rise from remote serfdom.

Raymon's son, Grimon, increased the family fortune, enlarged its holdings in houses and land, and enabled Pierre, the father of our Montaigne, to free himself from the merchant's desk.

Pierre Eyquem, 'squire, and lord of Montaigne,' acquired the privileges due his title of petty nobleman by taking up arms under Francis I. For more than twenty-five years he served Bordeaux in various public capacities: prevost, *jurat,* vice-mayor, and finally mayor. Though he continued to use the family mansion in Bordeaux and traffic in wine, he was the first to devote himself to the estate up the valley of the Dordogne; and he practically rebuilt—and, with an eye to political bad weather, fortified—the château where Michel was born.

Altogether, the Eyquems, like France itself ever since the victories of Joan of Arc, followed an ascendant star. By dropping the name, Michel merely confirmed its success.

Of his mother, Montaigne says nothing. Yet she lived under the same roof with him all his life, and survived him by a number of years. His silence may mean little, for he was reticent in writing about his living relatives and friends—his father, whom he adored, and his friend La Boétie, whom he loved more than a brother, were both dead before he published his affection for them. Still, in this case, there could be other grounds.

His mother was, by blood, a Jewess. She was born Antoinette de Louppes of a Toulouse and Bordeaux family of converted Jews—part of a considerable group of Spanish refugees who settled north of the Pyrenees after the establishment of the Inquisition in Spain and the expulsion of the race in 1492. She was a convert to Protestantism, and two of her children—a brother and a sister of Michel—were likewise followers of the new religion.

Montaigne's Jewish blood has provoked the customary speculation: vague guesses that he owed to it his restlessness, sensitivity to suggestion, wariness, and even his tolerance and skepticism. It is, of course, too simple to lay these traits to his individual character, to his 'master form' as he calls it. Yet if they must be credited elsewhere, it would be more reasonable to trace them to the atmosphere of his home, which permitted extreme and burning differences in religious belief without destroying the 'brotherly concord' of the family. Indeed Montaigne's pride in this concord was more than justified. His casual remark that 'when religion serves us as a cloak for war, even your own relatives may, with an appearance of justice, become unreliable' takes its point from innumerable domestic dramas. From the royal household down, families were on all sides splitting into hostile factions. Brothers and cousins—so Henri of Navarre tells us—used to watch one another out of the corner of their eye and carry a dagger up their sleeve.

At home and at school Montaigne was exposed to a novel air, the full breath of the Renaissance. His baptism at the hands of poor peasants, his babyhood in a village hut, the highly original course he and the whole household received in Latin, all the Shandean whims of his father, were enough to encourage in him something of an open mind and the ability to question custom and usage.

Sooner or later he must have heard talk of the scholars who frequented his father's house or tutored him at school. Pierre Bunel, who gave that copy of Sebond to his father, was suspected of Protestantism. Andreas Goveanus, the principal of the college where Michel received his formal education, as well as a number of its instructors, were of the same Jewish origin as his mother. One of his tutors, the Scotch poet Buchanan, owed his flight abroad to an imputed taint of Calvinism. Another tutor, the orator Muret, was facile enough to lose caste for free thinking and win applause for eulogizing the Massacre of Saint Bartholomew. Castalio, one of the 'estimable' scholars who Montaigne regretted to learn had died of starvation and whom apparently he would have rescued, was ostracized by Catholics and Protestants alike for publishing, in 1554, a tract in favor of tolerance.

Notable among his schoolmates at the College of Guienne were the three sons of the Count of Foix, cousins and cordial friends of the house of Navarre. In later years Montaigne was to arrange the marriage of one of these sons and dedicate his essay on education to the young wife, Diane de Foix. His many relations with Henri of Navarre, twenty years his junior, probably sprang from his intimacy with the family of Foix.

Upon completing his course at the College of Guienne, he was put to the study of law. Then his father bought him, when he was twenty-one, a magistrate's seat. In that century, as Montaigne complains, a judge bought his office and a litigant bought the right to have his case heard. He first served in the Cour des Aides, a king's court, newly established in Périgueux. When it was dissolved a few years later, he was transferred to the Cour de Parlement at Bordeaux—the highest tribunal in the province, and for the character of its membership one of the most distinguished and influential in France.

These *cours* were more than judiciary bodies. Through their privilege of registering a royal edict before it could become effective law, they wielded considerable political power. The chancellor L'Hospital in fact complained that 'the Cours de Parlement, especially the one at Bordeaux, occupy themselves more with political than judicial affairs.' Religious offences, and all the violence that arose from them, likewise came under their jurisdiction. While Montaigne was a member of the Parlement of

Bordeaux, men were fined, imprisoned, and burned on religious grounds, and riot quelled and punished.

He held his office until, in 1570, following the death of his father, he sold it to a friend of boyhood days. In all he served—with many absences—fifteen years on the bench. Yet aside from references in a family diary, he never mentions his term of office and seldom his personal experiences in it. Although for different reasons—reasons which he makes plain in his opinions on lawyers, judges, legal procedure, torture, and capital punishment—he apparently thought as little of the law as he did of herrings.

Meanwhile the world at large was completing his education. At twenty-two he accompanied his father, then mayor of Bordeaux, on an official visit to Paris, the first of many and prolonged stays in the city which, above all others, won his love. 'It is Paris alone,' he writes, 'which makes me French.' And he knew it, too, from the intrigues of the Louvre to the scoldings of the fish wives on the Petit Pont.

Two or three years later he met Etienne de la Boétie, likewise a member of the Bordeaux Parlement, the man to whom he gave his heart as to no other being. La Boétie was a rich youth, born in Sarlat (1530), and steeped in law and Renaissance learning at the University of Orleans—a conscientious and rising littérateur, political thinker, and magistrate.

The two young men dressed their friendship in classical tags and paraded it before their own admiring eyes. Yet as we come to know its force in Montaigne's life—hardly a train of thought or turn of events but leads him back to La Boétie—we realize how little of it was literary. 'Forever on his funerals' Montaigne made his friend immortal; and only the man who 'knows how rare such friendships are' can truly gauge its passion.

In the Latin 'satires' La Boétie addressed to his friend we learn something of the relation between them: Montaigne the intellectual and La Boétie the moral mentor of their common life. The grave young magistrate from Sarlat roundly lectures Michel on his intrigues with women, on deserting Pallas and Apollo for the goddess with the yielding girdle.

Even allowing for the exaggeration of a 'satire,' the Montaigne we see through the eyes of a friend rather differs from his own view of his youth. 'My only vices,' Montaigne believes, 'were sloth and poor mettle—the danger was not that I should do wrong, but nothing.' La Boétie was of another opinion. 'You who are gifted—we, your friends, all know it—for either great virtues or great vices, you will have a harder struggle.' And the victory, La Boétie candidly adds, 'will fill me with joy—and astonishment.'

There is one strangely familiar note in these poems, a note unheard in the detached beauty of a Ronsard or even in the personal lamentations of Du Bellay. Younger than these poets and aware of the tarnish gathering on the new age, La Boétie already talks like a lost generation.

'What think you,' he asks Montaigne, 'of the dire fate that has brought us to birth in these times, and what are you resolved to do? My country's ruin lies before my eyes—but why disturb her poor ashes! For myself, I see no other course than to emigrate, forsake my home, and go wherever Fortune bears me. Long now the wrath of the gods has warned me to flee—showing me those vast and open lands beyond the ocean. When, on the threshold of our century, a new world rose from the waves, the gods—we may well believe—destined it as a refuge where men shall till free fields under a fairer sky, while the cruel sword and a shameful plague doom the ruin of Europe. Over there are fertile plains awaiting the plough, a land without bourn or master—it is there I will go.' La Boétie and Montaigne expatriates in the as yet invisible village of Manhattan—or shall we call them parlor pioneers?

But not Montaigne. Throughout his life he threatened flight;

but while house after house fell to ruin on all sides of him, he stood his ground 'gaily and with a steady foot,' his door open and the porter at the gate. As for La Boétie, he was soon to embark—but on an unknown sea.

The sword and the plague La Boétie foresaw were not slow in disclosing themselves upon the rise of Protestantism. 'If anything could have tempted my youth,' Montaigne writes in later years, 'it would have been the ambition to share in the risks and dangers of this new enterprise.' What, as his youth could have heard of them, were these risks and dangers?

He was ten years old when the ' good' Marot was driven from Paris for translating the Psalms into French, and Pierre Ramus, the most eminent professor of philosophy in his day, was forbidden to criticize Aristotle—the same Ramus whom the Protestants prevented from teaching at Geneva in 1570 and, two years later, the Catholics murdered on the signal of Saint Bartholomew. The year Montaigne left the College of Guienne, Etienne Dolet was burned for an atheist in the Place Maubert, Paris. He was twenty-six when Du Bourg, once a teacher of La Boétie, went to a similar death. Closer home, in Bordeaux, two youths went to the flames in 1556 and—while Montaigne was a member of the Parlement—a merchant was condemned to the fire in 1559, and six more victims met the same fate in 1561. And thereafter in France the hangings and burnings grew beyond count.

We may have forgotten, as Montaigne could not, that the risks were not all on one side. A Protestant was as quick as the next man when it came to piling fagots. While Michel and the Reform movement were still young, Calvin drove Castalio into exile and starvation for denying the doctrine of predestination (1544), and secured the execution of Jacques Gruet for writing a book that never existed (1550); Servetus was predestined to burn in Geneva (1553); Valentius Gentilis mounted the pyre in Berne (1566); and under the English—whose change of religion 'mortified' Montaigne—five Catholics vanished in smoke. Admiral Coligny, idol of the Huguenots and the most distinguished victim of Saint Bartholomew's Eve, a man 'whom nothing pained so much as bloodshed,' put two hundred and sixty prisoners to the sword in Perigord.

Nor was the question confined to dogmas and ritual. Though it took both its reasons and fervor from matters of belief, the Reform was rooted in grave economic and political abuses, and inevitably became the occasion of a struggle for money, prestige, and power.

To put into effect the religious reforms they devoutly proposed and which they felt to be the true road to salvation, the Protestants were compelled to take possession of—'confiscate' the Catholics called it—churches and church revenue, part of which was due the state. They had, perforce, to abolish—'destroy' said the Catholics—monasteries, religious orders, and their property. They had to assure security for their cult by seizing town fortresses—'sedition' was the Catholic word for it; and win themselves posts of power in the government—'plotting' claimed the Catholics, and 'usurpation.' Church property, one of the greatest stakes in the game, was estimated by Bodin, a contemporary of Montaigne, to comprise over half the wealth of the kingdom.

In these circumstances, politics and greed quickly dominated the entire issue. Henri II, who saw to it that hundreds of French Protestants were burned, did not recoil from aiding German Protestants against his enemy Charles V, at the price of receiving Toul, Metz, and Verdun. To further their aspirations to the throne, the Guises embraced the Catholic, and the Bourbons the Protestant, cause. Yet when ambition demanded it, Francis of Guise could dicker with Protestant Wurttemberg, and his brother, the Cardinal of Lorraine, could flirt with the Confession of Augsburg; while Anthony of Navarre complacently deserted the Protestants when a bit of Spanish territory was dangled before his grasp. Coligny was all for war against Spanish Flanders in order to appease the civil strife at home—the sort of opportunist war which Montaigne viewed with horror. Smaller fry, with an eye on a province, a city, a castle, or even a neighbor's château, began spilling blood for and against the right to read the Bible in private and confess their sins in public.

Every selfish chord was touched, except the social. From nobility down to peasantry, the classes of society were divided among themselves as venomously as in any individual family. There was no chance or hope—if indeed there ever is one—that by a shift in social power, peace and unity might be achieved.

And the outlook was utterly blackened by the absence on either side of any effective desire or understanding of tolerance. Even those who strove for it, a Catherine de Medici and her chancellor L'Hospital, considered it at best a device to gain time until the Council of Trent or some national French conference should work out a single acceptable and obligatory form of faith for the entire people. The notion that any minority group — Jews, Anabaptists, Atheists, what not—should, even when unarmed, be granted a secure place in society, was abhorrent to Catholic and Protestant alike.

To anyone living in France through the decade after 1560, if he was at all interested in prophecy, the time must have seemed ripe for a Jeremiah. It is something to the credit of humanity that it was neither dolorous harangues nor bitter imprecations, but the smile of a little man in a tower and his apparently private and innocent preoccupation with his own imperfections which ultimately helped bring the world to its senses. But not, it must be added, before it had drunk deep of the futility of war.

III

IN 1559 MONTAIGNE was in Paris, and, in view of his distaste for the law, presumably exploring the chances for a political career. He accompanied Francis II to Bar-le-Duc, where he remarked a portrait King René of Sicily had drawn of himself. Nothing seems to have come of his political explorations; but the portrait lingered, germinating, in his mind.

The Parlement of Bordeaux sent him back to Paris in 1561 on an errand pertaining to religious affairs in Guienne. He remained at the capital through most of 1562, seventeen months in all—whether further exploring his political chances cannot be said. But the mere march of events was enough to root to the spot a spectator possessed of political curiosity, access to the Court, and concern for his country's welfare.

In these two years, 1561–62, the fate of France was decided. Francis II had died and was succeeded by the ten-year-old Charles IX. The public was given a great theological conference in Poissy—a 'comedy' the historians describe it. Meanwhile, behind the scenes, the rival parties manœuvered to control the Queen Regent, Catherine de Medici, herself no awkward hand at manœuvering.

Catherine and the chancellor L'Hospital—one of the few men independent of party—thought they could put an end to manœuvres by issuing in January, 1562, an edict of limited tolerance. It had the effect one might expect on men who had not yet tested their arms nor sickened themselves with blood. The Protestants were disappointed that the privileges they got were so few, and the Catholics enraged that privileges were granted at all. A massacre of Protestants took place at Vassy. In alarm the Protestants seized a dozen towns and the Catholics seized the royal family. And the country plunged, with brief intermissions, into forty-six years of civil war.

Meanwhile, our spectator possessed with curiosity and ambition—who was gaining the friendship of the Queen and some
insight into the business of political intrigue—appears in two
incidents. Following L'Hospital's edict, Montaigne presented
himself in July, 1562, before the Parlement of Paris, and in his
capacity as a member of the Parlement of Bordeaux took the
required oath of loyalty to the Catholic cause. Because the oath
need not have been taken until his return to Bordeaux, a great
amount of futile conjecture has been devoted to his apparently
precipitous zeal—futile, because his motives are no longer
known. Certainly neither then nor at any time during his life was
there ever, in his own mind, a doubt as to his loyalty to Catholi-
cism and the Catholic state. Indeed the virtue of his claim and
plea for tolerance lay, as we shall see, in his conformity to the
established order.

In the same year Montaigne accompanied the Court and the
boy king to Rouen after its capture by the Catholics—one of the
first victories of the war. There he had his curious talk with the
cannibal chieftain from Brazil, and with his usual disarming
smile gives you to understand that he cannot understand why the
poor continue to tolerate the cruelty and injustice of the rich.

A year later he is seated at the deathbed of La Boétie. The letter in which he relates to his father the last hours of his friend is
the earliest literary morsel we have from his hand. It is literary
not because it employs a calculated style, but records the spirit of
a man—a 'soul of the old stamp.' Something, Montaigne felt, of
antique virtue passed with his friend. Not only his words but his
life shows that he buried with La Boétie his own youth. No more
dreams of ploughing fields in the new world, or by disinterested
public service setting the old to rights.

After a last plunge into lovemaking, which we gather was the
favorite sport of his youth, he consented to marriage. Françoise
de la Chassaigne, the daughter of a fellow magistrate in Bor-

deaux, brought him a sizable dowry. Though he is hardly reticent on the subject of marriage, almost the same reserve he maintains in speaking of his mother is shown in his allusions to his wife; and it, in turn, has given rise to speculative gossip. At any event, the union fulfilled what Montaigne gives as the common definition of a happy marriage: it appeared to be one.

Whoever is curious to learn all the 'humors' of Montaigne the husband can be referred to Florimond de Ræmond—the friend who succeeded him in the Parlement of Bordeaux. 'I have often heard the author say,' writes Ræmond in a margin of his copy of the *Essays*, 'that although he married a beautiful and attractive woman when he was still full of love, ardor, and youth, he never approached her except with the respect and honor which the marriage bed requires, never uncovering to his gaze anything but her hands and face, not even her bosom—yet among other women he was madcap and licentious enough.'

He was married three years when his father died (1568) and left him lord of Montaigne and a wealthy man. An elaborate contract with his mother assured her a home in the château, all the comforts she was accustomed to enjoy, not omitting the service of 'two maids and one man' and, for pocket money, "100 Tournay *livres* a year."

With a wife, a mother, and two younger sisters under his roof—with, for his own part, a dislike for household management and a supreme ignorance of it—he tried to settle down to the life of a country gentleman. And somehow his fondness for books grew apace, and he installed his library in the old lumber-room of a tower, at once 'remote and rather of a climb.'

Some while before, he had completed, at his father's request, a translation of Raymond Sebond's *Natural Theology*—a popularly written, rationalist defence of Christian orthodoxy. He now prepared the book for its publication in Paris (1569). Sebond's arguments in behalf of Christian dogma incited Montaigne to undertake a long and detailed examination of human belief, its vagaries and limitations.

This was for him—who was, as he said, 'an unpremeditated philosopher'—no detached and abstract preoccupation. Beyond his door men and women were dying, France was dying, for all sorts of beliefs. His researches into the nature of the mind, his meditations on human character, and the groping growth of his own thought covered a span of years each marked by the destruction of neighbors, friends, and compatriots, by the crash of falling houses and the rising fumes of cruelty, anarchy, and greed—all the manifest harvest of dogma. When, a decade later, his conclusions were printed in his longest essay, *The Apology of Raymond Sebond,* itself a fair-sized book, it became the core and key of his life's work.

In 1570, freed from his office in the Parlement, he went to Paris and supervised the publication of La Boétie's literary remains—poems, translations, the sweepings of a young author's desk. But the only works of consequence which his friend had written, Montaigne withheld from print. By way of explanation he said that he found their spirit 'too dainty and delicate to be exposed to our present inclement weather.' One of these dainty morsels was the essay on *Voluntary Servitude,* a republican attack on the tyranny of kings. The other delicacy was a memoir (written on the occasion of the Edict of 1562) which denounced Catholic abuses and violence as the origin of the religious reforms, condemned largely on political grounds the toleration of more than one cult, and proposed that peace and unity be restored by abolishing the abuses in the Church and reforming many features of its ritual. 'Dainty and delicate'—the reader of Montaigne may as well learn at the outset what the vocabulary of an ironist has in store for him.

A brief peace was tempering the inclemency of the weather. On the political stage new actors were playing the leading roles or training for them. Young Henri of Navarre was now head of the Huguenot party, with Coligny the brains; and the Catholic faction was led by the young Henri of Guise. And Catherine was as ever shrewdly and dispassionately manœuvring for her own party, which was limited to Catherine.

In the halls of Saint-Germain and the Louvre, Montaigne developed a friendship with both Henri of Navarre and Henri of Guise, without neglecting Catherine. Court life and service to the state had a fascination for him which he could never wholly extinguish. It even brought him rewards. Before the year was over, he received the coveted collar which made him a Knight of the Order of Saint Michael, the highest order in the land— though, as he wryly observes, fast becoming the most common; and he was appointed Gentleman in Ordinary to the Chamber of the King.

But the cost, so he tells us in scathing detail, was too great for the simplicity of his manners and integrity of character. As he describes it, his behavior at Court, his attitude toward politics and government, his methods of serving the bigwigs—*les grands*—would make, and he admits it, a complete manual on 'How Not to Succeed in a Public Career.'

A touch, too, of the sound sense for which many of his political-minded contemporaries were later to praise him, gave him perhaps an inkling of the extremely 'inclement' weather ahead. The Massacre of Saint Bartholomew was not a year away. Lying, betrayal, and massacre—he found—were inevitable, and hence 'necessary' to public business; 'but we will leave them to more supple and obedient men.'

IV

LEAVE THEM HE DID—and Paris, the Court, and the world of affairs as well. He retired to his château and his books for good, or so he thought. And he set about creating for himself and future generations the legend of the gentleman in the ivory tower.

To demonstrate his intentions, which indeed are not to be doubted, he had painted above the mantelpiece in his study the well-known inscription: 'In the year 1571, at the age of thirty-eight, Michel de Montaigne, long weary of the servitude of the Court and of public employments, betook himself to the bosom of the learned Virgins, where, if the fates permit, he may pass, in calm and freedom from all cares, what little shall remain of his allotted time now more than half run out. . . .'

Above the doorway, the same painter—whom Montaigne introduces to us as a craftsman worth following when you come to write an essay—represented a scene of shipwreck with survivors painfully struggling to the shore. A verse from Horace indicates that the scene symbolizes an escape from the perils of love and the world.

Of the old château nothing but the tower survives to give us a word of its master. But in those days a house reflected the whims of the owner more than of an interior decorator. So the remaining frescoes in the study had, we may be sure, their meaning for Montaigne. The picture of Mars and Venus surprised by Vulcan is taken from Ovid and recalls, if nothing else, the first book that charmed his boyhood. Cimon nursed by his daughter hints of Montaigne's love, almost a cult, for his father. The doorway is very low, even for a 'little man,' and his good-humored sensitivity to his small stature is caught in the one word he had inscribed above the lintel: *Brevis*. A generous display of his crest and the collar of Saint Michael reminds us of his vanity which, like his size, set him smiling at himself.

The library proper, which adjoins the study, was dedicated by a formal inscription to La Boétie, whose books were now on its shelves. The ceiling beams preserve some fifty-four inscriptions which, since they are his own choice, speak for the man who used to sit with his back to the only straight wall in the room and look across his desk at the 'thousand volumes' curving before him.

Taken chiefly from the ancient skeptics and the Bible, the mottoes express either the vanity of human reason or the wisdom of confining our grasp to things which lie in our reach. The Scriptures are quoted copiously, but not a passage exalting religious faith or devotion; *Ecclesiastes* predominates, and even Isaiah and Saint Paul are put to the service of philosophic doubt. The place of honor, on the two traverse beams, is reserved for the keywords of the Greek skeptical schools: 'I stop—I examine—I do not understand—I remain poised in the balance—I take for my guide the ways of the world and the experiences of the senses.' The first inscription to be seen upon mounting to the library is of Montaigne's own composition, and fairly interprets the spirit in which he understood and applied the others. 'For men,' it reads, 'the height of wisdom is to take things as they are, and look upon the rest with confidence.'

Below stairs, in the chapel, will be found an age-old symbol of things as they are: Saint Michael attacking the dragon. And we remember that Montaigne would burn a candle, in case of need, to one as readily as to the other. But only, we must not forget, 'so far as duty gives me rope.' As to the 'rest'—the things that are not yet but may be tomorrow—he remains true to the motto on the beam. 'Seeing the miseries which have overwhelmed us,' he will write in bitter days, 'I do not conclude we are at the last gasp . . . I do not despair.'

In this tower he began to write the *Essays*—the first pieces of literature to bear that name. In the beginning they were, as he explains, essays of his judgment on the world. Failing to penetrate, as wise men fail, much of the world beyond its infinite variety, and being wise enough not to try to arrange its contradictions into a forced pattern of his own, he gradually turned the essays of his judgment on himself. Again for the first time in literature—the ancients of whom he speaks are as little known to us as to him—a man tried to put on paper not what he did, but what he was. And here in this tower you may believe that the author, who speaks volubly of his solitude and retirement, spent the remainder of his days.

The truth is, as the reader of the present *Autobiography* has ample means to learn, Montaigne never abandoned his interest or his hand in public affairs. To a certain degree his withdrawal sprang from unrequited love. He wanted to serve, but his integrity would not let him bend to the service the world required; and, added to this, a genuine urge toward solitude and meditation hindered him from freely spending himself on others, even when opportunity and conscience permitted. Then, too, the opportunity may have dodged him in those younger years: he failed to click.

His restlessness, brooding, and the melancholy which sometimes stole upon him and which he declared most alien to his nature, could well have risen from this inner disharmony. No chagrin is more rankling and yet less apparent to a man than the disappointment which lies in knowing his own capacities and feeling the world will not or cannot employ them. Montaigne retired partly by choice, but partly from necessity; and the sting lay in not knowing which.

So his retirement was largely a myth. He tells us as much when he says that his *Essays,* written over a period of twenty years, were done 'in scraps and intervals, often interrupted by long months of absence.'

Three years after he had withdrawn to his tower for life, he was undertaking in Bordeaux a diplomatic affair for the Duke of Montpensier. In the same or the immediately succeeding years (1574–76) he was at Paris trying to negotiate an understanding between Henri of Navarre and Henri of Guise, whose personal feud and rival hopes for the throne had cast additional fuel on the flames of civil war. The negotiations failed; Henri of Navarre escaped from Paris and set himself at the head of the Protestant army; and the Duke of Guise took control of the newly formed Catholic League—fanatic last-ditchers.

Montaigne's friendship with the Protestant chief—or his services toward peace—won him, in 1577, the appointment of Gentleman to the Chamber of Henri of Navarre. He notes in his diary that the honor came 'without his knowledge and during his absence'—another absence from retirement, but one on which we have no information. The same year he suffered his first attack of the ultimately fatal nephritic colic, and then or after visited the baths at Bagnères. In 1579 he helped arrange the marriage of Diane de Foix Candale with his old friend, Louis de Foix. A few months later (March, 1580), the first edition of his *Essays*, comprising the first two books, appeared in Bordeaux.

These years may have been comparatively secluded, but they were hardly tranquil. The war had come to his gate. He saw his 'neighborhood grown so old in riot' he wondered how the social fabric held together. 'I saw,' he says, 'common and general behavior so ferocious, above all in inhumanity and treachery, that I cannot think of it without blenching in horror.' Contemporaries estimated that 128,000 houses were destroyed by this 'general behavior.' And Montaigne's province of Guienne, with its nearly balanced Catholic and Protestant population, furnished more than its share.

Civil war, household cares, ill health, and inner restlessness proved too much for the old recluse. Toward the end of June; 1580, he left home, with a supply of *Essays* in his baggage. His first stop was Paris, where he was received by the king, Henri III, to whom he had previously sent a copy of the *Essays*. Either because he had not read the passage in which the author denounced the morals of His Majesty or because he thought it was a perfect characterization of someone else, the King said he liked the book. 'If you like the book,' answered Montaigne, 'you must like me, for my book and I are one.'

He next took part in the siege of La Fère, and accompanied the body of a friend, the Count of Grammont, to its burial in Soissons. Then he set out on a grand tour of Germany, Switzerland, and Italy. Altogether he was gone from his bed in the tower for a year and a half.

On his travels as in his essays Montaigne shows us the man he knew himself to be—'essentially communicative and born for society.' Our record, unfortunately, is confined to a journal which he half dictated and half jotted for the private benefit of his weak memory. In it much of his grace and edge of style is therefore lacking, but the loss is more than made good by an exuberant wealth of detail.

His communicative nature, the curiosity of a philosopher of men, led him to take note of anything human and converse with everyone in his path. Catholics and Protestants, dukes and peasants, theologians and courtesans, papal censors and Jews; machinery, farming, cookery, church-going, street-loafing, libraries, table linen, ancient ruins, modern art, heating, ventilation, plumbing, women's hats—he has an eye and a word for them all. The man who wishes to travel through sixteenth-century Europe can do no better than embark on the complete *Diary of Montaigne's Journey,* of which the present *Autobiography* must content itself with merely suggestive morsels.

While taking the waters at Bagni della Villa, his curiosity, wanderlust, and colic still unabated, he received word that he was elected mayor of Bordeaux. Duty, he realized, had given him all the rope it could; and reluctantly, after a final fling at Rome, he returned home.

V

BORDEAUX was the third largest city of France, and its ticklish situation 'in the very mine' of Protestantism gave considerable importance to the office of its mayor. Gaston de Foix had worked for Montaigne's election, the *Essays* had begun to show him as a man not pontifically yet candidly above the battle, and the memory of his father still worked in his favor. Even royal politics saw fit to interpose the king's command in overcoming his reluctance.

He anticipated harder work than he was called upon to do, and well he might. The civil wars, now moving toward their thirtieth year, had spawned new parties reflecting new shades of conflict. A truce reigned between them, and the skill and tact of such local officials as the mayor of Bordeaux were decisive in keeping the peace.

Luckily, Bordeaux had in Montaigne a man who 'was no friend of noise' and who appreciated that his task 'was to continue and preserve things' as he found them. His first term of office (1581–83) passed off quietly in routine achievements which, as the mayor said, 'vanish in the first telling.' But even if his work was silent, it must have pleased; for he was reelected.

In 1583 things began to happen. As a manœuvre in the armed peace, Henri of Navarre proceeded to occupy a village which threatened the commerce of Bordeaux. The escapades of his wife, Marguerite, who was a sister of Henri III, increased the strain. Montaigne had enough to do, with letters and visits to Henri of Navarre and Matignon, governor of the province, in order to prevent a resumption of bloodshed.

The tension was renewed when the brother of Henri III died, and Henri of Navarre became heir apparent to the French throne (1584). Navarre and his court visited for two days at the château of Montaigne—an obviously political move. Here was cemented the friendship between the philosopher and just such a young prince to whom he would like to tell the truth. He even took occasion to address his candor to the young prince's mistress of the moment—La Belle Corisande, widow of his old friend the Count of Grammont—whom he urged not to ruin the career of

Navarre. The royal visit was repeated in 1587. It is easy to see the attraction Montaigne felt for a king who could say, 'Everyone who follows his conscience belongs to my church, and I belong to the church of any and all decent men.'

Meanwhile, in 1585, the three rivals—Henri III, Henri of Navarre, and Henri of Guise—came to an open break. At any moment, from one quarter or another, the blow was expected to fall in Guienne.

With Matignon marching and dickering in the province, Montaigne held Bordeaux. A threatened revolt of the troops was averted by his cool behavior. He supervised the defences by land and sea. 'I have passed every night under arms,' he wrote Matignon, 'either within the gates or down at the port . . . there is not a day I have not been at the Trompette fortress.'

But the plague struck Bordeaux before any of its other enemies. The château of Montaigne, despite the 'healthy air' of its site, was not spared. For 'six miserable months' he led his family over the countryside, a caravan of wanderers in a vain search for shelter.

Then the renewal of the war brought its usual horrors. La Noue, a chivalrous Protestant warrior whom Montaigne ranks among the notable men of his day, probably maligned the beasts when he said that the war turned most Frenchmen into tigers. 'A thousand times' Montaigne went to bed expecting to be murdered before morning. A scheming neighbor made himself master of the château, only to retire before the aplomb of its owner. The philosopher learned what it meant to be suspected on all sides, to owe his life to the charity of friends who were his religious opponents and to foes who professed his own faith. In desperation he resolved—as he said he should have done in the first place—to trust solely to himself. And with deeper purpose than ever, he worked on the study of himself and his portraiture.

Despite the 'troubled times,' a third volume of essays was written. In them the portrait is brought fairly to completion. It was a dramatic labor—a man painting himself while the heavens fell, painting in order to master himself and, so he hoped, offer amid the fall mastery to others.

Fresh efforts toward peace brought another lull in 1588. Montaigne went to Paris—attacked and robbed on the way by free-booters of the Catholic League. He published a new edition of the *Essays*, which included the third book, richest of all in its personal revelations, and many additions to the previous books. He visited the Court of Henri III at Rouen, where it had fled from the League; and, returning to Paris, he was imprisoned by the forces of Guise. After some hours in the Bastille, he was released upon the persuasion of Catherine. A severe attack of his chronic disease brought him close to death; and his friend, Pierre de Brach, who sat by his bed, tells us that he faced the next world as he did this, and as La Boétie had done before him—'gaily and with a steady foot.' Recovering his strength, he attended the political conferences at Blois.

But, for him, the memorable experience of the year was Marie de Gournay. A girl of eighteen, of a severe classical education and a severer resolve to live a learned virgin, she had fallen in love with the *Essays* and, through them, with their author. She sought him out in Paris; and the fifty-five-year-old philosopher felt he had reillumined with her some embers of that 'sacred friendship' he had lost with La Boétie. He spent several months at her home in Gournay, and called her his adopted daughter, an affectionate and purely honorary title. Later, she was to win additional fame as one of the first feminists in modern times.

Returning home, he was employed by Matignon, now mayor of Bordeaux, in a move against the League. But the long agony of the wars was nearing its final crisis. Henri of Guise had been assassinated, and in 1589 Henri III met the same fate. Navarre was at last King of France. And victories were joining with exhaustion to usher in a genuine peace.

Two letters to Navarre, now Henri IV, tell how Montaigne regarded the triumph of his favorite prince. 'In conducting your affairs, not common means must be used, but clemency and magnanimity. . . . I expect from the coming summer not so much the ripening of the fruits of the earth, as those of our public tranquillity.' And then to the man himself—for no office could make him neglect the man—a word begging him to cherish the gay and careless honesty of his youth, to remain the *Vert-Gallant*.

The King invited him to serve at his side in Paris. But it was too late—'mustard after dinner.' Montaigne was ready to consign to newcomers whatever wisdom he had gained. Now he had other appointments: he was busy 'finishing this man.'

So, between the encroaching attacks of the stone, he put what finishing touches he could to his life and his portrait. The touches—changes, insertions, additions—ran into the hundreds. And September 15, 1592 he died as he had hoped to die— 'patiently and tranquilly.'

Pierre de Brach and Marie de Gournay prepared a final edition of the *Essays* and unveiling of the portrait, which appeared in 1595. Shortly after, the spirit of the book and the man were written by his prince into the Edict of Nantes, a bill of Protestant rights which ended the horrors of civil war.

VI

THE DEAD BONES of an age and a man, as hastily resurrected in the preceding pages, will be given breath by my collaborator. And the many strands of his sinuous thought can be left to his own telling. I merely wish to suggest how the master strands, which guided his life, grow plain and pertinent against his background.

The dominant issue of his times—the validity of religious

beliefs—led Montaigne to wrestle with it as a man today might wrestle with social or economic beliefs. He reached the conclusion that all beliefs are guesses. Either they are the guesses of an individual; or, enshrined in custom and habit, the guesses of society.

His whole age thought differently. For the mass of men and the leaders in it, beliefs were truth; and truth must be made to prevail—if need be, by fire and sword. Entire nations were laid waste to save the world for truth.

No, said Montaigne quietly, your truth is a guess, and it is setting too high a price upon a guess to burn a man alive for it.

Ceasing to pin his faith on dogma, what remained for a man living in a world where dogmas were held to be the essential of life? Here Montaigne, like all skeptical thinkers, was no skeptic. Life remained. The experience of the senses, the ways of the world, the joys and sorrows of existence, these things, whether they are 'true' or not, are real. The essential of life is not what we believe about it, but how we live it. And the way to live it is upon its own terms.

Montaigne was born and raised a Catholic. For him, then, the terms were to live and die a Catholic. This was a matter of birth and custom, not of belief and truth. We are Christians, he said, for the same reason we are Frenchmen or Germans. So far as his belief went—a guess on which he would stake neither his own life nor the life of another—he looked upon all men as his fellow countrymen and all faiths as a guess as fair as his own.

When the issue came to bloodshed and war, when it threatened the ruin of his country, again he took life on the terms it offered him. 'A man,' he declared, 'must take sides.' He took the side he was born in; but in itself, this is of little importance. No matter which side he would have taken, his conduct, believing as he did, would have been the same.

Life and its immediate and unquestionable values were paramount. We may debate what is truth, but no one can debate what is treachery, cruelty, inhumanity, and death. With these a man loyal to life can hold no traffic. So far, therefore, as Montaigne could serve his cause without violating his integrity and decency as a man, he did it. Beyond that point he would not go. And once that point was passed, he was merciless in his denunciations of his own party.

He finally came to see that nothing could save society but the willingness of men to live and let live. Only if others became as doubtful of their own dogmas as he was of his, only by communicating to others his own feeling for the sacredness of life, could he hope to make substantial decency rather than will-of-the-wisp truth prevail. To make decency prevail—that is what is meant by tolerance.

But how to do it? There are men who propose to gag others in order to make them speak as they ought. There are others who will kill a man to teach him how he should live. There are still others in all parties, and too many of them, who would destroy their country in order to convert it into a Paradise.

This was not Montaigne's way. I must begin, he thought, with myself. When I have drawn a portrait of this self, with all its vanities, follies, and imperfections, others may recognize themselves in it. When I have shown them how, in order to live, I must tolerate myself and others, perhaps infection will lead them to a similar course. And together, all of us confessedly open to error and weakness, we can build a world more to our liking, without murdering men in the task.

Today we may think it futile to imagine that men will cease resorting to force in the defence or realization of their rights, their property, and their most cherished convictions. It will certainly be futile unless the party of men who have most to lose, the men who wield the powers that be, the men of Montaigne's party—for he stood squarely for the established order—can see into themselves as he did, and be prepared, as he was, to meet the world halfway.

The sixteenth century was not prepared. It needed two hundred years and more of bloodshed to 'weaken' men to the point of conceding peacefully what they might have conceded at the outset. But, eventually, concede they must and did. And are we to bleed another century or two? If we do, is this not also a futility?

The year after the final edition of the *Essays* went to press, a man was born in France who took up the work where Montaigne left it. Descartes, and with him modern science, has shown us how to build without dogma and slaughter, with merely a trust in the experience of the senses and in the ways of the universe. And in two hundred years they have built more than have a millennium of men fired with religious and social faiths.

— MARVIN LOWENTHAL

An Editorial Note

The sources used in compiling the *Autobiography* are the *Essays* of Montaigne, in their earlier and later form as well as in the edition of Bordeaux; his *Letters* as collected in the standard editions of his works; the *Diary* of his journey to Italy; the notes he wrote in the *Ephemerides* of Beuther, a family journal; the inscription he had painted on the wall of his study; and—the only words for which he is not directly responsible—De Thou's account of a conversation with him concerning his negotiations between Henri of Navarre and Henri of Guise.

The translation is based on the Cotton-Hazlitt version, as edited by O. W. Wight (Boston, 1887); but my modifications of it are so numerous I must relieve Cotton and Hazlitt from all responsibility. Since the *Autobiography* comprises hundreds of passages brought, some of them into a single sentence, from widely separated sources, I should warn anyone who wishes to turn to the French that he will often be baffled by my juxtapositions. In a very few cases, notably from the travel diary, I have changed the tenses, and the use of the third person for the first. Yet it is my belief I have nowhere betrayed Montaigne's thought or intention.

I hope the present book will lead the reader to the full-length portrait of the author as it appears, without my bold shifting and cutting, in the *Essays* and the *Diary*. The time-honored translations of the *Essays* are by Florio and Cotton, both available in numerous editions. The best modern translations are by E. J. Trechmann (London, 1927), and by Jacob Zeitlin (New York, 1934): the latter, when completed, will be indispensable for its editing and its wealth of notes. For Montaigne's travels, the reader is recommended *The Diary of Montaigne's Journey to Italy*, translated by E. J. Trechmann (London and New York, 1929). — M. L.

CHAPTER I

𝕿𝖍𝖊 𝕭𝖊𝖘𝖙 𝕱𝖆𝖙𝖍𝖊𝖗 𝕿𝖍𝖆𝖙 𝕰𝖛𝖊𝖗 𝖂𝖆𝖘

HEN I AM DEAD I shall no longer have a handle to grip hold of fame, or enable it to catch and cling to me. ¶ So far as expecting my name to do this service I have, in the first place, none sufficiently my own. Of the two I possess, one is common to all my line and, indeed, to others as well. In Paris and Montpellier is a family surnamed Montaigne; and another in Brittany and Saintonge called De la Montaigne. The shift of a single syllable will so tangle our web that I shall partake of their glory, and they perhaps share in my shame. Moreover, my people were formerly called Eyquem, a name still borne by a well-known family in England; there remain on our side some traces of our ancient kinship. As for my given name, it belongs to anyone who wants to take it—in this way I may do honor to a porter instead of to myself.

Secondly, names are so many pen-scratches common to a thousand men. How many are there, in every family, of the same name and surname? And how many more in different families, centuries, and lands? Who will stop my groom from calling himself Pompey the Great?

Coats-of-arms offer no more security than names. I bear an azure field sown with gold trefoils, and traversed by a lion's paw likewise in gold, armed with gules. What privilege does this figure possess to remain exclusively in my house? A son-in-law will carry it to another family, or some paltry upstart will buy it for his first crest. Nothing is more subject to change and confusion.

I come from a family that has lived without tumult or lustre, but, since time out of mind, particularly set upon integrity. I have had the best and most indulgent father that ever was, even to his extreme old age, and who descended of a line famous from father to son for brotherly concord.

My father, Pierre Eyquem de Montaigne, was born September 29, 1495, at Montaigne.

You can't imagine what strange stories I have heard him tell of the chastity of the age in which he lived. It was for him, too, to tell them, being by nature and art cut out and finished for the service of ladies. He said that in whole provinces there was hardly one woman of quality with a bad name. He would tell of queer intimacies, some of them his own, with virtuous women, yet free from any suspicion of ill. For his own part, he swore he was a virgin at marriage.

Yet he did not wed until after a long term at arms beyond the Alps. Of these wars he has left us a journal written in his own hand, which gives a detailed account, point by point, of everything that happened both concerning the public and himself. I have heard my father say that during the campaign against Milan, when towns were repeatedly taken and retaken, the people became so overwrought by the turns of fortune that he saw a list of twenty-five heads of families who had killed themselves in a single week.

He was married, moreover, at a well-advanced maturity, in 1528, during his thirty-third year, on his way home from Italy.

His manner was grave, mild, and very modest. He was most solicitous of neatness and decency, both in his person and clothes, on horseback or on foot. He was monstrously true to his word, and of a conscience and religion inclining more to superstition than the other extreme.

For a man of small stature he was well proportioned, close knit, and full of vigor. He had a pleasant face, rather brown; and he was adroit and exquisite in all the manly sports. I still have about the house some canes loaded with lead, with which, they say, he exercised his arms for fencing, throwing the bar, and putting the shot—as well as some leaden-soled shoes to harden him for running and leaping. Of his vaulting he has left little miracles behind him. I have seen him, when over sixty, laugh at our exploits and throw himself, furred gown and all, into the saddle, or resting on one thumb swing himself in a sort of half-somersault over a table. He seldom mounted the stairs to his chamber without bounding up three or four steps at a time. There was hardly to be found a man of his condition who equalled him in bodily exercises—just as I have met hardly anyone who couldn't surpass myself, except in running, at which I was fairly good.

He spoke little and well, always spicing his talk with some illustration out of authors most in fashion, especially the Spanish. Guevara's *Marcus Aurelius* was very often in his mouth.

My house has long been open to men of learning, and is very well known among them. For my father, who ruled it fifty years or more, was fired by the new ardor with which Francis I embraced and honored letters, and he sought out the acquaintance of learned men at great pains and expense. He received them in his home like saints blessed with some marked inspiration of divine wisdom. He collected their words as so many oracles, and with more reverence and religion as he had less authority to judge them by—for he had no knowledge of letters, no more than his forbears. As for myself, I love but do not worship letters.

Among others, Pierre Bunel, a man of great reputation for learning in his time, spent several days in the company of my father, together with more of his kind. Upon leaving, he gave my father a volume entitled *The Natural Theology of Raymond Sebond*. Since it was written largely in Spanish corrupted by Latin endings, he hoped that my father, who knew Italian and Spanish, could with a little help draw some profit from it. He therefore recommended it as a useful and timely work, for the novel doctrines of Martin Luther were then beginning to come into vogue and, in many localities, rock our ancient faith.

Some days before his death my father accidentally stumbled on the book among a mass of discarded papers, and requested me to translate it for him into French. It was a new and strange occupation, but having by chance the leisure for it and not being able to refuse the best father that ever was, I did it as well as I could. He took a singular delight in my work and ordered it to be printed—which was done after his death.

I remember, when a youth, to have seen him in his old age cruelly tormented with the rack of public business as Mayor of Bordeaux. He forgot his health, the management of his own affairs, and the gentle repose of his house to which the ravages of age had attached him for several years before—even despising his life, verily threatened by the long and painful journeys he took in their behalf. Such was the man. This humor of his sprang from the great goodness of his nature; never was there a more charitable and public-spirited soul.

A man of clear judgment, despite the aid of nothing but his experience and natural gifts, my father once told me he had thoughts of trying to introduce in our cities a designated place where anyone who needed something could come and register his wants with an official appointed for the purpose.

For example: 'I want,' says someone, 'to sell pearls'; or 'I want to buy pearls.' Someone else seeks a companion to go with him to Paris, a third is looking for a servant with certain qualities, a fourth for a master or a workman, this man one thing and that another, each according to his needs.

Doubtless, this means of information would furnish no light service in our daily business. At every turn there are conditions which seek a common contact, and for the lack of which men are left in dire distress. To the great shame of our century, I have heard that before our very eyes two most estimable scholars died of hunger—Lilius Gregorius Giraldus in Italy, and Sebastianus Castalio in Germany. Yet I believe there are a thousand men who would have taken them into their homes on excellent terms or relieved them where they lived, if their plight had been known.

In his domestic economy my father followed a rule which I know enough to praise, but not to imitate. Besides the business ledger, in charge of an accountant, which recorded the small items, payments, and transactions not in need of a notary, he ordered one of the men who did his writing for him to keep a journal, setting down in it any event of note and, day by day, the memoirs of his house—very pleasant to read when time began to dim their memory, and often useful in sparing us the pains to recollect when a certain work was begun or finished, what cavalcades passed our gate and which of them entered, as well as our travels, absences, marriages, deaths, the receipt of good or bad news, the changes among the more important servants, and similar matters. An old custom which I hold it wise to revive, each one in his own home, and which I think myself a fool for neglecting.

My father delighted to build up Montaigne, where he was born; and in all domestic affairs I love to follow his example and rules. I shall pledge my successors, as much as in me lies, to do the same. If I could do more for him I would, for I glory in feeling that through me his will still moves and acts. God forbid that my hands should fail at giving to so good a father any semblance of life within my power. When I have undertaken to finish an old stretch of wall or repair a bit of ramshackle structure I have done it, in truth, more out of respect for his desires than my own satisfaction. I berate my laziness for not bringing nearer to completion the handsome beginnings he made in his house—the more so because it looks as though I shall be the last of my line to own or put a hand to it.

It is likely I inherited the gravel from my father, for he died sadly afflicted by a large stone in the bladder. He did not become aware of the disease until his sixty-seventh year. Before that, he felt neither menace nor pain in his reins, sides, or elsewhere. He had lived in robust health and seldom subject to illness. Then, for seven years he endured this affliction, painfully dragging out the end of his days.

I was born twenty-five years or more before the disease appeared, when he was in his prime—the third of his children in order of birth. While he was still so remote from the disease, how could the light trifle of his substance out of which he built me convey so deep an impress? And how could it have remained so hidden that I did not perceive it until forty-five years later? Moreover, I am the only child among many brothers and sisters born of one mother that was ever troubled with it. Where could the propensity have been brooding all this while? The doctor who can satisfy me on this point I'll believe as many miracles of as he pleases, provided he does not give me—as they usually do—a theory more intricate and fantastic than the thing itself.

My antipathy against their art is hereditary. Medicine is grounded on experience and examples. So is my opinion. My father lived seventy-four years, my grandfather sixty-nine, my great-grandfather—born in 1402—almost fourscore, without one of them tasting medicine of any kind. Anything out of the ordinary diet they held to be a drug. Is not this an appropriate and telling experience?

I do not know if the doctors can find me in all their records three men born, bred, and dying under the same roof, who lived so long by following *their* rules. They must confess that if I haven't reason on my side, at least I have luck; and with doctors luck is worth a whole lot more than reason.

My ancestors hated medicine by some occult and natural instinct. The Seigneur de Gaviac—my paternal uncle and a churchman—a born invalid who nevertheless made his puny life stretch for sixty-seven years—once fell into a high and dangerous fever. The doctors ordered him to be bluntly told that if he did not take recourse to their aid (so they call it, though it is most often a handicap) he was a dead man. Despite his fright at this dreadful sentence, the good soul replied, 'Well, then, I am dead.' But, soon after, God set the diagnosis at naught. (He died, years later, in 1573 and bequeathed me one-third of his estate.)

By far the youngest of these uncles—there were four of them—the Sieur de Bussaguet was the only one to submit to medicine, perhaps because of his familiarity with the other arts, for he was a magistrate in the Court of Parliament. And though outwardly vigorous, he died long before the rest—except the Sieur de Saint Michel.

My father died July 18, 1568, aged seventy-two years and three months, and left five sons and three daughters. He was buried at Montaigne in the tomb of his forefathers.

How happy I should be to hear someone tell me about the manners, air, and looks, the daily life and common talk of my ancestors! How closely I would listen! Truly, it takes an evil nature to despise so much as the portraits of our friends who have gone before us, the cut of their clothes, and the fashions of their arms. Of my predecessors I have preserved the writing desk, seal, and breviary, as well as a peculiar sword they liked to use. And I have not chased from my study the long staffs my father always carried in his hand.

If my posterity is of another mind, I shall have a neat revenge; for they will never be able to be so indifferent to me as I shall then be to them.

CHAPTER II

My Most Tender Years

 WAS BORN, an eleven months' child, between eleven o'clock and noon, the last day of February, 1533—as we now reckon the calendar, beginning the year with January.[1] ¶ If I had sons I would readily wish them my own fortune. The good father whom God gave me and who received from me nothing but the acknowledgment of his goodness—hearty though it was—sent me straight from the cradle to be reared in a poor village of his, and kept me there all the while I was at nurse, and for some time after, in order to harden me to the lowest and most common manner of life—thinking it better for one to rise from hardships than fall to them. His whim had still another aim—to bind me to the class of people who need our aid. He felt I ought to have greater regard for the man who holds out his arm to me than turns his back. For this reason he had men of the most miserable condition hold me over the baptismal font, in order to oblige and attach me to them.

Nor has his design altogether failed. Whether because it is more to my credit or because of a natural compassion which dominates me, I give myself most readily to the small and weak. The faction I should condemn in our civil wars, I would condemn more sharply if it were flourishing and successful. And I'd be half-reconciled to it, if I saw it miserable and overwhelmed.

---

1. Before 1563, the calendar year began at Easter.

Indeed, it is strange that men esteem no other creatures but themselves for qualities alien to them. We praise a horse for its strength and not its harness; a greyhound for its speed and not its collar. Why don't we, in a like manner, value a man for what is properly his? The pedestal is no part of the statue. Let a man lay aside his revenues and titles, and stand in his shirt. When we consider a king and a peasant, a nobleman and a villein, a rich man and a poor, we are immediately taken up by the disparity between them—though the only difference is the cut of their breeches.

My father had been advised to make me relish knowledge and duty of my own free will and desire, and to educate me in all gentleness and liberty. He carried the matter, I may say, to a point of superstition. Because some people claim it harms the tender brains of children to rouse them suddenly in the morning and violently tear them at a stroke from sleep (in which they are plunged deeper than we), he had me wakened by the sound of a musical instrument, and always kept a man on hand to render me this service.

What they most had to correct in me was my refusal of things which are generally loved at this age: sugar, jams, and cookies. My tutor fought this hate of tidbits as a kind of over-nicety. Indeed, it is nothing else but a defect in the sense of taste. Whoever cures a child of a stubborn fondness for brown bread, garlic, and bacon, cures him as well of pampering himself with delicacies.

They tell me that in all my childhood I never tasted the whip but twice, and then lightly enough.

Passing along our streets, how many times have I wished to kick up a farcical row in order to avenge the lads I have seen attacked, beaten, and flayed by some father or mother insane with wrath! You see them sally forth, their eyes on fire and their throats aroar, often against a babe just come from the breast.

And, behold, the little fellow lamed and stunned with blows, while our courts take no notice of it—as though these maimed and crippled victims were not members of our commonwealth. No one would hesitate to send to the gallows a judge who had condemned a criminal out of anger. Why, then, are parents and teachers permitted, out of the same passion, to lash and punish their children? It is no longer correction, but revenge. Chastisement is a medicine for the young; and would we tolerate a doctor who raged against his patient?

I was brought up to walk the straight and open road, and it went against me to juggle or cheat in my childhood play. In truth, the games of children are not games, but should be looked upon as their most serious business. Even now, there is no pastime so trivial I do not bring to it a natural and extreme aversion to deceit. I handle my cards and keep the score as strictly when I play for farthings as doubloons. It is the same for me if I win or lose with my wife and daughter, or if I play in deadly earnest. At all times my eyes have enough to do in remaining glued to my hand; no one watches it more closely than I, and there is no one for whom I have greater respect. As a child I was mortally offended if anyone, contending with me in games or sports, held himself back because he thought me unworthy of his best efforts.

I remember that from my most tender years there was remarked in me I don't know what carriage and behavior smacking of vain and silly pride. It is not extraordinary, let me say, to possess leanings and dispositions that are so much a part of us that we lack the means to recognize or describe them, and which give the body a certain quirk, without our knowledge or consent. Because of his beauty, Alexander cocked his head a little to one side; and Cicero, as the sign of a man given to scoffing, was wont to pucker his nose. Such gestures may pass imperceptible to us.

There are other and artificial gestures of which I shall not speak—bows and curtseys which give men the reputation, often unwarranted, of being modest and polite. I am always doffing my hat, especially in summer, and I return every salutation no matter from whom, except my own servants.

I do not know whether my childhood gestures belonged to the first sort, and whether I really had an innate tendency toward pride; it may be so. I can't answer for the reflexes of my body.

I do find that our worst vices take their bent in our earliest infancy, and our main education is in the hands of our nurses. Mothers are amused to see a child wring the neck of a chicken or enjoy himself tormenting a dog or cat; and there are fathers foolish enough to think it a sign of a martial spirit when they see their son bullying a peasant or lackey who can't defend himself; and they look upon it as a stroke of wit if the lad overreaches or cheats his playmates. Yet these are the true seeds and roots of cruelty, tyranny, and treason.

It is a dangerous mistake to excuse these first sprouts of villainy because of their triviality, or the tender age of the child. First, the treachery does not depend upon the difference between pins and crowns. Parents argue that the child is only playing for pins, and would therefore never cheat for crowns; but I hold it more likely he will later cheat for crowns, since he already does it for pins. Secondly, it is Nature that speaks: and her voice is more frank and undisguised as her mouthpiece is weak and young. Children should be taught to hate vice for its own texture, so they will not only avoid it in action, but abominate it in their hearts—that the very thought of it disgust them, whatever mask it takes.

CHAPTER III

My Peculiar Education

 SEE BETTER than anyone that what I am writing here are only the reveries of a man who has, in his youth, barely nibbled at the outer crust of the sciences, and retained nothing more than a vague and rough image of them—a snatch of everything and the whole of nothing, *à la française.* ¶In sum I know there are such things as medicine, law, and the four branches of mathematics; and what by and large they aim at. It is possible, too, I know what purposes in life the sciences claim to serve. But to dive deeper than this—to have cudgelled my brains over Aristotle, the master of modern learning, or stuck it out in any one science—I have never done. Neither is there any art of which I can draw the first outlines.

There is not a schoolboy in the lowest grade who cannot call himself more learned than I. For I would not know how to go about examining him in his first lesson. If I am put to it, I find myself compelled to ask him, irrelevantly enough, such general questions as may test his natural intelligence: a lesson as strange to him as his to me.

Greek and Latin are no doubt useful fixtures, but we pay too much for them. I will tell you a way to get them cheaper than usual. It was tried out on me, and you may adopt it if you wish.

My father made every inquiry among scholars and men of understanding as to the choicest method in education. He was warned against the drawback in the prevalent system, and told that the length of time we take to learn the languages of people who got them for nothing was the only reason we could not attain the grandeur of soul and knowledge of the ancient Greeks and Romans. I do not think this is the sole reason.

Anyway, my father hit upon the following expedient. When I was still at nurse and before my tongue was loosed in speech, he placed me in charge of a German who knew nothing of French, but was deeply versed in Latin—he has since died, a well-known physician in France. The man was brought, at great cost, expressly for the purpose; and he had me continually in his arms. He was aided by two other scholars, of lesser learning, who looked after me and came to his relief.

None of them spoke to me in anything but Latin. As to the rest of the household, it was an unbreakable rule that neither my father nor mother, manservant nor maid, should speak anything in my presence but such Latin words as they had scraped together in order to prattle with me.

The harvest was astonishing. My parents learned enough Latin to understand it, and to speak it well enough for all ordinary purposes, as did the servants who were closest about me. In short, we Latined it at such a rate that it overflowed into our neighboring villages, where many Latin names for workmen and tools took root and may still be heard.

As for myself, I was over six years old before French or Perigordin meant any more to me than Arabic. Without artifice, books, grammar, rules, whipping, or tears, I had by that time learned to speak as pure a Latin as my teacher himself. For I had no means of confusing or spoiling it with another language. If, for example, they wanted to test me with a theme, school-fashion, what they gave to others in French for translation, they had to give me in bad Latin, to turn into good.

My private teachers—Nicholas Grouchy, author of *De Comi-*

tiis Komanorum; Guillaume Guerente, who wrote a commentary on Aristotle; George Buchanan, the great Scotch poet; and Marc Antoine Muret, hailed in France and Italy as the best orator of his day—often told me I had my Latin so well in hand and ready on my tongue, they were afraid to begin talking to me. George Buchanan told me—when I saw him afterwards in the retinue of the late Mareschal de Brissac—that he was about to write a treatise on education patterned on my example.

As for Greek, of which I have only a smattering, my father planned to have me learn it by an artifice—but a novel one—as a sort of game. We pushed the declensions to and fro, much as those who learn arithmetic and geometry on a kind of checkerboard.

By this you may judge of the rest; as well as the prudence and affection of so good a father. He is not to be blamed for failing to reap the fruits appropriate to such excellent culture. The reasons were two.

First, a barren and unsuitable soil. Though I possessed a sound and healthy constitution and a tolerably gentle and amenable nature, I was with it all, so heavy, limp, and drowsy I could not be roused from my sloth—even to get me out to play. What I saw, I saw clearly enough; and under this sluggish cast I nourished bold imaginations and opinions beyond my age. But I had a slow wit that would go no faster than it was led, a tardy grasp of things, a slack invention, and, to cap it off, an incredibly poor memory. It is no wonder that out of all this my father was able to extract very little of worth.

Secondly, the good man was extremely afraid of failing in a matter on which he had so set his heart. As sick men in a frenzy to be cured submit to all sorts of prescriptions, he let himself at length be overruled by common opinion—which, like cranes, ever follows those who go before. No longer having about him the men who had first suggested the new course, which he had brought from Italy, he yielded to the custom of the day. He sent me, at six years of age, to the College of Gujenne—then most flourishing and reputed the best in France.

Nothing could add to the pains he took in providing me the ablest tutors or in arranging the other details of my upbringing. As to the latter, he insisted on many particulars contrary to the practice of schools. But despite everything, it remained a school.

Among other things, the strict discipline of our schools has always displeased me. They are little else but jails for our imprisoned youth. The inmates are debauched by being punished before they ever become so. Enter one of them when the lessons begin, and you will hear nothing but the cries of tortured children and the noise of teachers drunk with wrath. A pretty way this, to waken in tender and timorous souls an appetite for learning! How much decenter it would be to see the classrooms strewn with greens and posies than with the bloody stumps of birch and willow! If I had my way I'd paint the walls—as did the philosopher Speusippus—with pictures of Joy and Gladness, of Flora and the Graces. Where children go for profit, let them also find their pleasure.

In truth, there is nothing more charming than the little children of France. But they generally deceive our hopes and, grown up, show no particular excellence. I have heard men of understanding claim it is our colleges (and we have plenty such!) which turn them into dullards.

Be that as it may, my Latin quickly sank into a bastardly corruption. By disuse I have since lost all power to wield it. I have not spoken it, and scarcely written it, in forty years. Yet in the two or three emotional crises of my life—once when I saw my father, apparently in perfect health, swoon in my arms—the first words wrung from my bowels were Latin. Thus nature, in the face of long disuse, gushes forth and asserts itself.

So my peculiar education served no purpose except to push

me rapidly through the lower classes. When I left the college at thirteen I had 'finished my course' (as they call it); but, to tell the truth, without any fruit I can now put to account.

My first taste for books came from the delight I took in the fables of Ovid's *Metamorphoses*. Though only seven or eight years old, I slipped away from every other pleasure to read it; the more so because it was written in what, after all, was my mother-tongue, it was the easiest book I knew, and its contents best suited to my tender age. As for *Lancelot of the Lake, Amadis of Gaul, Huon of Bordeaux,* and such trash as children relish most, I never even heard their names, and to this day do not know what they are about. So exact was my discipline.

But this made me more negligent in my other studies. Here I was lucky to have an understanding teacher who knew how to wink discreetly at this and other truancies. For it was in this way I sped without stopping through Virgil's *Æneid,* then Terence, then Plautus, and then some Italian comedies—always lured along by the sweetness of the subjects. If he had been so foolish as to balk me, I believe I would have brought away from school nothing but a hatred of books, like most of our youth.

Instead, he handled himself cleverly, pretending to see nothing of what was going on. Thus he sharpened my appetite by holding me gently to my other lessons and letting me devour these books in undisturbed secrecy. For the chief thing my father wanted developed in me by my schoolmasters was a pleasant disposition and an easy manner.

In truth, my only vices were sloth and poor mettle. The danger was not that I should do wrong, but do nothing. Nobody predicted I would become wicked—but useless. They foresaw laziness, not malice.

And I find they were right. People buzz in my ears, 'He is idle, cold to his friends and family, and in public affairs too offish and finicky.' The most insulting of them never say, 'Why did he take that? Why won't he pay for this?' But they do ask, 'Why doesn't he send a receipt?'

Nevertheless, if I were a brilliant hand at touching up my own portrait, I could perhaps cut under these reproaches and make some of my critics understand that they are less offended at my not doing enough than at my capacity for doing much more.

Shall I put to my credit one talent of my youth? I had a bold countenance and supple voice and gestures which I applied to any rôle I undertook to act. In my twelfth year I played the leading parts in the Latin tragedies of Buchanan, Guerente, and Muret, which were handsomely presented in our college. Our rector, Andreas Goveanus, the best in France, was a master at this as at everything else in his profession; and he looked on me as one of his star performers.

Acting is an exercise I find not unworthy of our wellborn youth; and I have seen our young princes give a good account of themselves at it. In Greece, even men of quality were permitted to adopt it as a profession. Those who condemn such entertainment I have always thought impertinent; and those who refuse to admit worthwhile players into our good towns are, I claim, unjust in begrudging the people this public diversion. Large cities should provide theaters for the purpose, if only to lure people from worse actions, and secret.

To return to our mutton, there is nothing like whetting the appetite. Otherwise, in education, you turn out asses loaded with books. By dint of lashes we give our pupils a school-bag full of knowledge to take home with them. Whereas, to do well, learning must not be merely installed in the house, but married.

Agility and address I never had, though I am the son of a very active and sprightly father. I could never be taught anything in music or singing, for which I had no gifts, or in playing any sort of instrument. In dancing, tennis, and wrestling I could never attain to more than an ordinary pitch; in swimming, vaulting, fencing, and leaping, to none at all.

My hands are so clumsy I cannot write so as to read myself what I have written, and I'd rather scribble it over again than take the trouble to decipher it. I read little better than I write, and feel that I soon tire my listeners. Otherwise, a good clerk.

I cannot decently fold up a letter, and I could never trim a pen, or carve at table worth a pin—or saddle a horse, fly a hawk, or speak to dogs, birds, or horses.

In fine, my physical gifts are well suited to my mental—there is nothing nimble in either, only a firm and full vigor. I am patient enough at labor and pains, but only when I go to work of my own will. Otherwise, if I am not enticed by some pleasure, I am good for nothing. I am of a mind that, life and health apart, there is nothing for which I will bite my nails or buy at the price of torment and constraint.

Extremely idle, and given over to my own inclinations both by nature and training, I would as willingly bleed for a man as worry over him. I have a soul free, entirely its own, and used to guiding itself as it pleases. Never having had, to the present hour, master or ruler imposed on me, I have gone as far as I wished at the pace that suited me best. This has made me soft and unfit for the service of others—and of use to no one but myself.

Nor was there any need to force my sluggish and lazy temper. I was born with money enough to content me (though thousands of others would have used it as a springboard from which to leap into the tumult and worry of gaining more), and with as much sense as I required. I sought nothing, and found what I sought.

The man to whom Fortune has denied a footing and the means to lead a tranquil and settled life is to be excused if he risks what he has, because, come what will, he must of necessity shift for himself. I have found the easier way by following the advice of the good friends of my youth, which was to rid myself of ambition and sit in my corner. I judged rightly enough that my strength was not capable of great things, remembering the words of the late Chancellor Olivier that 'the French are like monkeys that swarm up a tree, from branch to branch, till they come to the top, and once there show the world their backside.'

Whoever wants to raise a boy to be good for anything when he grows up, must not spare him when he is young, and must often violate the rules of medicine. It is not enough to strengthen his mind; his muscles must be strengthened as well. For the mind will be too sorely pressed, if not aided by the body; and will have too heavy a task, if it must carry the burden alone. I know how much my own mind has been winded by a tender and sensitive body, which is forever leaning on it for support. In my reading I often notice that what our mentors treat as examples of courage are nothing but toughness of hide and hardness of bone. I have known men and women, so equipped, to whom a good drubbing meant less than the flick of a finger to me.

Moreover, a boy must be hardened to the roughness and labor of physical exercise in order that later in life he may be able to stand up under broken limbs, cholic, cauteries—and even prison and torture, which, as the times go, are visited on both the just and unjust. We have proof enough in our present civil wars that whoever draws his sword against the laws threatens the best of us with the whip and the noose.

I loved to dress in finery when I was still under age, for lack of other ornament; and it became me well. There are some people upon whom their rich clothes weep. I was always ready to imitate the negligent garb still to be seen among our young men—my cloak across one shoulder, my hood to one side, and a stocking in disorder, all of which was meant to show a proud disdain for these exotic trumperies and a contempt for everything artificial.

But I find this negligence put to much better use in speaking.

The way of talking I love best is natural and plain—a muscular expression of a man's self, not so eloquent as prompt and brusk. Just as in our dress it is the mark of a small mind to set ourselves apart by an eccentric fashion, so in our language to dig up new phrases or obsolete words shows a childish and pedantic ambition.

May I be bound to speak no other language than you may hear in the markets of Paris! The lackey or fishwife on the Petit Pont will, if you listen, give you a bellyful of talk, and make as few slips as the best Master of Arts in France. The least contemptible class of men seems to me those whose plainness and simplicity have put them at the bottom of the ladder. I find the rude manner and language of the peasants more in accord with the teachings of true philosophy than those of the philosophers themselves. 'Common folk,' says Lactantius, 'are much wiser for only knowing what they need to know.'

My French is corrupted in pronunciation and otherwise by the barbarism of my province. I never knew a man in these parts who hadn't the twang of his birthplace, or who failed to offend your truly French ears. Yet I am not very good at my Perigord dialect, for I use it no more than German, nor do I much care. It is a puling, drawling, scurvy language like all others in my belt of France. True, there is spoken above us, towards the mountains, a Gascon which I find singularly handsome, blunt, and pithy—as manly and soldierly a speech as I know of. Most of my neighbors speak the same language as I am writing here; but whether they think the same thoughts I cannot say.

A young man should be whipped who plays at being a connoisseur of wines and sauces. At that age there was nothing about which I knew or cared less. Now I begin to learn. I am ashamed enough, but what can I do? I am even more ashamed of the circumstances which push me to it. It is for us old fellows to dream and putter away our time; and it is for the young to put their best foot forward and think upon their reputation. They are going towards the world and its opinion; we are on our way back.

I find fault that society does not employ us early enough. Augustus was master of the world at nineteen, and yet wanted a man to be thirty before he could be entrusted to decide where to lay a gutter. For my part, I believe our minds reach maturity at twenty, and are as fit then as ever. A mind that hasn't given a token of its powers by that age will never prove itself thereafter.

I am confident that since that age both my mind and body have decayed rather than improved. For those who use their time wisely, it is possible that knowledge and experience may increase with years. But vitality, alertness, hardihood, and those other parts of us more essential, important, and truly our own, languish and wither.

Sometimes the body yields first, sometimes the mind. I have seen plenty of men whose brains weakened before their stomachs and legs. Because this infirmity causes the victim no pain and its symptoms are hard to detect, it is the more dangerous. Therefore I complain of our laws, not that they keep us too long at work, but that they set us to work too late. Considering the frailty of life and its natural hazards, we ought not to give up so large a share of it to childishness, idleness, and apprenticeship.

A friend of mine, Madame Diane de Foix, told me the other day I ought to write a little further on the education of children. Certainly, Madame, if I had any proficiency in this subject, I could do no better than make a present of it to the little man who is threatening you with his happy birth (for you are too generous not to begin with a male). Since I had so large a hand in bringing about your marriage, I feel I have a certain right and interest in the greatness and prosperity of all that comes from it.

In truth, however, all I understand of the matter is that the gravest and hardest of human sciences is the rearing of children.

It is easy enough to beget them; but once you have them, then the cares, troubles, and anxieties begin.

Their inclinations in babyhood are so obscure, their promise so uncertain and deceptive, it is mighty difficult to have any solid conjecture or judgment about them. Cubs and puppies quickly show their natural bent; but men, as they grow up, fit themselves so readily into received customs, opinions, and laws, they soon change or at least mask their true nature. Hence it happens that by not guessing their real road, we waste our time and pains in educating them to things they are hardly fit for. As to this difficulty, I believe they should be set upon the best and most profitable highway, without bothering too much about the hints and signs they give in childhood—to which Plato, I think, credits undue weight.

Learning, Madame, is a fine ornament and marvellous tool, especially to persons of your rank. While I am sure that you, who have tasted of its sweets, will not omit this necessary ingredient in the education of your child, I will nevertheless presume to tell you a crotchet of mine, which runs contrary to the common usage. It is about all I can offer you on the subject.

A boy of good family, then, who seeks in letters not a livelihood or outer adornment, but something for his personal use to furnish and enrich his inner being, who wants to make of himself an able rather than a learned man—for such a boy I would have his friends select a teacher who had a well-turned rather than a well-filled head. We need a man with both, but preferably with manners and understanding than with learning. And we want him to do his work in a new way.

Teachers are forever thundering in our ears, as though pouring into a funnel; and our business is merely to repeat what they tell us. I would have our tutor reform this altogether.

At the very outset he should put the pupil on his own mettle. Let him taste things for himself, and choose and determine between them. Sometimes the teacher should break a new path, and sometimes the pupil. It is well to make the boy, like a colt, trot before him, so he can judge the pace and by how much to abate his own speed. This is one of the hardest things I know of. Only the most disciplined and finely tempered souls know how to slacken and stoop to the gait of children. I walk firmer and surer uphill than down.

Our schoolmaster should judge what his pupil has gained by the testimony of his life, not his memory. Let the boy examine and sift everything he reads, and take nothing on trust or authority. Then Aristotle's principles will be no more principles to him than those of Epicurus or the Stoics. The diversity of opinions should be laid before him. If he is able, he will make his choice; if not, he will remain in doubt. And if he adopts the principles of Plato through his own reasoning, they will no longer be Plato's but his. The man who follows another follows nothing, finds nothing, nay, seeks nothing.

Who dreams of asking a pupil what he thinks of grammar and rhetoric, or of this and that sentence in Cicero? No, our teachers hammer them, with all their feathers, in our memory—like oracles, in which the letters and syllables are the kernel of the thing. But to know by heart is simply not to know. What a man truly knows he can toss about at will, without regard for the author or need to fumble in a book.

Book knowledge is mere nuisance. It may do for an ornament, but never for a foundation. I wish that Paluël or Pompey, those beautiful dancers of my day, could have taught us how to cut capers only by watching them, without budging from our seat, as our schoolmasters pretend to instruct our understanding without setting it to work. I'd be glad to find someone who could teach us to toss a pike or play the lute without practice, as these men try to make us think and speak well without exercising either our judgment or our tongue.

If our pupil really has something stocked in his mind, the words will come only too fast. He will drag them after him, if they don't follow of their own accord. When you see people stammering to give birth to a sentence, you realize that they do not understand themselves what they are after. Their difficulty is not in the delivery, but the conception—they are straining at an abortion.

In plain truth, our education, its pains and expenses, aim at nothing but to stuff our heads with facts—of judgment, prudence, and virtue, no word. And it has succeeded altogether too well. Instead of teaching us prudence and virtue, it gives us their etymology. We learn how to decline Virtue, but not to live it. If we don't know what Prudence is in effect and by experience, we know it by jargon and rote.

Yet we are not content to know our neighbors by their family trees and marriage connections. We want them for friends, to enjoy their society and mind. But our education has taught us the declensions and divisions of Virtue as so much genealogy, without a care for cultivating our familiarity and friendship with it. It selects for our schooling not the books which contain the soundest opinions, but those which speak the best Latin and Greek, and by their fine words plant in our fancy the vainest humors of antiquity.

We greedily ask of a man, 'Does he know Latin or Greek? Does he write poetry or prose?' But whether he has become better or worse—the main thing in education—we never give a hang. We ought to ask, not who knows the most, but who knows the best.

In true education, anything that comes to our hand is as good as a book: the prank of a page boy, the blunder of a servant, a bit of table talk—they are all part of the curriculum. When he is in company, our lad should have his ear and eye in every corner; for I find that the best chairs are usually sat in by the least capable men, and that high station is seldom accompanied by good sense. I have been present when those who sat at the head of the table talked of nothing but the beauty of the linen or the bouquet of the wine; meanwhile, many a fine thing said at the foot was thrown away or lost.

Let our pupil examine every man's talent: a peasant, a bricklayer, a passerby. One may learn something from them all, each in his own line. Nay, the folly and impertinence of others will add to his own wisdom.

In this converse with men, I mean also those who live in the records of history. Here he will talk with the great and heroic souls of the best ages. What profit he will reap, as to the business of men, by reading Plutarch's *Lives!* But let our teacher remember the true purpose of this instruction. He is not to stamp in the pupil's memory the date of the fall of Carthage so much as the manners of Hannibal and Scipio—not where Marcellus died, but why it was unworthy of him to die there. It is not the narrative of history he must learn, but the judging of it.

A pupil should be taught what it means to know something, and not to know it; what should be the design and end of study; what valor, temperance, and justice are; the difference between ambition and greed, loyalty and servitude, liberty and licence; the marks of true and solid contentment; the extent to which we should fear disgrace, affliction, and death; the true springs of our actions and the reasons for our varied thoughts and desires. Our first lessons, I think, should teach us how to rule our behavior and understanding, how to live and die well.

Among the liberal sciences let us begin with the one that truly liberates us. Once we learn how to keep the functions of life within their natural limits, we shall find that most of the other sciences in use are of no use to us. It is nonsense to teach our children the behavior of the stars before they understand their own.

After you have taught the science that will make him wiser

and better—which is philosophy—then you may entertain him with logic, physics, geometry, and rhetoric. Having already learned to form his own judgment, he will rapidly progress in whatever branch he chooses.

It is a thousand pities that, as matters stand today, philosophy is considered a useless, vain, fantastic thing. I think this is because petty quibbling and sophistry have seized upon all its approaches. It is logic-chopping that makes her disciples so filthy, not she. Certainly, people are much to blame for making children believe it is a difficult thing.

There is nothing in the world more airy, gay, frolicsome and— I might say—wanton. Philosophy preaches nothing but feasting and merriment. A cold melancholy face shows she is absent. What! it is she who calms the storms of the soul, who teaches hunger and fever to laugh and sing—and not by any imaginary mechanics of the stars, but by natural and palpable reasons.

Now, philosophy has virtue as her end. And virtue is not lodged, as the schoolmen claim, on the peak of a rugged inaccessible mountain. Those who have approached her say she dwells in a fair and fruitful plain, open to anyone who knows the way, through shady, green, and sweetly flowering avenues, of pleasant and smooth ascent, as is the vault of heaven.

Our tutor will therefore make his pupil digest this new lesson—that the worth of virtue lies in its usefulness and pleasure. So far from thinking it a difficulty, boys as well as men, simple minds as well as subtle, will make it their own. And it is to be had, not by force, but by gentle habit.

Since philosophy shows us how to live, and since children need the art as well as adults, why don't we teach it to them at an early hour? We learn how to live when life is fairly over. A hundred students get the pox before they ever come to Aristotle's treatise on temperance. Our boy has only fifteen or sixteen years to give to education—the rest to action. Let us therefore devote that span to indispensable teachings. Away with the thorny subtleties of dialectics!—they are abuses which can never mend our minds. Take, instead, the simple discourses of philosophy: learn how to choose and apply them. They are easier than a story of Boccaccio. A child at nurse can grasp them more readily than learn how to read or write.

To our little lad, a study, a garden, a table, his bed, alone or in company, morning or evening: all hours shall be his lesson time and all places his classroom. For it is the privilege of philosophy—which shall be his chief study for it forms the judgment and manners—to have a hand in everything.

Just as the steps we take in pacing up and down a hallway, though three times as many, do not tire us so much as a set journey, so our lessons—met as it were by chance—will insinuate themselves without his feeling it. Thus his very sports and games will prove a good part of his study. For I would have his limbs trained no less than his brains. It is not a mind we are educating, nor a body: it is a man. And we must not split him in two.

Young bodies are pliant and therefore should be bent to all sorts of fashions and customs. Provided a youth can hold his will and appetite to their proper bonds, boldly train him to fit into all nations and companies—even, if custom demands it, to debauchery and excess. A young man ought to break the rules in order to rouse his vigor and keep it from rusting. There is no course of life so stupid and weak as that governed by inalterable rule and discipline. If he takes my advice, he will occasionally kick over the traces. Otherwise, the slightest debauch will put him flat on his back and make him a social nuisance. The nastiest quality in a decent man is fastidiousness and a stubborn devotion to eccentric behavior—and all behavior is eccentric if it is not pliable and supple.

Our young man should be able to do everything, but love to do nothing but the good. Let him laugh, play, and wench with his prince. I would wish that even in debauchery he outdid his companions, so when he refused to indulge in vice, it was not because he lacked the knowledge or power, but simply the will. A man should be ashamed not to dare or to be able to do what he sees his companions doing. Such a one should stick by the kitchen fire.

When Socrates was asked, 'What is your country?' he did not answer 'Athens,' but 'the world.' His fuller and wider imagination embraced the universe for his city. He extended his knowledge, his society, and his friendship to all mankind—unlike ourselves, who look no farther than the end of our nose.

This vast world—which some men now think is but one among many of its kind—is the mirror in which we must look in order to know ourselves in our true scale. And this world, in short, is the book my young scholar must study.

The pageant of its humors, sects, opinions, laws, and customs will teach us to judge rightly of our own, and enable our understanding to recognize its own weakness and shortcoming—no trivial speculation. Its endless shift of states and kingdoms, its turns and revolutions of public fortune will make us wise enough to raise no great fuss about ours. Its famous and mighty conquests buried in oblivion will reduce to ridicule our hope of immortalizing our name by the capture of a corporal's guard, or a henroost remembered only for its fall. The pride of foreign pomps, the swollen majesty of countless courts and grandeurs will accustom us to look at the brilliance of our own without blinking. That millions of men have already gone to their grave will encourage us not to fear joining such goodly company.

Pythagoras used to say life resembles the Olympic Games: a few men strain their muscles to carry off a prize; others bring trinkets to sell to the crowd for a profit; and some there are (and not the worst) who seek no further advantage than to look at the show and see how and why everything is done. They are spectators of other men's lives in order better to judge and manage their own.

These are my lessons. The man who applies them will profit more than the man who merely knows them. When you see such a man, you hear him; when you hear him, you see him. 'God forbid,' says someone in Plato, 'that philosophy should mean learning a pack of facts and discoursing on the arts!' Hegesias once begged Diogenes to read a certain book. 'You are jesting,' Diogenes replied, 'surely you prefer real to painted figs—why then don't you choose living lessons rather than written ones?'

It may happen that our pupil will prove to be a contrary fellow. He may prefer to hear a silly fable rather than a wise discourse or the true story of a notable voyage. While his playmates fire to the beat of a martial drum, he may respond to the tub-thumpings of a circus clown. Perhaps he will find it less delightful to return dusty and victorious from a battlefield than stroll home after winning a match at tennis. In that case, I see only one remedy. Even though he be the son of a duke, either his teacher should strangle him at an early hour, or if that can't be done without witnesses, he should be apprenticed, in some nice town, to a pastrycook.

CHAPTER IV

A Friend I Cannot Find Again

HE MOST GIFTED MAN I ever knew—I mean
for natural endowments—was Etienne de la
Boétie. His was truly a full nature, beautiful in
every aspect, a soul of the old stamp. If Fortune had
granted it, he would have achieved great things, for he had
roundly developed his talents through learning and study.

When he was a mere lad, before he was eighteen, he wrote by
way of essay a discourse which he called *La Servitude Volontaire*,
in honor of liberty and in protest against tyrants. For if he had
had his choice, he would rather have been born in Venice than in
Sarlat, and rightly so. This work passed through the hands of
men of great learning and discernment, not without remarkable
and merited praise, for it was finely written and as meaty as
could be. Yet it fell far short of what he was able to do; and if in
his maturer years (when I had the happiness of knowing him) he
had undertaken—much as I am doing—to put his thoughts in
writing, we would have seen things fairly rivalling the best works
of antiquity.

I owe a particular debt to this treatise. It gave me my first
knowledge of his name, for it was shown to me long before I met
him. And it proved to be the source of a friendship which we
afterwards deepened and, as long as God was pleased to continue us together, kept so spotless and whole that the like of it is
hardly to be found in story. So many happy chances must join to

build it that it is a great deal if Fortune bring it to pass once in any three centuries.

There was a fatal power beyond all telling which drew us together. Before we had met we sought one another by the accounts we had heard, which worked more strongly upon us than, in reason, mere report should do. We embraced each other in our names.

Our first meeting came about by accident, among the throng of a great city entertainment. At once we found ourselves so taken, so intimately known and endeared to one another, that from this time forward nothing was so near to us as we were to each other.

He wrote an excellent Latin poem, since printed, in which he explains and excuses the rapidity with which our souls united and their union reached perfection. Having met so late—we were both grown men, he a little older—and having so short a while before us, we had no time to lose. Nor were we bound by the example of ordinary friendships which need cautious sparring and long preliminary intercourse.

Our friendship had no other end than itself. It referred to nothing without. It had neither one ground, nor two, nor a thousand. It was I know not what quintessence of them all which absorbed my soul and plunged it and lost it in his, which seized upon his and made it lose itself in mine. I can truly say, lose; for we kept back nothing of all we had and were.

If you should press me to give the reason why I loved him, I feel I could only answer by saying: because it was he, because it was I!

Nature seems to have inclined mankind to social intercourse above all else. And its supreme point of perfection, I find, is friendship.

The name of brother is indeed beautiful and full of sweetness; and for this reason he and I gave it to the bond between us. But the clash of interests and the division of property, whereby the wealth of one brother means the poverty of the other, goes far towards weakening this natural tie. Besides, there is no reason why the congeniality of manners, gifts, and tastes which creates true friendship should exist between brothers—or fathers and sons. He is my son, he is my brother: yes, but he may also be ill-tempered and a fool. Moreover, in so far as law and duty enjoin these family ties, there is less play for choice and freedom. And freedom has no sphere more properly its own than in affection and friendship.

Though it, too, is voluntary, our love for women cannot stand comparison. It likewise found a place in my youth, no less than in his—as his verses plainly confess. But I could always distinguish between the two. Its fire more restless, scorching, and sharp, a feverish fire which holds us only by one corner, love is scarcely more than a frantic desire for what eludes us. Fruition destroys it; having only a fleshly end, it vanishes with satiety. As soon as it enters upon the terms of friendship, it droops away. Whereas friendship—a temperate, constant, and firm heat—thrives on enjoyment. For it is of the spirit, and the edge of the spirit is sharpened by use.

As for marriage, if a voluntary union could be contracted, in which soul and body reached complete fruition and a man be engaged throughout, doubtless the friendship it attained would be even fuller and more perfect. But women have never yet reached this perfection. The ancients rejected the possibility of it out of hand.

That other Greek licence is justly abhorred by our manners. Moreover, the necessary difference in age and function between its lovers—'Why,' asks Cicero, 'don't they ever love a handsome old man?'—makes it lag far behind the perfect union and harmony of which I speak.

As for the rest, what we commonly call friends and friendship are nothing but acquaintances and social intimacies formed for convenience or by chance. I have had as much experience with them as anyone, and with the best of their kind. In these ordinary friendships you must walk softly, bridle in hand; for the knot is so loose, at any moment a man may fear it will slip. 'Love a man,' says Chilo, 'as though you knew that one day you will hate him; and hate him, knowing that one day you will love him.' This precept—however abominable in the friendship of which I write—is sound enough in the usual run of intimacies, to which indeed one may apply the words so often on the lips of Aristotle: 'o my friends, there is no friend.'

Let no one, therefore, rank common friendship with ours. Not all the eloquence in the world could make me suspect the intentions of my friend. Nay, not a single action of his, however dubious it might look, could be revealed to me without my understanding it at once. Our souls had grown so completely into one being, had loved each other with such warmth, and with the same affection had uncovered the depths of our hearts, I not only knew him as well as myself, but I could have trusted him with my own interests more readily than myself.

In this master friendship, gifts, favors, and services do not even deserve to be mentioned. I am not obliged to myself when I do myself a good turn. So in the union of true friends, they lose any sense of duty, and loathe and banish from their talk all words suggesting division or difference, such as kindness, obligation, gratitude, request, thanks, or the like. All things—their wills, thoughts, goods, wives, children, honors, and lives—are common to both of them; and being nothing else but one soul in two bodies, they can neither lend nor give to one another. This is why lawgivers, in order to honor marriage with some semblance of this divine union, forbid gifts between man and wife.

To let you see how this works out, I will cite an ancient and singular example. A Corinthian had two friends, Areteus and

Charixenus. On his deathbed he drew up his will in this manner: 'I bequeath to Areteus the maintenance of my mother, and to Charixenus the dowering and marrying off of my daughter.' The people who read the will thought it was a jest, but the legatees accepted it with great content.

The example is perfect, barring one objection. There were two friends. But true friendship is indivisible. Each party to it gives to the other so completely of himself he has nothing left to bestow elsewhere. On the contrary, he is sorry he is not double or treble so as to give still more to his one and only friend.

I am like the man whom an acquaintance was surprised to find perched on a hobbyhorse, playing with his children. He begged the acquaintance to say nothing until he, too, became a father. So I, in turn, would like to speak with someone who has had my experience.

But knowing how rare such friendships are, I despair of meeting the man who can understand me. Even the discourses of antiquity seem to me flat and poor when compared with my own feelings. For once the effects of philosophy surpass its precepts.

Although one of the fittest and most needed men for high office in France, my friend spent his life crouched by the cinders of his hearth, to the great loss of the commonweal. But I have always been consoled by the knowledge that, so far as he was concerned, he was abundantly furnished with the treasures that mock at fortune and never a man lived more satisfied and happy.

He left nothing behind him but this treatise on voluntary servitude (and that by chance, for I believe he never saw it after it passed from his hands); some observations on the Edict of January made famous by our civil wars; and certain verses, of which twenty-nine sonnets were written in the green of his youth while enflamed with a noble passion, and the rest written later, when he was a suitor for marriage, in honor of his wife and smacking of I know not what matrimonial chill. For my part, I agree with those who claim that poetry is never so gay as in a wanton and illicit subject.

As to his last hours, no one can give a better account of them than I. Throughout his illness he spoke more readily to me than anyone else, and our close friendship gave me the most intimate knowledge of what was passing through his mind.

When I returned from the courthouse, Monday the ninth of August, 1563, I sent word asking him to come and dine with me. He answered, thanking me but saying he was somewhat ill, and asked me to pass an hour with him before he left for Medoc.

I called on him shortly after dinner. He was lying down, clothed, and showed a vague alteration in his looks. He told me he was suffering from an intestinal flux, with cramps, which he had caught the day before while playing, lightly clad, with M. d'Escars, and that chill often affected him in this way.

I counselled him to leave as he had planned, in part because his lodgings adjoined some houses stricken with the plague, which made him uneasy as he had just come from Perigord and Agenois, both badly infected. Moreover, I found that horseback riding is excellent for what ailed him. But I advised him to go no farther than Germignan, which is only two leagues from the city. Accordingly, he set out accompanied by his wife and his uncle, M. de Bouillhonnas.

Early next morning one of his men came from Madame de la Boétie and told me he was seized during the night with a severe dysentery. She urged me to send him a physician and apothecary, and come myself.

On my arrival he appeared overjoyed to see me; and when I made to leave, promising I would return the following day, he asked with more than his accustomed warmth that I remain with him as much as I could. This moved me rather strangely. And when I was nevertheless on the point of going, his wife—

touched with a presentiment of evil—begged me with tears in her eyes not to stir that evening.

When I saw him next, on Thursday, his condition had worsened. His pains and discharges of blood, which had already weakened him, were increasing hourly.

On Saturday I found him very low. He then told me his malady was somewhat contagious and, in any case, disagreeable and depressing; and knowing my temperament he begged me to drop in only for brief visits, but as often as I could. I never left him again.

Sunday he sank into a coma. When he came to himself he said he seemed to have been lost in a universal blur, in which everything swam pell-mell and in which he could distinguish nothing but thick cloud and mist—nevertheless he had felt no acute discomfort. 'Brother,' I said, 'death is no worse.' 'Nay,' he replied, 'not so bad.'

Because he had not slept since the onset of his illness, and his medicines, even the most drastic, proved unavailing, he began to despair of a cure and told me so. At this I made bold to suggest that he put his affairs in order—which he took with a brave countenance.

He bade me summon his wife and uncle. I told him not to frighten them. 'No, no,' he said, 'I will hearten them. I will give them better hopes for the outcome than I have myself.' Then he inquired if his fainting spells had not alarmed us. 'They are nothing,' I assured him, 'they are common to the disease.' 'You cannot call it nothing,' he said, 'when the thing you fear most stares you in the face.'

'It would bring nothing but happiness to you,' I told him, 'the pain would be ours who would lose the companionship of a friend so wise and good I cannot hope to find his like again.'

'Possibly so,' he replied, 'and if I do not hasten through the passage in which I have already gone halfway, it will be for the sake of your loss and theirs'—meaning his wife and uncle—'who are all that I love most.'

At this point I left him to call them. They composed themselves as best they could. When we were seated about his bed, the four of us alone, he spoke in a calm and cheerful voice.

'I am feeling very well,' he said, 'and, God be thanked, full of hope. But we know the insecurity of human affairs and how even our life, which we hold so dear, is but vapor and nothingness. And since I am, after all, a sick man, I am by that much threatened with death. So I think it wise to put my house in order.'

Turning to his uncle he continued, 'My good uncle, if I had to give an account of all I owed you from infancy I should never be done. You have been a real father to me, and as a true son I feel I have no right to dispose of anything without your consent.' Then he stopped and waited until the sobbing and tears of his uncle let him answer that anything he did would be approved. Whereupon he made his uncle heir to the residue of his estate.

He next addressed his wife. 'Likeness mine,' he said—for he often called her 'Likeness' because of the long bond between them—'I have loved you with all my heart, and I know you have done as much for me, and I can never be grateful enough. I beg you to accept the share of my goods I am giving you and rest content with it, though I know it is a poor token of your merits.'

'Brother,' he then said, turning to me, 'whom I have loved so dearly and chosen to renew with me that noble and true friendship alien to our times, and only a few traces of which linger from our memories of antiquity, I beg you to take my library and books—a sorry gift, but it comes with a good heart and belongs to you as a lover of letters. It will be for you μνημόσυνον tui sodalis.'[1]

Then, addressing himself to all three of us, he blessed God

---

1. A souvenir of your comrade.

that in this hour of extremity he was surrounded by those dearest to him, and said it was a goodly sight to see four persons so united in friendship, not doubting, he said, that we loved one another each for the sake of the other. He continued to speak with such a firm voice, renewed color, and strengthened pulse I thought he had been revived by some miracle; and I even made to compare his pulse with mine.

At that moment my heart was so low I could scarcely answer him; but some hours after I told him I had blushed for shame to think my courage failed me on hearing what, in the midst of his sufferings, he had had the courage to say. Hitherto, I told him, I had thought that God seldom gave us such mastery over human accidents and could hardly believe the accounts I had read of it in history, but now having seen proof of it I praised God to have found it in a person by whom I was so much loved, and this would serve me as an example to act the same part when it came my turn.

Taking me by the hand he said, 'Brother, I assure you that many things in my life have been as hard and troublesome to do as this. It is time I was ready, and I have long had my lesson by heart. After all, isn't it enough to have lived as long as this? I am near to beginning my thirty-third year. God has graciously given me up till now nothing but health and happiness. In the inconstancy of human life it could not have lasted much longer. Now I shall be spared the malice and duplicity which come when a man seeks to enrich his fortune, and the pains of old age. And I am sure I will enter the abode of the blessed.'

Because I showed the trouble his words awoke in me, he exclaimed, 'What! you wish to make me afraid? And if I were, to whom would I turn for courage but to you?'

That evening the notary came to draw up the will. I had him prepare it in writing and then asked my friend to sign it. 'No,' he said, 'I will draw it up myself, but you must give me a little respite, for I am exhausted.' I wanted to change the subject, but he suddenly pulled himself together and told me, a man doesn't need much time to die in. When he was through dictating he turned to me, saying, 'And that is what men call their possessions!'

Monday morning he was so ill he abandoned all hope. When he saw me, he called me to his side. 'Brother mine,' he said, 'have you no pity on my suffering? Can't you see that everything you do to aid me will only prolong my agony?' Soon after, he fainted. When he revived he asked me for a little wine. Feeling better, he said it was the best drink in the world. 'No,' [said, to keep his attention, 'water is best.' 'Yes,' he replied, 'ΰδωρ ἄριστον.'[1] His limbs were already cold, a mortal sweat rolled from his body, and his pulse could barely be felt.

Tuesday he made his last communion. 'I want to say in your presence,' he told the priest, 'that I wish to die as I was baptized and have lived, in the faith Moses planted in Egypt, the fathers received in Judæa, and from hand to hand has come down to France.'

In the afternoon, starting suddenly out of a doze, he exclaimed, 'Well and good, let it come when it will; I await it gaily and with a steady foot'—words which he repeated two or three times during his illness.

Towards evening he began to show the unmistakable print of death. As I sighed he called me to him. No longer but the shadow of a man, he whispered, 'Brother, friend, please God I shall see in reality what I have just seen as in a dream.' After a moment of silence I asked him, 'What did you see?' 'Great things, great things,' he responded. 'You have never,' I protested, 'concealed anything from me—will you begin now?' 'True,' he replied, 'and I should like ... but I can't. Oh, they were marvellous, infinite, but not to be said.'

---

1. Water is the best thing' (Pindar).

Hearing the tears of his wife, he called her and sought to reassure her. 'Good night, dear wife,' he said, 'you may leave now, for I am going to sleep.' It was his last farewell to her.

When she had left, he said to me, 'My brother, stay, I beg you, by my side.' As the thrusts of death grew sharper, he began to implore me over and over again to give him room. I feared for his mind, and trying to reason with him I heard him say, 'Brother, brother, then you refuse me room?' I tried to convince him that since he still lived and breathed and had a body, it must perforce be occupying its proper place. 'In truth, yes,' he replied, 'but it is not the place I desire—besides, when all is said, I no longer have a being.' 'God,' I told him, 'will soon give you a better.' 'Would I already had it,' he said, 'for three days now I have panted to leave.'

In his distress he kept calling to know if I were near him. At last he composed himself; and feeling more hopeful, I rejoined his wife.

An hour later, after calling my name once or twice, he uttered a deep sigh and gave up the ghost—towards three o'clock on Wednesday morning, the sixteenth of August, fifteen hundred and sixty-three, having lived thirty-two years, nine months, and seventeen days.

In good earnest, if I compare all the rest of my life—and I have passed my time not unpleasantly—with the four years in which I enjoyed the sweet companionship of this man, it is nothing but smoke and a dark and tedious night. From the day I lost him I have had but a languishing existence. My very pleasures, instead of consoling, double my grief.

We were halves throughout, and by outliving him I feel I am defrauding him of his share. I had grown so accustomed to be his double in all things, times, and places, I now feel I am not more than a fragment of myself. I think or do nothing without missing him—as I know he would have missed me. For even as he surpassed me in virtue and all other accomplishments, so he did in friendship.

> *Never shall I speak to you again nor hear your voice*
> *Nor see you, brother dearer to me than life,*
> *But I shall love you forever.*
> —CATULLUS

CHAPTER V

I Set Myself to Making Love

ERHAPS I WOULD have never recovered from my sorrow if I had trusted to my own strength. To rescue me I needed a powerful diversion, and so by art and study I set myself to lovemaking—in which my youth aided me. And love relieved and drew me from the pain in which friendship had plunged me.

In everything else I am the same. A violent imagination grips me, and I find it easier to change than to tame it. If I can't fight, I run away; and in the crowd of other thoughts and amusements, it loses the scent and I am saved. Even a philosopher sees his friend dying hardly less vividly after a lapse of twenty-five years as of one. But so many other occupations intervene that grief droops and tires at last.

In my youth I had to watch and control myself to keep in the path of virtue: good health and abundant spirits are a poor help in the matter. I am now in another state: old age does the watching and controlling—and only too well. From an excess of sprightliness I have fallen into an excess of sobriety, which is much more troublesome.

For this reason I am permitting myself a little dissipation, by diverting my mind with thoughts of my days of youth and wantonness. Of late I've become too dull and sodden. Every day my years lecture me on temperance and frigidity. It is now my body's turn to reform my mind, and it performs the task more rudely and imperiously than when matters were the other way around. Sleeping or waking there is not an hour when it lays off sermonizing me on patience, repentance, and death. As I once had to guard myself against indulgence, now I must defend myself from continence, which is pushing me into a sort of stupor.

But I propose to be master of myself in all things. Virtue has its excesses, which stand in need of moderation, no less than vice. Therefore, lest I altogether wither and dry up with prudence, I shall step softly aside and, turning my eyes from the grey sky ahead, amuse myself with the memories of my youth. Let the years haul me along as they will—but backwards!

What if I have a mind to play at knucklebones or spin a top? Even together, wisdom and folly will have their hands full to support me in this calamity of old age.

I know perfectly well that few of the people who will complain of the licence of my writings could not be better employed complaining at the licence of their own thoughts. I suit their desires, but I offend their eyes. I hate these carping and morose fellows who dodge all the joys of life but glue themselves to its evils—like leeches that suck nothing but bad blood.

I am resolved to dare to say all I dared to do. However, if it is an indiscretion to publish one's own missteps, there is small danger it will be imitated. As Ariston said, the winds men fear most are those that blow open their cloaks.

Like the Huguenots who condemn private auricular confession, I do my confessing in the open. I am hungry to make myself known, provided it be truly; or, more accurately, I hunger for nothing, but should mortally hate to be misknown. Men who are ignorant of themselves may be fobbed off with false praise; but not I, who examine myself to my very bowels and well know what is due me. I shall thank no one for recommending me as a good pilot—or as modest and chaste.

I am vexed that my *Essays* have served the ladies only to decorate their parlor table. This chapter will send me to their boudoir. Very well, talk in public is without spice or favor, and I prefer to deal with them in private. These are my last embraces.

But to come to my subject. Why is the act of generation—natural, necessary, and just as it is—never spoken of without a blush? We say boldly enough, 'Kill, rob, betray'; but this other we whisper under our breath. Do we mean that the less energy we spend on it in talk, the more we'll have for thinking about it? Certainly, the words least often spoken are the best and most widely known. And the sex that practices it most mentions it least. Is it not the same with books, that sell faster for being suppressed?

I have not been so long discharged from the army of Venus that I can't recollect her force and worth. There still remains a spark of the fire and a twitch of the fever. And I'll take Aristotle at his word when he says that bashfulness is an ornament of youth, but a reproach in old age.

When I was young I gave myself over to the desires that ruled me as licentiously and recklessly as anyone else. The close kisses of youth, luscious, devouring, and moist, used to keep their perfume on my lips for hours afterwards. Like Horace, I can say, 'I too fought not without honor'—though much more in the duration than number of my exploits. It is both a sad thing and a miracle to confess, as I must, the early age at which I first tasted the subjection of love. It was, to be sure, by chance and before the years of choice or knowledge. In fact I can't remember when. My lot may well be compared with that of Quartilla, who could not recall ever being a virgin.

The society of beautiful and well-bred women was always dear to me. But a man must stand a little on his guard in it, especially if his body has a way of getting the upper hand, as does mine. I scalded myself properly, and suffered all the torments poets say befall to those who fling themselves headlong into love.

Since then, it is true, the lash of the whip has made me wiser.

It is folly for a man to fix all his thoughts on it, and expend on it a furious and unmeasured passion. On the other hand, to engage in it without will or fervor; to play a part, like actors, suitable to one's years and the conventions of the game, putting into it nothing but words; this is indeed to play safe—but in as cowardly a way as the man who abandons any honor, profit, or pleasure, because of the risk. Nothing of such behavior can satisfy a man of high spirit. We must in good earnest desire what we expect in good earnest to enjoy.

The result is much as we should anticipate, and can see on all sides. The lack of earnestness among the men has driven the women to take refuge in themselves; or else, imitating our example, play their part in the farce as we do ours and give themselves up to the business without fire, care, or love. It becomes a comedy in which the spectators have as much pleasure as the performers, or more.

For myself, I can no more recognize Venus without Cupid than any mother without a child. One connotes the other. The man who cheats at this game cheats himself. It costs him little but he gains less.

Though I do not wish myself better thought of than I am, I will say this for the slips of my youth. Not only because of the danger to my health (though I didn't know enough to escape two attacks, both light and transitory), but even more because of contempt, I seldom gave myself to common and mercenary embraces. I preferred to heighten my pleasure by difficulty, yearning, and a touch of triumph. I like the taste of Tiberius, who looked for modesty and gentle birth as much as for any other quality; and that whim of the courtesan Flora, who never sold herself to anyone less than a dictator, consul, or censor. There is no denying that pearls and brocade, titles and a retinue of servants, add something to it.

I held a good mind in high account, provided there was nothing to be said against the body. For to tell the truth, if I had to do without one or the other of these attractions, I would have renounced the former, which has its place in better things. But in the business of love, which is concerned principally with the sight and touch, something can be done without the graces of the mind: without the graces of the body, nothing.

As to physical beauty, before I proceed further, I wonder if we can agree on a description of it. Likely not; for we ascribe to it a multitude of different forms, which we manufacture to suit our appetite. Indians paint it black, with great swollen lips and big flat noses; they load the cartilage between the nostrils with rings of gold to make it hang to the mouth, and the lower lip with hoops that weigh it down to the chin. In Peru the biggest ears are the most beautiful. Mexicans hold large breasts in such esteem that they boast they can suckle their children over the shoulder. The Italians fashion beauty massive and sumptuous, the Spanish peaked and slender; and among us, one makes it white, another tan, one soft and delicate, another strong and robust. But in all, there is not a woman, however ill favored, who doesn't think herself worth loving and pride herself either on her youth, the color of her hair, or the grace of her step. Indeed, there is no such thing as an altogether ugly woman—or altogether beautiful.

I have often heard women describe this commerce as purely spiritual, and disdain to bring the senses into consideration. Both serve in the matter; but while I have frequently seen a man pardon the weakness of a woman's wit for the sake of her beauty, I've yet to see them welcome a body that was never so little on the decline, because of her mental charms.

If anyone should ask me what is the first thing to be considered in love affairs, I should answer: to know how to seize the right moment. The second thing, I may add, is the same as the first. And the third is the same as the second. Ah, the outrageous advantage of opportunity! It does everything.

I have often had bad luck—and sometimes been wanting in myself as well. (God keep it from the man who can still boast in this respect!) Our young men show greater boldness today, which they lay to greater passion. But if the women looked into the thing, they would find it came from a greater disrespect.

I was always superstitiously afraid of giving offence, and gladly respected the woman I loved. Besides, the man who discards reverence from this business removes its lustre. I like a man to play somewhat the child and servant.

I don't know which ancient wished he had a throat like a crane's, so that the taste of his food might last longer. He had done better to wish length in this quick and precipitous pleasure—especially for a man like myself who has the fault of being too prompt. To stay its flight and dally with preambles, all things—a glance, a flutter, a word, a sign—favor and reward one another.

Would it not be a handsome saving if a man could dine on the steam of a roast? Our love is compounded less of solid substance than of vanities and fevered dreams: we should serve and pay it in kind. Let us teach the women to set a higher value on themselves in toying with and fooling us. We give the final charge at the first onset—the impetuosity of the French. If they will but spin out their favors and display them in small parcels, we can all, even in old age, reap a little reward according to our merit.

The man who has no game except when he wins, who wins nothing unless he sweeps the stakes, ought not to join our school. The more tiers there are, the higher is the top seat. We should delight in being led to it, as in a great palace, by various portals, devious passages, long and pleasant galleries, and many detours. Thus we can linger, we can love, longer. Without desire and hope, our performance is worthless. Conquest and possession we should dread most. Women who completely surrender themselves to our fidelity run a grave risk; for fidelity is a rare and difficult virtue. A woman is no sooner ours than we are no longer hers.

Dearness is a good sauce to the meat. Do but observe how our custom of promiscuous kissing has brought it to no esteem. It is a disgusting fashion and very damaging to our ladies, who must submit their lips to every fellow with three footmen at his heels. And we, too, gain little enough. As the world goes, for every three beautiful women we must kiss threescore ugly ones. And to a tender stomach, as mine is now, a poor kiss is too big a price to pay for a good one.

Love among the Spanish and Italians pleases me. It is more courteous, timid, secret, and coy. In Italy they court even the women who sell themselves. 'There are degrees,' they say, 'in enjoyment, and by paying court we seek to gain the highest; these women sell nothing but their bodies—their will you must woo.' Indeed, it is the will we must win by courtship. Wasn't it lunatic of the Moon to put Endymion to sleep and please herself with a motionless boy?

There is a proverb in Italy—the regent of the world in affairs of love—that a man does not know Venus in her supreme sweetness unless he has lain with a lame mistress. I thought that perhaps the limp of such a woman added some new pleasure to the performance. But I have recently learned that ancient philosophy has decided that since the legs of a lame person do not demand the normal amount of nourishment, more strength is available to the parts above; which is also the reason why the Greeks decried women weavers as hotter than others of the sex, because of their sedentary trade. I might add of the latter that the joggling about, as they sit at work, provokes their desire, as does the swinging and jolting of a coach to our own ladies. But where won't reasoning carry us, at this rate? Our minds are so ready to credit false and frivolous impressions that merely on the authority of this proverb I at one time convinced myself I had more pleasure in a woman because she was crooked, and counted this defect among her charms.

But all enjoyments are not alike. Consent and good will alone are not sufficient warrants of affection. Treachery may lurk there as elsewhere. Some women go to it with only one thigh. Others would rather lend you that than their coach. You must look to it whether you please them on some other account, or whether you suit them for that alone, like a robust stableboy. And what if they eat your bread with the butter of a more pleasing imagination? 'She holds you in her arms, but another in her thoughts.'

The difficulty of meeting together, the danger of surprise, the shame of the morning after—'languor, silence, and sighs,' says Horace—it is these which give tang to the sauce. How many pleasant wanton games are born of our decent and reserved manner in speaking of the works of love! Even pleasure seeks to augment itself by pain: it is sweeter when it smarts and rasps. The rigor of our mistresses is annoying, but their easy surrender is, to tell the truth, more so.

Why did Poppea mask the beauty of her face, except to enhance it in the minds of her lovers? Why do women veil, even below the heels, those charms which everyone desires to show— and see? Why do they cover with so many hindrances, one on top of the other, those parts where our desire is mainly lodged—and theirs? What purpose serve that virginal blush, studied coldness, severe countenance, that profession of ignorance of the things they know better than we who would be their teachers, if not to whet our desire to conquer, devour, and trample underfoot all these ceremonies and obstacles?

There is not only pleasure but glory in making them give way to folly, in debauching that tender sweetness and childish modesty, and in reducing a proud and haughty brow to the mercy of our ardor. It is a glory, say the men, to triumph over modesty, chastity, and temperance; and any man who persuades the women to give up these virtues betrays both them and himself. We want to believe their hearts flutter with fright, that our words wound the purity of their ears, that they hate us for the way we talk, and yield only by sheer force.

Beauty, powerful though it is, cannot make itself relished without these little arts. You may see in Italy, where the most and rarest beauty is for sale, how it is compelled to use other devices to make itself desirable and how, despite these wiles, it remains poor and feeble, since it is, after all, a beauty any man can buy.

In my day I have conducted my love affairs with as much conscience as in any other contract. I never pretended to a passion I didn't have. I always told my mistress its birth, strength, decline, its fits and intermissions—a man does not always keep the same pace.

If there were still preserved all the paper I scribbled to the ladies at a time when my hand was really carried away by passion, there might perhaps be found a page or so worth handing over to our young idlers who are besotted with this madness.

I was always sparing with my promises, but I think I did better than my word. The women found me faithful even when they were inconstant—a confessed and sometimes wholesale inconstancy. I never broke with them as long as I had any hold at all; and when I did break, never with hatred and despite. For I felt that these intimacies, obtained on no matter what scandalous terms, obliged me to a certain goodwill. True, I sometimes showed a little anger and impatience at their tricks and evasions; for I am given to rash emotion which, though brief and light, often, I confess, spoiled my market.

If at any time they asked my opinion and judgment, I never hesitated to give them fatherly and sharp advice and pinch them where it smarted. Their only complaint might be that, in comparison with our lovers of today, I was a little too conscientious. I have kept my word when I could easily have broken it. They have sometimes capitulated on terms they would have liked to see me disregard. More than once I have armed them against myself, so they were safer in following my rules than their own.

The raptures of Venus—say her critics—put us out of our mind. Yet I know otherwise. I know that even at the most critical moment a man may master himself and think of something else. In my own experience I have found that Venus is not the almighty goddess that many men—more virtuous than I—claim her to be. I do not hold it a miracle, as does the Queen of Navarre, to pass whole nights with a long-coveted mistress, enjoying all the liberty and opportunity a man could want, and yet be true to his pledge of pushing the matter no further than kisses and embraces.

Whenever I could, I took on myself the risks of the rendezvous. I always arranged our meetings in the most difficult and unlikely fashion—as least open to suspicion and, in my opinion, most accessible. Places least feared are least observed. You may freely dare what nobody thinks you will dare: the difficulty makes it easy.

Never a man was less frankly genital in his approaches than I—though no one knows better how ineffectual it proved. Yet I do not repent of it, for now I have nothing more to lose. And if I could begin over again, it would be by the same method, however fruitless. Folly and insufficiency are worthy in an unworthy action.

Finally, I did not allow myself to be wholly carried away. I pleased but I did not forget myself. I kept what little sense and discretion Nature had given me—a touch of emotion, but no infatuation. And never treachery, ingratitude, malice, or cruelty. I would not purchase the pleasure of this vice at any cost, but contented myself with its simple and proper price. A man must stop there: it hurts nobody but fools.

Conducted in this manner, I look on it as wholesome, and fit to enliven a heavy mind and body. As a physician I would prescribe it to a man of my temperament and condition, to rouse and preserve his years. While we are still at the suburbs of old age and the pulse still beats, we need to be nipped and tickled.

But may I say—without having my throat cut—that, in my belief, love is out of season except in youth. And beauty too. In maturity it is already somewhat dated, though not so much as in old age. Marguerite of Navarre, like a woman, extends its claim for her own sex, and rules that not until thirty need a woman cease to call herself beautiful, and begin to call herself good.

For me who have no other title left in these things except by hearsay, it is enough if our daughters retain me for counsel. I advise them then—and the men too—to be abstinent; but if the age won't permit it, to be modest and discreet. As Aristippus said when his pupils blushed to see him enter a house of ill fame: 'The vice lies not in going in, but in not coming out.' If a girl has no care for her conscience, she should still regard her reputation.

I commend them a gradation and delay in bestowing their favors. They more allure our desires by concealing their own. Like the Scythians, they conquer us more easily by running away.

We train our women from infancy to the enterprises of love. Their grace, dress, knowledge, talk, and education have chiefly this end. Their governesses impress on them nothing but the image of love, if only by continually dwelling on it to give them a distaste for it.

My daughter—the only child I have—is now of an age that riper girls are allowed to marry at. But she is of a slow, thin, namby-pamby disposition; and she has been brought up by her mother in this manner, so that she is just beginning to be weaned from her childish follies. One day, while I was present, she was reading aloud from a French book when she happened to meet the word *fouteau*—the name of a well-known tree.[1] Her governess stopped her rather roughly and made her skip the awkward step. I said nothing, in order not to disturb their rules, for I never meddle in these affairs of state: feminine government has its own mysterious course which we had best leave to itself. But if I am not mistaken, the talk of twenty lackies could not have so impressed her with the meaning and use of these forbidden syllables as the single reprimand of that good old woman.

Let our women drop a little of their ceremony, let them give rein to their talk, and compared to them we shall find ourselves children in this science. I chanced one day to be placed where, unobserved, I could overhear their talk; but how can I repeat it? *Notre Dame!* I exclaimed, we needs must study up the phrases of Amadis and the tales of Boccaccio in order to cut a clever figure in their eyes: a fine use of our time! There is not a word, an example, a manœuvre they don't know better than our books. It is a knowledge born in their veins. Nature, youth, health—excellent schoolteachers—breathe it into their souls. They do not need to learn love: they breed it.

That good man who, when I was young, clipped off so many noble and ancient statues in his city, in order that they might not corrupt the sight of the ladies, wasted his time so long as he did not geld horses, asses, and all nature.

Perhaps it was chaster to let them know the fact as it is, rather than let them guess according to the heat of their fancy. Through hope and desire they substitute others three times as extravagant. A friend of mine lost his cause by producing his at a time and place when he had no opportunity to put it to better use. And what mischief results from those prodigious pictures our boys

---

1. The beech: in French, the sound of the word resembles a common obscenity.

scrawl on the stairs and walls of our public buildings! They give the ladies a cruel contempt for our real furniture.

It is folly to bridle this sharp and natural desire in women. When I hear them brag of their maidenly desires and retiring will, I laugh at them. They retire too far. If they were a toothless old hag or a young dried-up consumptive it might have some semblance of truth—though not, even then, altogether believable. But those still in life and breath who talk that way overreach themselves. Their self-praise becomes an accusation. It reminds me of a neighbor of mine who was suspected of impotence. To clear himself of the charge he went about swearing, three or four days after he was married, that he had ridden twenty posts in a night. The oath, I might add, was used to prove his ignorance of the whole business and win his wife a divorce.

I am told that during our civil wars a girl in my neighborhood threw herself out of a window, in order to avoid being forced by a rascally soldier quartered in her house. She was not killed by the fall and, undeterred from her purpose, tried to cut her throat with a knife. Nevertheless, after she had wounded herself, she confessed that the soldier had done nothing worse than court her with solicitations and gifts. She told the tale with such eloquence, and stained as she was with blood, you would have thought her a second Lucrece. Yet I know in sober truth that, both before and after, she was not so difficult a piece. Don't therefore conclude that if your mistress repulses you, handsome and worthy as you may be, that she is a model of chastity: it does not mean that the gamekeeper won't have his hour.

Naturally I am speaking only of those who boast in all earnestness of their insensibility and coldness and who expect to be believed. To talk that way means nothing: there is neither virtue nor continence without desires. Of course, when they talk with their tongue in the cheek and their eyes belying their words, when they rattle on in obedience to mere convention which always goes against the real grain of things, it is good sport.

If we can't curb their imagination, what would we have from them? The literal fact? Yet there are plenty of them who avoid any outside contact by which their chastity might be damaged—'doing what is done without a witness'—and those we suspect least are, perhaps, to be feared for most. Their silent sins are the worst. There are other ways, too, of losing one's virginity without shame, or even knowledge. 'By accident or awkwardness,' says St. Augustine, 'a midwife in testing a girl's virginity may shatter it.' Some by seeking their maidenhead have lost it.

We can't, in fact, prescribe with precision the actions we wish to forbid them. The whole idea we have for their chastity is ridiculous. They would have to become numb and invisible to please us. I don't know whether the exploits of Alexander and Cæsar really surpass the resolution of a beautiful young woman, bred up in the light and commerce of our society, who still keeps herself whole. There is no doing so hard as not doing. I hold it easier to wear a suit of armour every day of one's life than a maidenhead.

It may be an honor to us in future ages that a learned author of our time—a Parisian at that—has taken great pains to persuade our ladies to embrace death rather than submit to the outrage of their chastity. I am sorry he never heard the remark of a woman—it was told me at Toulouse—who had passed through the handling of several soldiers. 'God be praised!' she said, 'that for once in my life I had my fill without sin.' In truth such cruelties are not worthy of the gentle air of France, which, thank heaven, has been entirely purged of them since our author gave his good advice. It is enough now, following the rule of the good Marot, that the women say 'No' in doing it.

To add one word more, I do not advise women to call their duty 'honor.' Duty is the core, honor the rind. Nor would I advise them to bring their honor in as an excuse for their refusal. I presume that their desires and intentions—in which honor is not concerned, since there is nothing to show for them—are even better regulated than their behavior. 'She who refuses only because it is forbidden to consent . . . consents.' It is as great an offence toward conscience to desire as to do a thing. Moreover, these actions are so private they can easily be kept from the knowledge of others—and that is where honor lies. A woman should respect duty and love chastity for itself. And an honorable woman will rather lose her honor than wound her conscience.

Besides the fear of God and the value of so rare a glory, the corruption of our age should make them watch out for themselves. If I were they, I'd do anything rather than trust my reputation to our dangerous hands. In my time, the pleasure of telling what we did (a pleasure only a little inferior to that of the deed itself) was confined to our closest and most faithful friend. But now the common table talk is largely boasts of favors received and the secret liberality of ladies.

Science treats of things with too much refinement. My page makes love and knows what he is doing. But read to him Leo Hebræus or Ficino where they speak of the actions and thoughts of love, and he can't make head or tail of it. I can't recognize most of my daily doings when they appear in Aristotle. They are decked out or hidden in another cloak for the benefit of schoolmen. God grant they are in the right, but if I were in that business I'd do as much to naturalize art as they do to artify nature.

Well then, leaving books aside and speaking simply and substantially, I find that love in general is nothing but a thirst for enjoying something we desire; and Venus in particular is the pleasure of discharging our glands, similar to the pleasure Nature gives us in other discharges—which become vicious through either immoderation or indiscretion.

And when I consider the absurd titillation of this pleasure; the brainless motions it excites; the boundless rage, the countenance inflamed with fury and cruelty during its sweetest effects; the grave, solemn, entranced air in an action downright silly; the promiscuous shuffling together of our delights and excrements; and that the supreme moment of pleasure is bathed, like pain, in sighing and fainting—I then believe, with Plato, that the gods made men for their sport.

On one side, Nature pushes us to it, having tied the most useful, pleasant, and noble of her functions to this desire. On the other hand, she allows us to accuse and avoid it as something indecent, something to blush at and banish by abstinence. But are we not beasts to call the work that begets us, beastly?

Perhaps we are right to blame ourselves for making so foolish a product as man, and to call the act of production and the parts employed in the act shameful (mine are now shameful—and pitiful—enough). Everyone, certainly, flees from seeing a man born, and everyone rushes to see him die. To destroy a man we use a large field in open daylight. But to make a man we sneak into as dark and secluded a corner as we can. It is indeed our duty to hide ourselves and blush while we are creating life; but it is the fountainhead of many virtues and a glory to know how to destroy what we have created.

What monstrous animal is this who is a horror to himself, whose delights are a torment, and who dotes on unhappiness! Fanatics who think they are honoring Nature by denaturing themselves, who value themselves on their self-contempt, and who propose to grow better by being worse—we are ingenious only in misusing ourselves.

Alas, poor man, you have enough troubles that are inevitable, without increasing them by your own inventions. You are miserable enough by nature without adding to it by art. You have plenty of real blemishes without forging imaginary ones. Do you think you are too much at ease unless half of your ease annoys you? Do you think you have not performed all your duties to Nature unless you have manufactured new ones?

Come! you don't stickle for a moment to break her universal laws; but you cling to your own fantastic rules by just so much as they are fantastic. The laws of your parish occupy and bind you: those of God and the world leave you cold. But run over a few examples of this cloth—your entire life is of them.

But isn't it a great impudence on my part to parade my shortcomings when I most desire to please? For the little I am able to do now, I need trouble no one whom I wish to honor. Nature should be content in making old age miserable, without rendering it absurd as well. For the sake of one inch of puny vigor that comes to it thrice a week, I hate to see it strut and plume itself as though it had a big day in the offing.

This parade belongs to the flower of youth. Don't trust it to support that fine flame you think is burning in you: it will desert you in the middle of the road. The man who can linger till dawn and not die for shame at beholding the disdainful eyes of his mistress, witness to his fumbling impertinence, such a man has never known the glory of cudgelling them till they are weary, with the exploits of one heroic night. When I found a woman vexed with me, I did not hasten to accuse her of trifling; but I have rather turned my doubts on Nature, who in all probability used me unkindly and to my hurt.

To conclude this flood of babble, I say that males and females are cast in the same mold; and, except for education and habits, the difference between them is not great. Plato invites both sexes to partake in all the vocations of his Republic, whether in war or peace. The philosopher Antisthenes rejected all distinctions between their virtue and ours. It is much easier to accuse one sex than excuse the other. The pot likes to call the kettle black.

CHAPTER VI

This Discreet Business of Marriage

N 1565 I married Françoise de la Chassaigne. I was thirty-three years of age, and approve of thirty-five, which is said to be the opinion of Aristotle. Plato enjoins no one to marry before thirty. He is right at laughing at those who undertake the work after fifty-five, and he condemns their offspring as unworthy of food and life.

Thales gave the truest limits when, being young and urged by his mother, he said, 'It is too soon'; and when, along in years and urged again, he replied, 'It is too late.'

Marriage is more suitable nowadays for plain and common people whom pleasures, curiosity, and idleness are not likely to divert from it. But spoiled natures, such as mine, that hate every sort of bond and obligation, are not as fit for it. Of my own free will I would not have married Wisdom herself, even if she'd have had me. But we strive against it in vain—custom and the usage of daily life overpower us.

Most of my actions are guided by example and not by choice. As usual, I did not go into marriage of my own inclination. I was led and drawn to it by outer circumstances. For there is nothing so disagreeable, nay, ugly, vicious, and hateful, that may not become acceptable through some circumstance or accident—so vain is all human behavior!

I was persuaded to it when I was more unprepared and less amenable than I am at present, now that I have tried it out. Yet, licentious as I am held to be, I have in truth observed the laws of marriage more strictly than I either promised or expected.

It is too late to kick when a man has once put on his fetters. He must prudently watch after his liberty; but after having submitted to an obligation he should confine himself within the laws of common duty—or at least try to.

Those who engage in this contract intending to act with hatred and contempt for it, do an improper and unjust thing. And that fine rule which I hear the women pass from hand to hand as a sacred oracle:

> *Serve your husband as a master*
> *But guard against him as a traitor*

—a war cry and a defy—is equally damaging and destructive.

I am too mild for such deep designs. To tell the truth I have not achieved that cleverness and that refinement of wit to confuse reason with injustice, or to laugh at all rule and order that does not please my palate. Because I hate superstition, I do not throw myself willy-nilly into irreligion. If a man does not always do his duty, he ought at least to love and acknowledge it. It is treachery to marry your bride without espousing her.

Whoever seeing me now cold and again very fond towards my wife believes one or the other to be counterfeit, is an ass.

You know well, my wife, that according to the rules of our time, it is not proper for a gallant man to court or caress you any longer. They say that a clever man may contrive to win a woman, but to marry her proves him a fool. Let them talk. For my part I hold to the simple fashion of days gone by. In truth, novelties have cost so dear to our poor land (and I do not know if we have yet paid the final bill) that I have altogether quit them. Let us live, my wife, you and I, in the good old French manner.

Married men, time being their own, ought never to attempt or hurry their initial enterprise, if they do not find themselves ready for it. If a man discovers himself to be agitated and on edge, it is better to give up outright any attempt at marital commerce and await a further occasion when he is less upset, rather than to make himself unhappy ever after, at being taken by surprise and baffled at the first assault.

Women are to blame who receive us with that disdainful, squeamish, and outraged air which, while it kindles us, snuffs us out. The daughter-in-law of Pythagoras rightly said that a woman who goes to bed with a man ought to take off her modesty along with her petticoat.

Perturbed by so many different alarms, the mind of the assailant is easily dismayed. Once imagination has brought this shame upon a man—and it does so only at the first assaults because they are more eager and ardent, and because at this first account a man gives of himself he is much more fearful of failure—and once having made a bad start, he enters into a rage and despite over the accident, which dogs him on subsequent occasions.

I am inclined to believe that those amusing spells[1] which occupy our age—we hardly talk of anything else—are nothing but the result of apprehension and fear. For I know of the case of someone for whom I can answer as for myself—a man that cannot possibly be suspected of weakness or of being bewitched. He heard of the extraordinary predicament of a friend; and when he found himself in a similar posture, the tale sprang into his mind so forcibly that he fell into the same mischance. And from that time forward, the scurvy recollection of his own disaster gained complete mastery over him and left him continually helpless. However, he contrived a cure for this trick of imagination, by another trick. He openly confessed and declared his infirmity

---

1. Magical knots, tied in a strip of leather, cotton, or silk, which were supposed to prevent the consummation of a marriage.

beforehand. This appeased his agitation; and by reconciling himself to failure, the restraint upon his powers diminished. Finally, when he had regained control of himself—his fears at rest, his mind free, and his body relaxed—he found enough composure to allow handling and communication, and so effected a cure.

Once a man succeeds with a woman, subsequent failure with her becomes impossible unless through genuine weakness. Neither is the disaster to be feared except in adventures where our mind is overexcited by desire or reverence, especially when the occasion is unforeseen and time presses—there is then no means of defence.

I have known those who come half-sated elsewhere, purposely to lessen the ardor of their desire—and others who, grown old, have rendered themselves more potent by reducing their ambitions. I know one man who found relief in being assured that a friend had provided him with a counter-charm sovereign for these mishaps. But I had better relate what happened.

A count of a very great family, with whom I was most intimate, was marrying a fair lady who had formerly been courted by one of the wedding guests. The count's friends were badly disturbed; but especially an old lady, his kinswoman, at whose house the festivities were held, and who told me her fears of possible sorcery.

I bade her rely on me. I assured her that I had with me, by chance, a certain little gold medal. It was engraved with celestial signs, and when placed on the head and tied by a ribbon beneath the chin, it was in fact supposedly good against sunstroke or headaches—altogether a piece of nonsense akin to what we are discussing. Jacques Peletier, while living at my house, happened to give me this curio.

I thought to make some use of it, and told the count he might perchance run the same ill luck as others before him, especially as there were guests present who would like nothing better. But I urged him to go boldly to bed. For I would do him a friendly turn, even to working a certain miracle that was in my power, provided he would promise on his honor to keep the matter to himself.

I told him to give me a sign if, when the guests brought him the customary midnight broth, he found that matters were not prospering; and leave the rest to me.

Now he had had his ears so battered and his mind so filled with the eternal tattle of this business that when he came to it, he found himself sure enough thwarted by his troubled imagination. Accordingly, at the appointed moment, he gave me the sign. I thereupon whispered in his ear that he should arise from bed under pretext of driving us from the room and playfully pull my nightrobe from my shoulders—we were about the same build— and throw it over his own, and keep it there until he had fulfilled my directions.

The directions were as follows: when we had all left the room, he should withdraw to make water; repeat three times certain words and actions; each time wind the ribbon I gave him around his waist, and place the medal attached to it in a certain position across his reins. This done, and having fastened the ribbon snugly, he should confidently return to his business—not forgetting to use my robe as a blanket for both of them.

These monkey tricks are essential to success. Our fancy cannot rid itself of the notion that since the means are strange, they must come from a profound science: their very inanity gives them weight and respect. And certain it is, the figures on my medal proved more venetian than solar, and in their effect more stimulative than preventative.

It was a sudden whimsy, tinged with curiosity, which made me do a thing so contrary to my nature. I am an enemy to every subtle, covert, and deceptive action; and I hate all manner of trickery, though it be in sport and for a good purpose—for while the action may be innocent, its method is vicious.

Till possession be taken, our husband should leisurely and by degrees make several little trials and light offers, without obstinately committing himself to an immediate conquest. Those who know their members to be naturally obedient need only guard themselves against an overwrought imagination.

We are right in remarking the untamed liberty of this member. He puffs himself up most importunately when we do not need him, and swoons away when our need is greatest—imperiously battling the authority of our will and remaining proudly obstinate to every coaxing of the mind or hand.

Though his rebellion furnishes the ground for general complaint and proof enough to convict him, yet if he hired me to plead his cause, I should perhaps be able to cast suspicion upon all his fellow members for plotting this mischief against him, out of pure envy at the importance and pleasure lodged in his employment. They have, I suspect, conspired to arm the whole world against him by wickedly charging him with their own common fault.

I leave you to judge whether there is any one part of our body which does not, on occasion, refuse to function at the nod of our will, and which does not as frequently go its own way in defiance of our command. How often does the involuntary twitch of our features reveal our inmost thoughts and betray us to the first bystander! Are those veins and muscles the only ones that swell and flag without our consent or knowledge? We do not order our hair to stand on end, nor our skin to shiver with fear or desire. Our hands often betake themselves where we have not directed them. Our tongue will grow tied and our voice frozen at their own pleasure. When we have nothing to eat, our hunger and thirst do not for all that remain inactive, any more than that other appetite of which we are speaking;

and when they see fit, they as readily and unseasonably desert us.

The vessels that serve to relieve the belly and kidneys have their own proper dilations and compressions without asking our leave. Saint Augustine, in order to bolster his argument for the sovereign authority of the will, claims to have seen a man who could command his rear to discharge when he pleased; and Vivès, his commentator, goes Saint Augustine one better with an example, taken from his own time, of a man who could break wind in tune. But these examples hardly prove the case—for is there any member more rowdy and indiscreet?

When it comes to examples, I myself know one so rude and ungoverned that for forty years it has led its master in one continuous explosion, and is like to do so until he die of it. And it is not only by hearsay, God help me, that I know how often a man's belly, for the lack of a single puff, brings us to the door of a painful death. I could heartily wish that the emperor who gave us leave to let fly as we will, had given us the power to do so.

As to our will, in whose behalf we bring this accusation, how much more reasonably might we reproach herself with rebellion and sedition. Does she always want what we want her to want? Doesn't she often want what we forbid her to want, and to our manifest hurt? Does she allow herself to be any more readily governed by our reason?

By way of conclusion I would move in behalf of the gentleman, my client, that in view of the fact that his case is inextricably bound up with that of an accomplice; that, furthermore, he is charged with accusations which in their nature can never be laid to this partner; that, moreover, the business of the partner is to invite—often most inopportunely—but never to refuse; that finally, the invitation has a way of coming secretly and covertly—that, in view of all this, we consider the malice and injustice of his accusers to be proved beyond doubt.

Be this how it will, Nature protests that the lawyers and judges argue and sentence in vain, and goes her own sweet way. And she does well if indeed she has granted exceptional privileges to our client: the author of the only immortal work of mortals, a divine work according to Socrates—no other than love, himself the desire of immortality and himself an immortal demon.

But let us proceed.

Alive, naked, and panting, Venus is not so beautiful as she is in Virgil:

> The goddess spoke, and throwing around him her snowy arms in soft embrace, caressed her hesitating mate; suddenly he caught the wonted flame, the familiar heat pierced his marrow, he gave her the desired embrace and in the bosom of his wife dissolved away.

My only complaint is that he has pictured her a little too passionate for a married Venus. In this discreet business the appetites are not usually so wanton—they are graver and duller.

Love hates us to bide by anything than itself. It goes to work faintly in familiarities born of another title, such as marriage. For marriage is ruled by reason as much as by charm and beauty, if not more so.

Men do not marry for themselves, whatever they may say. They marry as much or more for their posterity and house. The custom and profit of marriage concern our race much more than ourselves. Therefore I prefer to have a match arranged by a third hand, by another's choice rather than a man's own—yet how far is all this from the conventions of love!

It is a kind of incest to employ in this venerable and sacred alliance the heat and extravagance of amorous licence. A man, says Aristotle, must handle his wife with prudence, lest in tickling her too lasciviously, extreme pleasure makes her exceed the bounds of reason. What he says upon the account of conscience, physicians say for the sake of health: a pleasure excessively hot, voluptuous, and frequent, spoils the seed and hinders conception. On the other hand, they say that in order to supply a needed and fruitful heat to a languid coupling, such as this naturally is, a man must come to it but seldom and at considerable intervals.

The love we bear our wives is lawful enough, yet theology too thinks fit to restrain it. I think I once read in Saint Thomas Aquinas, where he condemns marriage within forbidden degrees, this reason among others: that there is danger of such an attachment becoming immoderate.

Theology and philosophy are bound to have their say in everything. There is no act so private and secret as to escape their inspection and jurisdiction. The best pupils are those who have learned how to apportion their liberties wisely—it is womenfolk who are ready to expose themselves freely for the sake of a bout, but who are reduced to shame before a physician.

I would like, then, in behalf of these sciences, to teach husbands who are too vehement—if such there still be—that the very pleasures they enjoy in the company of their wives are reproachable if immoderate, and that an abuse of them is as reprehensible in marriage as out of it. Those shameless tricks that the first heat suggests to us in this game are not only indecently but injuriously practiced on our wives. At least let them learn impudence from another hand. They are, as it is, ever ready enough for our business. And I, for my part, always went the plain way to work.

Our poet, Virgil, describes a marriage blessed with concord and contentment, and yet not overloyal. Does he mean to imply that a woman may yield to the impulse of love, and still in some sort respect the duties of marriage? A servant, we know, may cheat his master without hating him. Beauty, opportunity, and destiny—for destiny likewise has a hand in it—may draw her to a stranger, though not so far that she will lose every bond holding her to her husband.

I am vexed to see husbands hate their wives only because they themselves do wrong. At all events we should not, I think, love them less for our own faults. Compassion and repentance should render them more dear to us.

Women are not to blame when they reject the rules of life introduced into society, for it is men who have made them without their consent. There is naturally contention and brawling between them and us in any case, and even the closest understanding we have with them is riotous and stormy enough.

We deal inconsiderately with them in view of our knowledge that they are, beyond comparison, more able and ardent than we in the practice of love—when, indeed, we may learn this from their own mouths. Take an emperor and empress of Rome, both renowned for their ability in this business. In one night he deflowered ten Sarmatian virgins. But during the same space, she engaged in five-and-twenty bouts—'stopping tired but not satisfied.' Or, again, the Queen of Aragon. When a woman complained of her husband's overfrequent addresses—less, I think, because she was inconvenienced by them (for I believe in no miracles outside of religion) than to curb the authority of men—the good Queen ruled six times a day to be a proper and necessary stint, disregarding, as she said, much of the needs and desires of her sex in order to establish an easy and therefore a permanent standard. At which the doctors cry out: what an appetite is this which, when it claims to be moderate and virtuous, demands such a price! Yet knowing and accepting all this, we proceed to allot continence as the woman's particular share of the bargain— and upon the direst penalties.

No other passion is so hard to combat; yet we want them alone to resist it, not merely as an ordinary vice, but as a hateful abomination worse than irreligion and parricide—while we, in the meantime, go to it without stain or reproach.

We want them to be at once healthy, plump, high fed, and yet chaste: that is to say, both hot and cold. For marriage, which we tell them will keep them from burning, is but a slight refreshment as we order the matter. If they take a husband whose vigor is still boiling, he will glory in sharing it elsewhere. If, on the other hand, they take a worn-out fellow, they are worse off, though married, than either maids or widows. We think them well provided because they have a man to lie with; but, on the contrary, we have only sharpened their need—for touch and companionship inflame desires that would remain quieter in solitude.

In brief, we allure and flesh them in all sorts of ways. We incessantly heat and incite their imagination. And then we find fault.

Let us confess the truth: there is hardly one of us who is not more afraid of being shamed by his wife's lapses than his own; who is not more solicitous (a wonderful charity!) in matters of conscience for his good woman than for himself; who had not rather commit theft and sacrilege, and his wife murder and heresy, than not have her more chaste than her husband. What an unjust scale of vices! Both we and they are capable of a thousand corruptions more damaging and unnatural than lust. But we weigh and grade our vices not according to their nature, but according to our interests.

Our exasperation at unfaithfulness springs from the vainest and most turbulent disease that besets the human mind—jealousy. She and envy, her sister, seem to me the most foolish of the troupe. As to the latter, I can say little about it. The former I know by sight, and that is all.

We have increased the fever of this disease through the influence of barbaric nations. Better disciplined peoples have been touched by it—reasonably so—but not carried away. Lucullus, Cæsar, Pompey, Antony, Cato, and other good men were cuckolds and knew it, without making a fuss. In those days there was only one idiot, Lepidus, who died of grief from it,

In judging, let us agree that the heart of the matter lies in the intent. Husbands have suffered cuckoldom without reproach or ill will towards their wives, but with great obligation and praise. I know men who have willingly acquired both profit and advancement from cuckoldom, the bare name of which frightens so many people. Do we not every day see women among us who surrender themselves for their husband's benefit and by his express command and arrangement—as Galba ordered it out of pure politeness? Entertaining Mæcenus at supper and noticing that his wife and the guest began to exchange nods and winks, he let himself sink back upon his cushions, as though in deep sleep, to lend countenance to their desires. With good grace he confessed as much when a servant made bold to remove a dish from the table. 'What, you rogue!' he frankly exclaimed, 'don't you see that I sleep only for Mæcenus?'

Curiosity is always bad, but here it is pernicious. It is folly to pry into a disease which every medicine inflames and aggravates, the shame of which grows greater and more public through jealousy, and of which the revenge wounds our children more than it heals ourselves. Those in my day who have learned the truth, how miserably have they achieved their knowledge! If the tattler cannot at the same time bring relief and apply a cure, he better deserves a dagger thrust than a denial.

We laugh as readily at the man who tries to prevent being a cuckold as we do at him who is one and doesn't know it. It serves no purpose to drag our private misfortunes out of obscurity and tragically parade them on the public block—misfortunes which hurt us only when they are known. For we call a wife good and a marriage happy not because they are, but because no one says to the contrary.

Men should be discreet enough to avoid this annoying and useless knowledge. The Romans had a custom, when returning from a voyage, to send someone on ahead to alert the wives of their arrival.

But the world will continue to wag its tongue. I know a hundred decent men who are cuckolds, but who are not regarded the less for it. A worthy man is not scorned, but pitied. Therefore, so order it that your virtue may smother your misfortune, that good men will curse its occurrence, and that the wrongdoer will tremble but to think of it.

Moreover, who escapes being talked about, from the least to the greatest of us? You hear how many good men are reproached with it in your presence—do not think that you, either, are being spared behind your back. Nay, the very ladies, they are laughing too. And what are they so apt to mock at, in this virtuous age of ours, but a peaceful and well-ordered marriage?

There is no man among you who has not made a cuckold of somebody else: and Nature is all for parallels, compensation, and tit for tat. The frequency of this accident ought long since to have softened its sting. It has almost become a custom.

A miserable accident which, what is more, must remain untold! For where is the friend to whom you dare unfold your grief, who will not laugh at it, or else make use of the occasion to get his own share of the quarry? The bitters as well as the sweets of marriage are kept secret by the wise. The custom which has rendered it indecent and harmful to tell others all that a man knows and feels—this is the chief of its inconveniences to a talkative fellow like myself.

It is a waste of time to give women the same counsel against jealousy. Their very being is so composed of suspicion, vanity, and curiosity that no legitimate cure can be expected. They often, it is true, recover by a form of health more to be feared than the disease itself—they shake off the fever by transferring it to their husband. Yet I know not if a man can suffer worse than from his wife's jealousy. It is a mischief that has no remedy but flight or patience—both very hard. It was, I think, a wise man who said that a blind wife and a deaf husband make a happy marriage.

Let us also consider whether the heavy duty we lay upon women does not produce two results contrary to our intention—that is to say, whether it does not tender the pursuers more eager to attack and the women more liable to yield. As to the first point, by increasing the worth of the prize, we sharpen the desire for conquest. Perhaps it is Venus herself who has cunningly raised the value of her wares by using our laws as pimps. In short, as the host of Flaminius said, it is all pork seasoned and varied by sauces. As to the second point, wouldn't we be cuckolds less frequently if we less feared to be—considering the nature of women, whom prohibitions incite and render more eager?

We almost always judge their actions as unjustly as they do ours. I confess the truth as readily when it tells against me as when it is on my side. It is, after all, a rascally intemperance that drives them on to a change, and will not let them limit their affection to any one person, no matter who he may be. Moreover, it is contrary to the nature of love not to be violent, and to the nature of violence not to be fickle. It would, perhaps, be stranger to see this passion constant. For it is not merely a physical passion: and if avarice and ambition have no bounds, there is doubtless none to lechery.

Women may plead as well as we to the love of variety and novelty, common to us both. But, further, they may plead—as we cannot—that they buy a pig in a poke; that more effort is required to do something than merely to submit to having something done; that they, for their part, are always provided with the necessity, whereas we are often not; and, finally, that when they come to try us out, they might not find us worthy of their choice. It is not enough that a husband's intentions be good. Therefore inconstancy is, after a fashion, more pardonable in them than in us.

Experience has taught us to rank the virtue of housekeeping above all others in married women. I put my wife to it, as her own concern, leaving her during my absence the entire government of my affairs. It is the most useful and honorable occupation for the mother of a family. Nevertheless, though I have seen many an avaricious woman, I have seldom known a good manager. It is the supreme quality a man should seek in a wife—the only dowry that can ruin or preserve our houses.

In several families of my acquaintance, I am vexed to see Monsieur come home around noontime, all jaded and ruffled over his affairs, while Madame is still prinking and combing herself in her boudoir. This is a business for queens, and that too is a question. It is ridiculous and unjust to maintain the idleness of our wives by our sweat and labor. No one, so far as I can help it, shall have a cleaner, quieter, and freer enjoyment of his estate than I. If the husband supplies the matter, Nature herself demands that the wife provide the form.

Yet women are ever prone to vex their husbands. No hand in the management of affairs seems to be of dignity enough if it comes from his assent. They must usurp it by insolence or cunning and always harmfully, or else it has not the grace and authority they desire.

The first excuse that comes to hand serves them for a complete justification. I know one woman who robbed her husband wholesale in order, as she told her confessor, to distribute alms more liberally. That religious liberality—you believe it! And when it is against a poor old man and for their children, they seize upon this pretence and make it serve their passion gloriously.

Even if I am not aware of being cheated, I cannot fail to see that I am very fit for it. Can a man ever overpraise the value of a friend in comparison with these legal unions? The mere shadow of friendship which I see in the simplicity of animals, how devoutly I respect it!

If others trick me, at least I do not trick myself into believing that I can defend myself against them, or in cudgelling my brains to that purpose. I guard against such treasons in my own home, not by restless prying and disturbance, but rather by diverting and fortifying myself.

I think it of poor advantage to a man whose affairs are in good shape, to seek a wife who will burden him with a large dowry. There is no obligation which will bring greater ruin to a family than this. My predecessors have always been on the alert against this danger, and so have I.

But those who dissuade us from rich wives for fear they will prove less grateful and manageable, are ill-advised in making a man forgo a palpable gain for a possible loss. It costs no more for an unreasonable woman to disregard a good reason as a bad. In fact she thinks better of herself when she is most in the wrong. The richer women are, the more they are apt to be good-natured—just as the more beautiful they are, the easier they can glory in being chaste.

I find that women are seldom born fit to govern men, except in their natural and maternal capacities—unless it be as a punishment for those men who, out of their minds with love, have deliberately subjected themselves to the sex. But this does not concern women along in years, of whom we are now speaking.

It is dangerous to leave to their judgment the distribution of our estate. Their choice of heirs is often fantastic and unjust. For they never entirely rid themselves of the eccentric appetites and unhealthy tastes they acquired when childbearing. We commonly see them dote on the weakest and most rickety of their children, or on those, if they have such, that are still hanging about their neck. Because they lack the strength of mind to choose the worthiest, they allow themselves to be carried away by the mere impressions of nature—like animals which recognize their young only as long as they are giving them suck.

It is easy to see from experience that this natural affection, to which we give so much authority, has very feeble roots. For a pittance, mothers allow us every day to tear their children from their arms and put our own in their place. And most of them show a greater solicitude for their foster children than for their own. It is common, all about where I live, to see the country women, when they want milk for their children, to call in goats to help them out. Two of my menservants never sucked their mother's milk more than a week after they were born.

It is, to be sure, reasonable to leave the administration of an estate to a mother, until the children grow of legal age to manage it. But the father has brought them up badly if he cannot hope that, coming to maturity, they will not show more wisdom and ability than his wife. On the other hand, it is unnatural to make a mother dependent on her children. She ought to be well provided for, enough to maintain herself according to her age and rank—since it is harder and more unbecoming for her to endure poverty than for them. The son should be cut short rather than the mother.

We have thought to tie the nuptial knot more firmly by removing all means of dissolving it. But the knot of our will and affection is loosened by just so much as the constraint is tightened. On the contrary, Roman marriages were kept in honor and inviolate by the liberty given to break them. The Romans held close to their wives because they could part with them when they pleased. With divorce completely free, five hundred years and more elapsed before anyone made use of it.

Good women do not come by the dozen, as everyone knows, and especially in marriage. It is a bargain full of so many thorny circumstances that it is difficult for a woman's will to endure the restraint of it for long. Men, though their terms in the deal be somewhat better, have it hard enough to stick it out. Time alone is the true touchstone and test of a happy marriage, of whether it has been uniformly gentle, loyal, and pleasant.

In our century women usually postpone the display of their affection and good works toward their husband until after they have lost him, or at least defer until then the outward proof of their goodwill—a bit too late and out of season! They prove, rather, that they only love him dead. Our life is laden with scolding; and our death, with love and courtesies. As fathers hide their affection for their children, so wives out of modest respect conceal their love for their husbands.

This mystery is not to my taste. In vain they scratch their cheeks and tear their hair. I whisper in the ear of a chambermaid or secretary, 'How were they, how did they live together?' I always remember that wise saying: 'They make most ado who are least moved.'

Their whimpering is offensive to the living and useless to the dead. We will gladly give them leave to laugh at us after we are dead, provided they will smile on us while we are alive. Isn't it enough to bring a man to life again out of pure spite, to see the woman who spat in my face when I was here, kiss my feet when I am gone? Let those who wept when their husbands were alive, laugh when they are dead—and laugh openly as well as to themselves.

Therefore pay no heed to those blubbered eyes and that pitiful voice. Look rather at her bearing, her complexion, the plumpness of her cheeks under all those thick veils—it is there she talks plain French. Few there are who do not improve their health in widowhood, and health is a quality that cannot lie. That ceremonious face looks not so much backward as on ahead—it is an advance payment on a new purchase rather than the settlement of an old debt.

When I was a youth, a beautiful and virtuous lady, who is still alive, wore somewhat more ornament on her dress than our laws of widowhood allow. Being reproached for it, she answered that she had resolved never to mate or marry again.

In a district near our mountains, the women play Father Martin: that is to say, both priest and clerk. They swell the grief for their departed husband by recalling his good and pleasing traits, but at the same time they note and publish all his faults—as though to compensate themselves for their sorrow. Yet this is done with nicer grace than we who when we lose a mere acquaintance, shower him with false praises: as if regret were enlightening, or as if tears by washing our eyes could clear our minds.

For my part, I here and now renounce all favorable report men might give me not for my merits, but simply for being dead.

I see no marriages fail sooner than those based on beauty and amorous desires. More solid and durable foundations are necessary, and greater precautions. A boiling dashing ardor is worthless.

Love and marriage are two goals approached by different and distinct paths. A woman may yield to a man she would by no means marry. Few men have married their mistresses without repenting of it. It is, as the proverb runs, to befoul your basket and then clap it on your head. In my time I have seen love, in a good family, shamefully and dishonestly cured by marriage. The considerations are too far apart.

Though the goals are different, they are in a sense compatible. Marriage has utility, justice, honor, and constancy for its share— a dull but uniform pleasure. Love builds itself wholly upon pleasure, and provides it too in a keener, livelier, and sharper degree. The bounty of women is too profuse in marriage, and blunts the edge of affection and desire.

Marriage is a solemn and religious tie; and therefore the pleasure we take from it should be restrained, serious, and seasoned with a certain gravity. It should be a sort of conscientious delight.

A good marriage—if there be any—rejects the company and conditions of love and seeks to reproduce those of friendship. It is a sweet companionship of life, full of constancy, trust, and an infinite number of useful and solid services and mutual obligations. No woman who has once savored its taste would wish to live as the mistress of her husband. When he raises a cry elsewhere and passionately pursues his game, let anyone but ask him, on whom he would rather a disgrace should fall, his wife or his mistress, which of their misfortunes would afflict him most, and for whom he desires the higher station—and the answer is beyond dispute in a sound marriage.

That few are observed to be happy is a token of its value and price. If well formed and rightly taken, there is not a finer estate in human society. Though we cannot live without it, yet we do nothing but decry it. We see the same with birdcages: the birds outside despair to get in and those within despair to get out.

CHAPTER VII

The Servitude of Courts

AM NO BORN ENEMY of court life. I have passed a good part of my own in it, and cheerfully frequent great assemblies provided it be at intervals and my own time. But at the Louvre and in the bustle of the court I press and shrink within my own skin. The crowd thrusts me upon myself.

Had I a mind to become rich, I would have served my kings—the most profitable traffic of all. But I never received any token of their liberality—indeed I neither asked nor merited it—or any pay for the steps I took in their service. I would not spare my purse where I should not spare my life. Princes give me a great deal when they take nothing from me, and do me good if they do me no harm: that is all I ask of them.

In my youth I was plunged to the ears in the business, and succeeded well enough. But I disengaged myself in good time. Since then, I have often avoided meddling in it when I feel the smoke of ambition rising in me; and I have rarely accepted and never solicited a commission.

In the little business I have managed between our princes, I have studiously avoided that they be deceived by me, or that they muffle themselves in my mask. I not only hate to deceive, but to have anyone else use me for deceiving another. I will never furnish the material or occasion for such a course.

Not that I wish to strip deceit of its laurels. That would show an ignorance of the world: for I know that deceit often renders a profitable service, and maintains and nourishes most of our trades and occupations.

Your professional diplomats go heavily cloaked and pretend to be, as nearly as they can, of the same mind as those they deal with. As for me, I disclose my frankest opinions and reveal myself in my own shape—a tender novice of a negotiator, who would rather fail in the affair than fail toward myself.

Yet so far I have had enough good luck (fortune doubtless deserves most of the credit) that few have succeeded better in dealing with one and the other of the two parties with less suspicion and more favor and intimacy.

I have a free and open way that easily ingratiates itself and makes men believe me at our first acquaintance. Truth and sincerity pass for cash in any age. Besides, the frank tone of a man who has no interest of his own at stake is never questioned or disliked. My frankness has likewise cleared me of any suspicion of dissembling by its very vigor, for I have left nothing unsaid however deep it bit and stung (I could have told nothing worse behind their backs); as well as my evident nonchalance and simplicity. I sought no other reward from my actions than to get the thing done. I added to it no long arguments and embellishments. Every action plays its own game for its own end, and gains it if it can.

As for the rest, I am not swayed by any passion towards the great, either of love or hatred; nor have I been throttled by any personal obligation or injury. I look upon our kings with simply a loyal and respectful affection, neither prompted nor restrained by my own interests; and I like myself for it.

I say nothing to one I would not, upon the proper occasion, say to the other with a slight change of accent. I cannot permit myself, under any consideration, to tell a lie. What is entrusted to my secrecy I religiously conceal, but I accept as few such trusts as

I can. The secrets of princes are a troublesome burden to those who have no personal interest in them.

I present them with this bargain: let them confide little to me, but rely on all I confide to them. I have always known more than I desired. Your own open speech opens the speech of others: it draws them out like wine or love.

When King Lysimachus asked Phillipides what he should give him of all his royal possessions, Phillipides was wise in answering, 'What you will, but none of your secrets.' I see everyone displeased if the bottom of an affair in which he is employed is not revealed to him. I am satisfied to know no more of the business than what I am entrusted to negotiate. If I must serve as an instrument of deceit, at least let it be with a safe conscience. I will not be reputed a servant so devoted and loyal I can be relied on to betray anyone.

But there are princes who do not accept men by halves, and refuse limited and conditional services. I cannot help it: I tell them how far I will go. A slave I will not be, except to reason— and even that is hard.

All this procedure is out of harmony with the current form. It would produce neither great nor lasting effects. Innocence personified could not, in this age of ours, negotiate without dissimulation, or traffic without lying. In all government there are necessary tasks which are not only abject, but vicious. They may be excusable because they are useful to us; but let us consign them to such citizens as will sacrifice their honor and conscience for the good of the country, as others sacrifice their lives. Public welfare requires that men betray, lie, and massacre: we will leave these commissions to men who are more obedient and supple.

I don't know what advantage men pretend to get by eternally counterfeiting, except not to be believed when they speak the truth. To brag, as some of our princes have done, that they would burn their shirt if it knew their real intentions, and that the man who can't dissemble doesn't know how to rule, is simply to give warning to all who have dealings with them.

I served at one time as mediator between the King of Navarre and the Duke of Guise when the two were at the Court. As to religion, of which both of them made a parade, it was a handsome pretext to keep the loyalty of their followers; but, as a matter of fact, neither of them was touched by it. Nothing but the fear of being abandoned by the Protestants prevented the King of Navarre from returning to the faith of his fathers. And the Duke would not have shied at the Confession of Augsburg—for which his uncle, the Cardinal of Lorraine, had given him a relish—if he could have followed it without damage to his interests. Such were the sentiments of these princes when I had to deal with them.

For my part, I would rather be a nuisance than a flatterer. I agree that something of pride and obstinacy makes me as forthright and open as I am—using the same liberty of speech and air towards the great as I bring with me from my own house. Sometimes I think I am a little too free.

But, in addition to my upbringing, I haven't a quick enough wit to evade a sudden question. Nor enough invention to improvise a lie. Nor enough memory to retain what I have improvised. Nor assurance enough to carry it off. So I am compelled to fall back on candor, to resign myself to speaking as I think, and leave the outcome to fortune.

Those who usually claim, in rebuttal, that what I call freedom and simplicity in my manners are really art and subtlety, and good sense rather than good luck, do me more honor than disgrace. But they make my cunningness a trifle too cunning.

I am sometimes asked what I should have thought myself fit for, had anyone undertaken to make use of me in my younger days. For nothing, I reply. And I am glad to profess my uselessness if it will save me from enslaving myself to a master.

But I would have told the truth to that master and king. I would have regulated his manners—if he had let me—not by scholastic lessons, which I don't understand, but by leisurely observing his ways and judging them one by one with my own eyes. And I would have given him to understand what common opinion thought of him, in contrast to what his flatterers thought. There is none of us who would not be worse than kings if we were infested, as they are, with this vermin.

To divert a young prince from revenge not long ago, I didn't tell him to turn the other cheek, or set about preaching to him the terrible consequences of this sweet passion. But I busied myself making him relish the beauty of the contrary course. By picturing to him the honor and esteem he would reap through a show of clemency and good nature, I won him over to another ambition. Thus is a man to deal in such cases.

My office would be a nameless one, or else it would lose its effect. And it could not be filled by everybody. It often happens that a man whispers something into the ear of a prince not only to no purpose, but unwisely. A virtuous rebuke can sometimes be viciously applied.

Yet a king is not to be believed when he boasts of his sturdiness in withstanding the charge of an enemy's onslaught, if he can't stand the liberty of a friend's advice—which has no other power but to pinch his ear. No man lives in greater need of advice: yet the men he favors most have commonly more regard for themselves than for him. They do well to look to themselves, for most services of friendship to a monarch run a rude and dangerous risk. That business requires not only freedom and affection, but courage.

I know how to speak only in plain earnest. I am totally lacking in that facility, which so many of my friends possess, to amuse the ear of a prince with all sorts of tattle. Princes don't enjoy serious talk, and I don't enjoy telling stories.

We owe loyalty and obedience to our kings, good or bad alike; for that is due their position. But as to esteem and love, these are only due their virtue. Let us aid them while their authority needs our support; but the relation of subject and prince brought to an end, there is no reason why we shouldn't express our real opinions on justice and liberty.

Since crowns and office are conferred more by fortune than merit, we are often wrong in condemning a king when these are misplaced. On the contrary, it is a wonder they have so much luck where there is so little skill. The secret is that most business gets done by itself. I was once deeply impressed by the grandeur of an enterprise of state; but when I made myself acquainted with the motives and skill of those who carried it out, I found very ordinary brains at work. The commonest methods are probably the best for accomplishing anything, though not for making a show of it. To maintain the authority of kings, it is wise that the plain man sees no farther than the outermost fence. When I have been consulted in an enterprise, I have sized it up by and large, and left the stress and main drive of the business to Heaven. For our wisdom itself, if you come to examine it, is mostly the child of chance.

Yet the hardest trade in the world is that of a king. I overlook their mistakes more readily than most men, in consideration of the intolerable weight of their task, which astounds me. But their good qualities are dead and lost, for they can be perceived only by comparison; and this we won't allow. Their ears are so deafened with approbation, they have little knowledge of true praise. We soothe and authorize their defects not only by applause, but imitation. Hernia has served to bring a courtier to favor, and I have seen deafness assumed; and what is more, debauchery, disloyalty, cruelty, superstition, effeminacy have been made fashions—and worse, if worse there be.

In truth, to see our king sit all alone at table, surrounded by a swarm of courtiers prating at him and a mob of strangers staring at him eat, I have often been moved to pity rather than envy. King Alfonso said that in this respect the asses of his kingdom were better off than he, for they could feed at their own ease and pleasure. And it has never struck my fancy that it could be of any great benefit to a man of sense to have twenty people babbling at him while he sat at stool.

The Emperor Maximilian had a humor quite contrary to that of other princes, who for the despatch of their most important affairs convert their closestool into a throne of state. He permitted no one to see him in that posture, and stole aside to make water as scrupulously as any virgin. I myself, who have an impudent way of talking, am naturally so modest in this respect that, unless it is a case of necessity or pleasure, I hardly ever communicate to another the sight of those parts and actions custom bids us conceal: I suffer from it more constraint that I think befits a man, especially one of my opinions. Maximilian, I may say, carried his modesty to the point of ordering in his will that he should be put in underdrawers as soon as he was dead. One thing was lacking: he omitted to add that those who pulled on the drawers should be blindfolded.

The advantages of kingship are imaginary: every human lot has in it some degree of princeliness. To speak the truth, our laws are easy enough, so easy that a gentleman of France hardly feels the pinch of monarchy above twice in his life. Real subjection comes to those among us who deliberately thrust their neck in the yoke. A man who loves his own fireside and can govern his house without falling about the ears of his neighbor or running into lawsuits, is as free as the doge in Venice.

I have picked up boys from begging and taken them into my service, who soon after left my kitchen and livery to return to their former mode of life. I found one of them, some while after, gathering mussels for his dinner; and neither entreaties nor threats could dissuade him from the sweetness he found in beggary. Beggars have their magnificences and delights as well as the rich; and, it is said, their titles and political orders.

Those who preach to kings a vigilant distrust under color of preaching them security, preach their disorder and ruin. Nothing notable can be performed without danger. I know one prince [Henri III?], a man of martial and enterprising courage, whose good fortune is continually marred through such persuasions: that he keep himself tightly guarded by his friends, that he listen to no reconciliation with his enemies, that he trust himself in no hands stronger than his own, no matter what promises are made him or what advantages he could reap. And I know another prince [Henri of Navarre?] who has unexpectedly advanced his fortune by following precisely the opposite course.

This prince once described himself to me in the following terms: that he foresees the trend of events as well as anyone; when there is no remedy for it, he resolves himself to suffer the outcome; when something can be done, he does it with all the wit and energy at his command and then sits back and waits. In truth, I have seen him maintain his freedom and poise in very difficult crises; and I find him much greater in adversity than prosperity—his defeats are more glorious than his victories, and he is more of a man in mourning his disasters than celebrating his triumphs.

Never was a time or place more favorable than today for a prince to reap a surer and greater reward for virtue. The first who will make it his business to push himself into esteem by this means will, unless I am mistaken, outstrip all his rivals. Force and violence can do something, but not always. We see merchants, artisans, and village magistrates go cheek by jowl with the highest nobility when it comes to military valor. On this score the renown of a prince is lost in the crowd. But let him try to shine in humanity, truth, loyalty, temperance, and especially justice—he will have little competition. He can do his business only through the goodwill of the people; and that can be won by no other qualities but these, which alone are of solid use to them.

Our kings can do what they please in external reformations at least. Their private taste becomes public law. Whatever is done in court passes for an ordinance in the rest of France. I wish, therefore, that our courtiers would develop a little distaste for those abominable breeches which reveal so much of the parts we wish to conceal; those great-bellied doublets which make us look like someone else and which are a nuisance when it comes to arming one's self; those long effeminate locks of hair and that foolish custom of kissing the lips and hands. Let them make it unseemly for a gentleman to appear in a courtly hall unbuttoned, untrussed, and without his sword at his side, as though he had just come from the privy. And contrary to the custom of our fathers that we must remain standing bareheaded before royalty, no matter where it be—and not only before royalty, but before all those thirdlets and quarterlets of kings we've got nowadays— as well as other similar novelties and degenerate manners. These are, it is true, only superficial defects; but they are omens of ill. When we see the plaster flake and split, we are warned that the whole structure is shaky.

Peoples who are bred up in liberty and to govern themselves, look upon all other forms of government as monstrous and unnatural. Those who are accustomed to monarchy do the same—though I think that popular government is the most equitable and natural of all; and when even with the greatest grievance and difficulty they have rid themselves of a troublesome king they proceed to create and accept another, for they are unable to hate servitude in itself.

We all behave in this way, for custom hides from us the true aspect of things. The very mask of grandeur represented on the stage in some sort moves and gulls us. What I myself adore in kings is the crowd of their adorers. All reverence and submission is due them, except that of the understanding. My reason is not obliged to bow and scrape: that is for my knees.

The virtue employed in affairs of state is a virtue of many pleats, corners, and elbows, so as to fit itself to human frailty. I tried to apply in these affairs rules and manners as rough hewn, fresh, and unpolluted as they were born and bred in me, and as I use in my own business. But I found them unsuitable and dangerous. He who joins a crowd must now go one way and then another, keep his elbows in, and duck and dodge in the shock of encounter. He must live not according to his own methods and what he proposes to himself, but according to the methods of others and what is proposed by time, men, and occasions.

Plato says that whoever escapes from the world's handling with clean breeches escapes by a miracle.

I find that if I had to apply myself wholly to such employments, I would need much remodelling before I would fit. With time and diligence I might accomplish the feat, but I do not wish to. The taste I had of it has by so much disgusted me. Laziness and love of liberty—my predominant traits—are diametrically opposed to that trade.

The best qualities I have would be useless in this age. My easy manners would be considered weakness and cowardice; my faith and conscience, superstition and finickiness. My frankness would be found annoying, inconsiderate, and rash.

But ill luck is good for something. It is not bad to be born in a depraved age: you will get a reputation for virtue at a bargain price. In our day, if you are only a parricide and blasphemer you are an honest and honorable man. By this standard I would be great and rare, just as I see myself vulgar and pigmy by the standard of some previous ages when—if nothing better concurred—it was not altogether uncommon to find a man moderate in his revenges, true to his word, neither slippery nor double-dealing, nor bending his beliefs to the will of others or the current of the times.

I am resolved to let the world of affairs break its neck rather than twist my faith to serve it.

CHAPTER VIII

My House on the Hill

EING LONG OUT OF PATIENCE with public duties and the servitude of the court, I retired to my own house in the year 1571, when I was thirty-eight and still in good health. I planned to pass in peace and security the days that remained before me in this sweet paternal abode, and consecrate it to my independence, quiet, and leisure.

I did not flee from men, but affairs. We have lived long enough for others: let us live the rest for ourselves. Since God has given us the leisure to order our departure, let us make ready, rope up our baggage, take leave of the company, and disentangle ourselves from the clutch of things which hold us elsewhere and keep us from ourselves. The greatest thing in the world is to know how to belong to yourself.

If you plan to withdraw into yourself, first prepare yourself a welcome. It is folly to trust yourself in your own hands if they cannot hold you. A man can fail in solitude as in society.

Yet, to anticipate misfortune, to do without the conveniences we still have, to lie on a hard bed, to throw our money in the river, to put out our eyes and wallow in discomfort—as religious men have done out of fervor and philosophers out of logic—this is to be overvirtuous.

A great deal less serves my turn. It is enough for me while I am in the good graces of Fortune to prepare my mind for the day I shall fall out of them; and, being at ease, to picture as far as my imagination can the ills to come. When I see a beggar at my door—often in better health and spirits than I am—I put myself in his shoes and try to dress my mind to his shape. And while I imagine poverty, disease, contempt, and death treading on my heels I resolve not to be frightened, since a lesser man than I accepts them with patience. I am not willing to believe that a weaker mind can do more than a stronger. And knowing how uncertain our comforts are, I never forget in the height of my enjoyment to make it my chief prayer to God that He render me content with what I have.

Wiser folks, possessed of great vigor of soul, can forge themselves a retreat altogether of the spirit. But I who have an ordinary soul must support myself with creature comforts. I do not think the philosopher Arcesilaus less virtuous for dining off gold and silver plate while he had it: I would have thought worse of him if he had denied himself the wealth he used with modesty and liberality. We ought to hold on, tooth and nail, to the pleasures of life, which the years snatch one after another from us.

My house is perched on a little hill, as its name indicates. Standing in a sweet and healthy air, it is sufficiently furnished and more than sufficiently large—royalty has more than once lodged there with all its train.

In 1584 the entire court was on my hands. The King of Navarre visited me at Montaigne, where he had never been before. For two days my people served him without the aid of any of his servants. He permitted no precautionary trial to be made of the food or the table appointments, and he slept in my own bed. The Prince of Condé, Messieurs de Rohan, de Touraine, de Béthune, de Haraucourt, the lieutenant of the company of the prince, his esquire, and about thirty-seven other gentlemen—besides the footmen, pages, and guards—were all lodged in my quarters. About as many more slept in the villages. On their departure I let loose a stag in my forest, which led His Majesty a two days' chase.

The employments a man should choose for a life of retirement should be neither hard nor displeasing; otherwise, there is no point in it. I have no fondness for husbandry—though gardening is pardonable; and those who have, should indulge it with moderation.

I was born and raised in the country and among farm laborers. I have had the business and management of an estate in my hands ever since my predecessors, who were lords of the land I now enjoy, left me their heir. Yet I cannot reckon up a column of figures either in my head or with a pen. I don't know the greater part of our common coins. I can't recognize the difference, unless it is very striking, between one grain and another, either in the fields or barn; and I can hardly distinguish cabbage from lettuce in my garden.

I do not so much as know the names of ordinary household utensils, nor the most elementary principles of agriculture, familiar to every child—much less the mechanical arts, commerce, and merchandise, or the variety and nature of fruits, wines, and foodstuffs. I can't doctor a horse or a dog.

Since I must wholly publish my shame, it was not a month ago I was trapped in my ignorance of the use of yeast for making bread, and why wine is kept in a vat. Give me the provisions and whole apparatus of a kitchen, and I would starve. I am not obliged to hide such absurdities as these, provided I recognize they are absurd. To know when I make a slip is so common with me that I seldom slip up by chance.

To tell the truth, I came so late into the management of a house, and my predecessors had spared me so long from the burden, that I had already taken another bent more agreeable to my tastes. Yet for all that I have seen of it, it is an occupation more absorbing than difficult. A man capable of anything is capable of this.

My presence, heedless and ignorant as it is, nevertheless lends a shoulder to my domestic affairs. I busy myself at them, though it goes against the grain. Neither the pleasure of building, which is said to be so fascinating, nor hunting, gardening, nor the other pleasures of a secluded life amuse me overmuch.

I am angry at myself for it, as I am for any distastes which deprive me of a harmless enjoyment. I do not ask that my occupations be learned or strenuous: they are true and sound enough if they are useful, convenient, and pleasing.

Those who whisper in my ear that my ignorance of husbandry comes from disdain, that I don't know the name and price of fabrics I wear or how to prepare the food on which I live, because my mind and heart are set on higher things—they as much as kill me. This would be folly and stupidity rather than anything to glory about. I would rather be a good horseman than a good logician.

We like to occupy our thoughts with the universe, which carries on very well without us. We worry over mankind—and not over Michel, who touches us more closely.

In the same way I do not pry irrelevantly into the character of my servants. I have a good lad as my tailor whom I never knew to be guilty of telling the truth, even when it was to his advantage. When I am hiring a footman I never ask if he is chaste—but if he is diligent. I am not inquisitive to know if my mulekeeper is a gambler so long as he is sturdy; or if my cook swears, provided he can cook. Precisely as in table talk I prefer wit to learning; and in bed, beauty before goodness.

I have just been talking with a steward, an Italian, who was in the service of the late Cardinal Caraffa; and I asked him the details of his work. Whereupon he began discoursing on this belly science with all the magisterial gravity of a man handling some profound point of theology. He laid out learned distinctions between the character of our appetite before we sit down to eat, and after we have finished the first course—and the second. He described the proper means for taking off its edge in the first instance, and stimulating it in the second and third; the ordering of his sauces, first in general, and then as to the particular qualities of their ingredients and the effects of each; the difference between salads according to their season, which should be served hot and which cold, and how to garnish them so they please the eye. After which he launched on the order of the whole service, full of delicate and weighty considerations. And all this swollen with lofty and magnificent words such as we employ when we descant on the government of an empire. I don't know whether it has the same effect on others as on me: but when I hear a builder puff himself up with such grand words as pilasters, architraves, and Corinthian and Doric cornices, I at once seem to see the palace of Apollidon—though all he is talking about are the paltry pieces of my kitchen door.

When I lace into my valet I do it with all my heart—not imitation but real curses. However, when the smoke of it has blown over, I will gladly do him a good turn if he stands in need of me. I turn the leaf at once. When I call him a lout and a donkey I don't mean to knight him forever with these titles, nor do I think myself a liar for calling him an honest fellow the next moment. If it were not the sign of a weak head to be talking to one's self, there would hardly be a day when I would not be heard grumbling to myself, 'Confound the jackass!' yet I don't suppose that to be my accurate description.

We incorporate our anger by hiding it: the more you hold back, the more you have to hold. I prefer a man to smack his servant's cheek, even if a little unjustly, than to rack himself in order to keep a grave and composed face. I had rather show my passions than brood over them to my own hurt.

In my own family, I counsel all those who have a right to express their anger, in the first place to economize it and not spill it on any and all occasions. This lessens its sting and weakens the effect. When you scold a servant for theft, it makes little impression on him if he has seen you do as much, a hundred times, for setting a stool out of place or not rinsing a glass. Secondly, that they make sure their wrath is confined to its mark and not wasted on the air: ordinarily they rail and scream before the culprit comes in their presence and for a century after he is gone. They fight with their own shadow and push the storm into parts of the house where no one is punished or annoyed except those who must listen to the uproar.

I have known hundreds of women, and people say that a Gascon woman has this prerogative: that you can more easily make her bite hot iron than pry her teeth from an opinion she has conceived in a temper. Compulsion and blows only make her worse. The woman who called her husband lousy, and being ducked for it, made the sign of scratching her head every time she came up out of the water, is a true image of their stubbornness—a stubbornness akin to their fidelity.

When I am angry, I make it as sharp but as short as I can. I altogether lose myself in violence and speed, and unconcern for what I say. I hurl indiscriminate insults right and left, and never trouble to aim my darts where I think they will wound the deepest—for I commonly use no other weapon but my tongue.

My servants come off better on serious than trivial provocations. Trivial annoyances catch me by surprise; and the worst of it is that once you are on the brink of the precipice, no matter who or what gives you the push, you go to the bottom. The fall itself carries you down. But in serious matters, I am satisfied in feeling the cause is so just that the offender obviously awaits a righteous explosion; and I enjoy the triumph of disappointing him. I stiffen and control myself, knowing that once the offence mounts to my head and carries me off, this time I will go a long way.

So I bargain with those who are liable to have a contention with me: 'If you see me stirred up first, right or wrong, let me be; and I'll do the same by you.' The real tempest only breaks when two angers collide; yet they seldom rise together, but one is usually born of the other. Give every man a free rein to his wrath, and we will all live in peace—good advice, but hard to follow.

As age sharpens my temper I study how to resist it; and I shall see to it, if I can, that in the future I am less peevish and hard to please, even though I shall have more excuse to be so. Up until now, however, I have been reckoned among the most patient of men.

I am afraid to confess that the tenderness of my nature is so childish that I cannot refuse to romp with my dog, even though he invites me at the most inopportune time. When I play with my cat, who knows whether I am not more of a toy for her than she for me? We equally amuse each other with our monkeyshines. If I have my hour for sulking or playing, so has she. When all is said and done, there is a certain respect and human duty which binds us not only to animals, that have life and sentiment, but even to trees and plants. We owe justice to men and kindliness to other creatures: there is an intercourse and mutual obligation between them and us.

As much as I can, I endeavor to reduce the ceremonies of my house: such as coming out to meet a guest when he has announced the time of his arrival, or receiving him at the door, or making sure I am at home. I often forget one or the other of these vain duties. If someone chooses to take offence at it, I can't help it. It is better to offend him once than myself every day, with this perpetual slavery.

Besides the care spent on it in my upbringing, I have moved enough in good society to know the formalities of my nation;

and I could give lessons in them. But there are some so trouble-some that, if a man omits them out of discretion and not ill-breeding, it will be every whit as handsome. I have seen people rude by being overpolite.

Ceremony forbids us to express natural and lawful things, and we obey it; reason forbids us to do unlawful and evil things, yet we will not listen to it. In my house there is a truce to ceremony. Everyone behaves in his own fashion. A man may talk or not, just as he pleases; I sit mute, musing, and wrapped in myself, without offence to my guests.

I love order and cleanliness more than abundance; and in my home I pay careful attention to the necessities, and little to out-ward show.

Few masters of a house (I speak of those in middling circum-stances such as mine) can so completely rely on another as to dis-pense with bearing the brunt of things on their own shoulders. This spoils a good deal of my ease in entertaining visitors. I'll wager that—like your common bore—I've detained not a few guests more through their hope of getting a good dinner than through the charm of my manners.

There is nothing more ridiculous than to see a host fidgeting about the house, whispering into the ear of one servant and glowering at another. Things ought to glide along imperceptibly, as though following their usual course. I hold it repugnant, as well, to keep talking to your guests about the details of your hos-pitality, whether by way of boast or apology.

If a footman falls to cuffing in another man's house or a dish spills, you only laugh. And you sleep soundly while your host is up arranging with the steward for your menu on the morrow.

I speak from my own experience, quite appreciating how pleasant the management of a house can be for some natures; and I have no desire to judge it by my own annoyances and blunders.

I pass most of my time at home, and I'd like to be better pleased there than anywhere else. I don't know whether I shall succeed. Rather than some other item in his legacy, I wish my father had bequeathed me the passionate love he had for household affairs. Your political philosophy could carp as much as it pleased on the pettiness and sterility of my occupation, if I could once relish it as my father did.

I believe that the most honorable calling of all is to serve the state and be useful to society. But for myself, I have renounced it partly out of conscience and partly out of indolence. I am content to enjoy the world without bustling my way about in it: to live a tolerable life that is a burden neither to myself nor anyone else.

CHAPTER IX

Concerning My Cashbox

 HAVE NEVER HAD any trouble except in the management of my own affairs. Epicurus says that to be rich is not the end, but only a change, of worries. I will give you my own experiences. ¶ Since my childhood I have lived in three different manners. During the first period, which lasted about twenty years, I depended upon an allowance and the aid of others—without any certain or fixed income. So I spent what I had, and the more freely and gaily as I felt it was all a matter of windfall. And I never lived better.

I found the purse of my friends always open to me, for I had resolved above everything else to pay what I owed the moment it was due. And I discovered that my readiness to pay won me a thousand postponements. In fact I practiced a thrifty and somewhat sly honesty.

However, I always borrowed at a great disadvantage. Lacking the courage to speak in person, I commonly confided my plea to the persuasion of a letter: in general a poor advocate and of great help to the man who is of a mind to refuse you.

I have a natural satisfaction in paying my debts, as though I dropped a load from my shoulders and redeemed myself from some shadow of slavery. Also, I tickle myself with a sort of flattery when I behave justly and please another.

But I make an exception of payments which involve reckoning and haggling. In such cases, if I can't find someone to relieve me of the task, I delay payment, no matter how scandalously, for fear of the inevitable wrangling, at which both my nature and manner of speaking make me a poor hand. I hate nothing so much as bargaining: it is a mere exchange of impudence and cheating, where after an hour of dodging and debate, both parties betray their word and oath for five sous difference in price.

In those days I usually left my affairs to the stars—and with a better heart than I now trust them to my prudence and judgment. Good managers will look with horror on this living in uncertainty. They do not stop to consider that, in the first place, most of the world lives no differently. Cæsar ran up above a million in debts, in order to become Cæsar. And many worthy merchants have begun their commerce by selling their farms and sending the proceeds 'across so many stormy seas' to the Indies. Secondly, they do not observe that the certitude on which they rely is hardly less uncertain and hazardous than hazard itself. I see misery as close to me when it lies two-thousand-crowns income away, as when it is at my heels. Besides, the more wealth we have, the more openings we give to chance to make a breach for poverty, and turn our bulwarks topsy-turvy.

My second state was to have money of my own. And I handled matters so that in a short while I had saved a notable sum out of a rather small income. I said to myself that the only money a man really has, is what he lays aside from his ordinary expenses; and that he can never rely on revenue to come, no matter how certain it may appear.

What—I asked—if I should be overtaken by this or that accident? Filled with these vain and terrifying imaginations I ingeniously proposed to put aside enough to cover any and all emergencies. And when anyone objected to me that the number of possible emergencies were infinite, I would reply that if I can't provide against them all, I mean to do so for as many as I could.

This was not accomplished without a great deal of care and anxiety. I kept my funds a secret; and, although I am aways talking of myself, I never spoke of my money, except falsely as others do—who when rich pretend to be poor, or when poor claim to be rich.

Was I going on a journey? I never thought I was providing myself with enough. And the more I loaded myself with money, the more I loaded myself with fear, now of the dangers along the road, again of the fidelity of the man who looked after my baggage—like so many others, I never felt safe unless I had my eye on him. And if I left my cashbox at home? Then I was torn with suspicions; and, what was worse, compelled to keep them to myself. My mind was always on that box.

Taking it all in all, I find it is more trouble to watch after money than get it. I reaped little or no advantage from what I had; and my expenses didn't seem smaller to me because my surplus was greater. For as Bion says, the fellow with a full crop of hair hates to have you pull one out as much as any baldhead. Once you have decided to keep a certain pile, it is no longer yours; for you can't spend it. I would sooner have pawned my clothes or sold a horse than made a breach in the beloved purse where I hoarded my reserves. You can't find it in your heart to open it. It becomes a fabric you fancy must crumble away if you so much as touch it.

The danger is that men who are intent on adding to their pile will in the end deprive themselves of the enjoyment of their own possessions. According to this, the richest people in the world are the police and night watchmen of a great city. All monied men, I conclude, are avaricious.

I continued this hoarding streak for some years, when I don't know what good demon fortunately threw me out of it, and cast my reserves to the winds. Then the pleasure of a certain journey I took at very great expense taught me to spurn this love of money. So I have now entered my third manner of living—certainly more enjoyable and more wisely regulated.

I live at the top of my income—sometimes a bit above or below, as the case may be. I live from hand to mouth, content to have enough for my ordinary expenses. As to extraordinary contingencies, not all the scrimping in the world would suffice. It is the maddest folly to imagine that Fortune will arm you against herself; indeed, we can fight her only with our own weapons—hers will betray us in the pinch of the business.

If I do save up something, it is for a definite and immediate purpose: not to buy lands, which I do not need, but pleasure. 'Not to be covetous,' says Cicero, 'is money in your purse; not to be eager to buy, is income.'

I have neither great fear of want nor great desire for more. And I am mightily pleased that this reformation has come to me when I have reached the years which naturally incline men to avarice. I see myself spared the imbecility most common to old men, and the last word in human folly.'

In the eighteen years I have my estate in my own hands, I can never prevail upon myself to read over the deeds or examine the transactions which should, by necessity, pass through my inspection and control. This is no philosophic disdain of worldly and transitory things. My nature is not refined to that degree; and I rate business affairs as high as they are worth. No, it is in truth an inexcusable, childish laziness and negligence. What wouldn't I do rather than read over a contract? Or, a slave to my business, go poring over dusty scraps of parchment? Or, what is worse, go poring over those of another man, as some do for hire.

Many fine opportunities in business have escaped me for want of proper management. Yet my deliberations were sound enough in view of the circumstances as I saw them. If my prudence can't see far enough, there is no remedy. I blame neither it nor myself; I accuse my luck and not my work.

I like to have my losses and business disorders concealed from me. I enter in my expense account what my negligence costs me in feeding and maintaining it. In the same way I like to be ignorant of how much I possess, in order that I may be less sensible of what I lose. Because I have not enough resilience to fight the shock of adversities, or patience to apply myself to my affairs, I resolve to leave them all to fortune—to take everything at its worst and bear that worst with good grace. I begrudge myself nothing but taking pains and care. All I seek is nonchalance and the quiet of cattle.

My friends put me to infernal trouble when they ask me to ask something of a third person. I find it hardly less expensive to write off a debt someone owes me by putting him to some use, than become obligated to someone who owes me nothing. With this exception, and so long as I am not asked to assume a lot of business and responsibilities (for I have declared war to the hilt against worry), I am always ready and glad to help anyone in need. True, I have oftener refused benefits than looked for chances to confer them—the easier way, says Aristotle. My fortune has seldom permitted me to do a good turn to others; and when I did, it was usually wasted effort. Yet if I had been born of high rank, I would have been ambitious to be loved, rather than feared or admired. Shall I put it with more insolence? I would have thought more of giving people pleasure than of doing them good.

Crates plunged himself into poverty to be rid of the cares of his house. But this I would not do. I hate poverty no less than pain. Still, I would be satisfied to change the life I lead for a humbler one and less bristling with business.

But, rich or poor, we need a palate in order to relish what we have. It is enjoyment, not possession, which makes us happy. No fortune can be enjoyed without good health and a sound mind. Otherwise a man becomes a dullard, his taste palls and grows flat: he no more enjoys what he owns than a fellow with a cold in his head can appreciate the bouquet of madeira, or a horse the rich harness he wears. At the first twinge of the gout, it signifies much to be called Sire and Your Majesty!

Now nothing is so clogging and killing to the taste as abundance. What appetite would not be baffled to see, like the Sultan, three hundred women at his disposal?

Since I am working for the reputation of having neither acquired nor dissipated anything—conformable to the rest of my life which is apt at doing neither good nor evil—and since all I desire is to slip by, I can accomplish this, thanks be to God, with little effort.

At the worst, I keep at forestalling poverty by trying to reduce my expenses. That is my chief concern, and I think I'll succeed before I am compelled. For my real needs do not consume what I possess. There is enough left for Ill-Fortune to bite at, without sinking her teeth to the quick.

CHAPTER X

My Library in the Tower

WHEN I AM AT HOME, I am more often than not in my library—as fine a one as you will find out in the country. It is situated above my gateway; and beneath me I can see my garden, courtyard, farmyard, and almost every part of the building—in a trice I can overlook all the concerns of my house. There you will find me thumbing one book after another in snatches, without method or plan. Sometimes I muse; sometimes—walking to and fro—I make notes and dictate such reflections as you now may read.

It is in the third storey of a tower, and was formerly a large storeroom and the most useless place in the house. The first storey is my chapel. The second, a bedroom with closet, where I frequently sleep in order to be alone. Every morning and evening a great bell rings out the *Ave Maria,* the noise shakes the very tower, and at first I thought I never could stand it. But now I am so used to it that I hear it without any manner of offence, and often without waking.

It is in the library I pass most of my days and most hours of the day. I am never there at night. Adjoining it is a rather decent study, very pleasantly lighted, and with a fireplace for winter. If it were not for the trouble, which I fear more than the expense, the trouble which frightens me from all business, I could easily build off from it—on each side and along the same level—a gallery about one hundred paces by twelve; a wall, already built for some purpose, rises to the necessary height. Every place of retreat ought to have a promenade. If I seat them, my thoughts go to sleep. My mind moves only when my legs set it in motion. Those who study without books are all in this plight.

My library is round in shape. The only flat stretch of wall is behind my table and chair; and so with one glance I can view all my thousand books about me, curving in rows five shelves high. The room is sixteen paces clear in diameter, and its three windows open on wide and noble prospects.

I am not there so continuously in winter, for it is the windiest spot in the house. But I like it for being remote and rather of a climb, both because of the exercise it affords, and the seclusion.

Not long ago I visited one of the most learned men in France, and rather well to do. I discovered him studying in a corner of his hall, partitioned off merely by a tapestry, and about him a rout of servants making what noise they pleased. He told me he found the uproar very useful; lashed by the racket he withdrew further into himself and his own thoughts. When he was a student at Padua, he said, his study overlooked a public square; and he grew so used to the clatter of coaches and the general hubbub that he became not only oblivious to noise, but needful of it. I am quite otherwise. I have a tender head and easily rattled; when it is occupied with something, the buzz of a fly assassinates it.

My library is my kingdom, and here I try to make my rule absolute—shutting off this single nook from wife, daughter, and society. Elsewhere I have only a verbal authority, and vague.

We should all of us set apart for ourselves a little back shop, wholly free and our own—there to establish our true liberty, our solitude and retreat. There we must entertain ourselves with ourselves—to laugh and talk as if without family, goods, train, or attendance; so if it comes to pass that we lose any or all of these, it will mean no new thing to do without them.

Unhappy is the man, in my opinion, who has no spot at home where he can be at home to himself—to court himself and hide away.

CHAPTER XI

The Days When I Read

T IS EASY ENOUGH for a man to walk who has a horse at his command. The invalid is not to be pitied who has a cure up his sleeve. And such is the advantage I receive from books. ¶They relieve me from idleness, rescue me from company I dislike, and blunt the edge of my grief, if it is not too extreme. They are the comfort and solitude of my old age.

When I am attacked by gloomy thoughts, nothing helps me so much as running to my books. They quickly absorb me and banish the clouds from my mind. And they don't rebel because I use them only for lack of pastimes more natural and alive. They always receive me with the same welcome.

Yet I make as little use of them, at most, as a miser does of his gold. Knowing I can enjoy them when I please, I am satisfied by their mere possession. I never travel without books, either in war or peace. Still, I often pass days and months without looking in them. 'I'll read by and by,' I say to myself, 'or tomorrow, or when I choose.' Meanwhile time slips away, and no harm is done. For you can't imagine how comforting it is to know they are by my side, to be opened when I will; and what a refreshment they are to my life.

They are the best provisions I have found for this human journey. And I am sorry indeed for the man of understanding who is deprived of them.

But reading books is as laborious as any other work, and can be as great a menace to the health. Neither should we be deceived by the pleasure of it, which is the same pleasure that traps the man of affairs, the miser, the libertine, and the ambitious. Books are pleasant enough; but if too much reading impairs the health and spoils our good humor—our most priceless possessions—we should drop it. Nothing we can gain from it will repay us for so great a loss.

In the days when I read a great deal, I used to lay a piece of glass on my page to remove the glare from the paper; and it gave my eyes considerable relief. Even now, at fifty-four years of age, I have no need of spectacles. I can see as far as I ever did, and as well as anyone else. True, if I read in the dusk I begin to notice that my sight is a little dim and weak. But, anyway, I always found reading a strain on my eyes, especially at night. They always tire quickly; and I could never stay long at a book, but was forced to have someone read aloud to me.

For my part, I like only easy and amusing books which tickle my fancy, or such as give me counsel and comfort. If I use them for study, it is to learn how to know myself, and to teach myself the proper way to live and die.

If someone tells me it degrades the value of the Muses to use them only for sport and pastime, I will answer that he little knows the value of pleasure—and it will be all I can do not to add that any other end in life is ridiculous. I live from day to day, and speaking with reverence, only for myself. When young, I studied for show; later, to make myself a little wiser; and now, for pleasure. And never for profit.

I do not bite my nails over the difficulties I encounter in a book. After one or two assaults I give them up. If I kept at them, I would only lose my time and myself as well; for my mind is good for only one jump. If I can't see a point at the first glance, repeated efforts will do nothing but make it more obscure.

If one book wearies me, I quickly pick up another. I never read except at such hours when the tedium of doing nothing drives me to it.

I am not much taken by the new books; the old ones seem to have more meat and sinew. Nor by the Greeks, for my judgment can't come into play when my knowledge of a language is rudimentary and weak.

Among merely amusing books, Boccaccio's *Decameron*, Rabelais, and the *Basia* of Johannes Secundus (if they are to be classed under this head) are worth reading for pastime. As for *Amadis* and novels of that stripe, they could not inveigle even my childhood. Moreover I must confess that this heavy old soul of mine is no longer tickled by Ariosto, no, nor by Ovid; and I have scarcely the patience to read them.

I have a particular fondness for poetry. As Cleanthes said, if a sound is forced through a trumpet, it comes out with more power and penetration; and to my way of thinking, a sentence pressed within the harmony of a verse darts into my ear and strikes my mind with keener and sweeter effect.

From my earliest childhood poetry had the gift to pierce and transport me. But this vivid and inborn feeling was played upon differently by different styles—not so much a matter of higher and lower, for each has its degrees, as of color. First I enjoyed a gay and ingenious ease, then an elevated and piquant subtlety, and lastly a ripe and sure power. But the examples will show better what I mean: Ovid, Lucan, Virgil.

I have always thought that in poetry Virgil, Lucretius, Catullus, and Horace held the first place by a long way—especially the *Georgics* of Virgil, which I look upon as the most accomplished work of a poet's art. In comparison with it, you may see that there are places in the *Æneid* which would have received a little more combing if the author had been given the leisure. Its fifth book strikes me as the most perfect.

As for my good Terence—the acme of Latin daintiness and grace—I think it astonishing how closely he portrays the motives and manners of our own day. Our present behavior is forever sending me back to him. And no matter how often I go, I always discover some new charm and beauty.

Those who lived shortly after Virgil's time were badly upset at any attempted comparison between Lucretius and him. I too believe they cannot be paired together; but I have a hard time defending my belief when I find Lucretius enthralling me with one of his beautiful passages. The ancients, I think, had more reason to be annoyed at those who ranked Plautus with Terence.

I have often remarked that our modern playwrights (in imitation of the Italians, who are happy enough at that art) take three or four plots out of Terence or Plautus to make one of their own, and crowd five or six of Boccaccio's tales into a single comedy. The reason, I believe, they overload themselves with matter is that they fear they cannot please by their own graces. Lacking any power in themselves to amuse us, they want the story to do it for them.

Much in the same strain, I observe that the good ancient poets keep clear of frills and search neither for those fantastic flights of the Spanish and Petrarchian schools, nor even for the gentler and more restrained conceits which adorn the work of the succeeding centuries. Yet no good judge regrets their absence; and he will admire the even polish, perpetual glow, and beauty-in-flower of Catullus' epigrams incomparably more than those of Martial, who sharpens their tails with a sting. The former make themselves felt without effort or incitement; without forcing themselves they furnish a suffused merriment. But the latter need outside help; they need body in the same measure as they lack wit. They mount on horseback because they can't stand on their own legs.

I have seen excellent clowns give us all the pleasure of their art, though dressed in everyday clothes and without makeup.

Whereas a duffer who does not know his business has to chalk up his face, disguise himself, and go through wild grimaces in order to make us laugh. Perhaps I can best illustrate what I have in mind by comparing the *Æneid* and *Orlando Furioso*. The first may be seen in high and firm flight, and moving ever towards its destination by sheer force of wing. The other flutters and hops from tale to tale, as from branch to branch, mistrusting its wing save for a brief flurry, and lands at the end of every field lest its breath and strength fail.

I am not one of those who think a perfect meter makes a perfect poem. Let a writer put a long syllable for a short if he will—it doesn't hurt. If he is happy in his invention, if his mind and judgment do their work, I'll call him a bad versifier but a good poet. This is what Menander meant when, as the day approached for finishing a comedy and a friend jibed at him for not having as yet put his hand to it, he replied, 'It is all composed and ready—all I have to do is add the lines.'

Since Ronsard and Du Bellay have set our French poetry in honor, there is not a fledgling who doesn't puff up his words and swell his cadences in their manner—'more sound than sense' as Seneca says. To the casual reader there never were so many poets as today. But by just so much as they copy the rhythms of these two, they fall short of the rich descriptions of the one, and the delicate fancies of the other.

Folk poetry, which is purely natural, has in it naïveties and graces which make it comparable in beauty to the highest poetry perfected by art. This may be seen in our Gascon *villanelles* and the songs that come to us from nations that possess no knowledge of science or even of the means of writing. The poetry which falls between these extremes is contemptible, and without honor or esteem.

It is curious that we have many more poets than judges and interpreters of poetry. It is apparently easier to write than to recognize. At the lower end of the scale, poetry can be judged by precepts and laws. But the real, the supreme, the divine is above rule and reason. Though you may see its beauty with a steady and knowing eye, you see no more than the splendor of a lightning flash. It doesn't work upon our judgment; it ravishes it.

My gaze is clear enough, but in poetry it is dazzled. I love it infinitely, and am able to give a fair account of it to others. But when I try to set my own hand to it, I play the child and am disgusted with myself. A man has the right to make a fool of himself in everything but poetry. 'Neither gods, men, nor booksellers permit mediocrity in poets,' says Horace. Would to God this sentence were written over the doors of our publishers!

As for my other reading, in which the pleasure is somewhat more tinged with profit and whereby I learn to order my opinions and behavior, the books which serve me best are Plutarch—now that he is translated into French—and Seneca. I never seriously settled myself to any works of solid learning except these. Like the Danaids, I am forever filling and pouring from them—a few drops splash on my paper, but little or nothing remains inside of me.

They both have this convenience: the knowledge I seek in them is treated in disconnected pieces which demand no sustained attention—of which I would be incapable. Such are the minor works of Plutarch and the letters of Seneca, the best of their writings. I do not have to sweat at them, and I can drop them when I please; for one part does not depend upon or follow the other.

There are in Plutarch many long discourses worthy of careful reading, for to my mind he is the master workman at this, and of all the authors I know, the one who best mingles art and nature, judgment and knowledge. But there are a thousand places where he merely skims and hints. He points with his finger, and it is for you to follow up the road if you wish. Sometimes he is satisfied with a single dig at the heart of the matter. We should learn to tear it from the page and exhibit it in our public squares.

As, for example, this one remark: 'That the inhabitants of Asia all became slaves to one man because they could not pronounce the one syllable, *No!*'—the sentence, perhaps, which gave La Boétie the theme and occasion for his *Servitude Volontaire*.

Plutarch and Seneca agree in most of their soundest opinions. Indeed, fortune brought them into the world at about the same period; both were tutors to two Roman emperors; both came from a foreign land; both were rich and influential. Their teachings are the cream of philosophy—at once simple and pertinent.

Plutarch is more uniform and constant, Seneca more undulant and varied. The latter puts himself in a sweat to arm virtue against weakness, fear, and vice. The former seems to hold the enemy in less esteem, and scorns to quicken his pace or set himself on guard. His views are Platonic—gentle and well adapted to polite society. Seneca's are Stoic and Epicurean, more removed from ordinary life, but in my judgment sturdier and more suitable to the individual.

Seneca seems to have lent himself to the imperial tyranny of his times; for I am certain he spoke against his better judgment when he condemned the generous assassins of Cæsar. Plutarch is a free man throughout. Seneca abounds in conceits and sallies, Plutarch in substance. The one fires and moves you, the other satisfies you more and pays you better. Seneca prods us, Plutarch guides.

The works of Cicero serving my purpose are those which deal with philosophy, and especially morals. But to confess the truth boldly, his style bores me. Prefaces, definitions, divisions, etymologies take up the bulk of his space. Whatever he has of pith and life is smothered by his long-winded preparations. When I have spent an hour reading him—a good deal for me—and try to recollect what I have extracted, I usually find it nothing but wind.

Since I only wish to become wiser and not more learned, this logical and Aristotelian apparatus is irrelevant. I want a man to begin with his conclusions. I know well enough what death and pleasure are: no one need give himself the trouble to dissect them for me. But right at the outset I want good and solid counsel on how to deal with them. Grammatical subtleties and an ingenious fabric of words won't do.

I like reasons which charge into the heart of a question: Cicero's beat about the bush. They are good enough for classrooms, lawcourts, and pulpits—where we have a chance to nap and can wake a quarter hour later still in time to pick up the thread. His manner of speaking is useful for winning over a judge by hook or crook, or dealing with children and ordinary people, to whom you have to say everything in the hope that something will stick.

I don't want an author to work at making me attentive—to shout at me fifty times, *Now hear! Now listen!* I left home prepared to listen. I likewise need no sauce or appetizer: I can eat my meat raw. Instead of whetting my appetite, these *hors d'œuvres* and curtain-raisers tire it out.

Will the licence of the times excuse me when I maintain that, in my opinion, even the *Dialogues* of Plato drag? That they are overwritten, and I regret that a man who had many better things to say wasted so much time in long and needless preliminary conversations? At least my ignorance will excuse me, for I do not understand enough Greek to appreciate the beauty of his style.

In general I choose books which use science, and not those which lead up to it. But I also delight in Cicero's letters to Atticus, because I discover in them much of his personal humors. I have a great curiosity to pry into the soul and real opinions of my authors. A man may judge of a writer's talent by the books he displays in the public market, but not of his manners or self. I would rather hear what Brutus said to his friends in his tent the night before a battle, than the harangue he gave next morning to his army.

Yet about the last word in cheapness is the endeavor of such gifted men as Cicero and Pliny to gain a morsel of fame from gossip and tittle-tattle, going so far as to publish their private letters to friends—even those which were never sent, because, forsooth, they did not wish to lose their labor and their midnight oil. Did it become two consuls of Rome, magistrates of a republic which ruled the world, to spend their spare time prettily stringing together a fine missive, in order to win the reputation of knowing the language of their own nurses? Could any schoolmaster have done worse? If the deeds of Xenophon and Cæsar had not far surpassed their words, I doubt if they would have troubled to write them down.

As to Cicero, I am of the common opinion that, apart from his learning, he had no great talents of mind. He was a good citizen; he was affable, as fat hearty men usually are; but he was weak and rather vain and ambitious. I don't know how to excuse him for having thought his poetry worth publishing. It is no disgrace to write bad verse, but it shows poor judgment not to have sensed how unworthy it was of his great name.

History is a ball straight to my racquet. It is my true game. For historians are pleasant and easy; and man in general, the object of my search, appears there more alive and entire than anywhere else—the truth and diversity of his inner nature, in gross and detail, the varied interplay of his motives and methods, and the fortunes that menace him.

Those who write biographies are my proper meat, for they dwell more on motives than events, more on what issues from within than happens without. That is why, above all others Plutarch is the man for me.

I am mighty sorry we have not a dozen like Diogenes Laertius, or that he is not more widely known or better appreciated. I am just as curious to know the lives and fortunes of the great teachers of the world, as their doctrines and ideas.

In this study of history we must thumb without distinction every sort of author, old or new, French or foreign, in order to get at their great variety of matter. But Cæsar, in my opinion, deserves particular study, not only for his knowledge and manner, but for himself. Aside from the false colors with which he seeks to paint over his bad cause, and the filth of his pestilent ambition, the only fault I can find with him is that he spoke too little of Cæsar.

I have just run through Tacitus' *History* without a break (something that seldom happens to me—it is twenty years since I have read an hour at a stretch). It is more a judgment than a narration of history. There are more precepts than stories. It's not a book to read, but to study and learn.

However, he always clothes his solid reasoning with subtleties and conceits, writing in the affected style of that age. They were so fond of inflated language that when there was neither point nor intricacy in the things, they borrowed them in words.

He writes somewhat like Seneca, but there is more flesh to him. He is better adapted to a sick and troubled world like ours. You might often think he was portraying us today, and pinching us.

He seemed to me to show poor mettle when he said that it was no spirit of ostentation which led him to mention his holding a high public office. This was a paltry remark, coming from a mind like his. A man should speak as frankly of himself as of anyone else. He must discard etiquette in favor of truth and freedom.

In reading history, I am accustomed to consider who and what the author may be. If he is a professional writer, I expect to learn from him mostly style and language. If he is a lawyer we should note what he offers on civil government, legal controversies, and the like; if an ambassador, what he says on the sources of information and the conduct of negotiations. We should always bring the cobbler to his last.

I like the historians who are either very simple or very capable. The simple ones make it their business merely to collect what comes to their hand and record it faithfully, without discrimination or contributing anything of their own mind—they leave us to our own judgment in getting at the truth. Such, for example, is honest Froissart, who is frank enough, when he is caught in an error, to correct it on the spot, and who gives us the varied accounts made to him of the same event, and even the rumors current in his time. His is the naked raw material of history, which everyone may profit by as far as he is able.

The really capable and excellent historians possess the judgment to sift the reports that come to them, and choose those most likely to be true. From the mind and character of a prince they deduce his intentions, and put the proper words in his mouth. But certainly this privilege belongs to very few.

As for the others, who fall between the two (and they are the majority), they spoil everything. They want to chew our meat for us. They assume the right to judge history and accordingly distort it to their own bias. They undertake to select what is worthy to be known, and often hide from us the very word and gesture which would teach us most. They omit as incredible anything they can't understand—and many things, perhaps, because they don't know how to express them in good Latin or French.

For the most part, but especially today, your historian or biographer is elected for the work because he knows how to handle language—as if we were to learn grammar from them! They are hired to weave the reports they pick up on the streets into a pleasant jingle of words, and sell us so much babble.

But good histories are those written either by men who commanded or participated in the events they describe, or at least have had similar experiences. Even so, the research for truth is very delicate. Asinius Pollio found mistakes in the histories of Cæsar himself, either because he could not have his eyes everywhere, or credited the false accounts of his lieutenants.

As a matter of fact, the knowledge we have of our own affairs is obscure enough. To aid my weak memory I have adopted a custom of late to note at the end of every book I read (and do not intend to read again) the date when I finished it, and what in general I thought of it. And yet it has befallen me time and again to open a book as new and untasted, which I had carefully read a few years before and scribbled up with my notes.

There are many books useful for their subject matter, but which earn little praise for their authors—and good books, as well as good works, which shame the workmen. I might write of how we dine and dress, and write it badly. I might collect the edicts of our time, and publish the correspondence of our princes, which would have a wide audience. I might abridge a good book (though every abridgement of a good book is a poor abridgement), and the book itself might become lost. Perhaps posterity would find these compositions very useful; but for myself, what honor would I gain—except by luck? A good number of famous books are in this class.

Most minds require outside matter to stir and exercise them. Mine needs it to tarry and settle down—'the vice of idleness must be shaken off by occupation.' For its main study, and hardest, is to study itself. Books scatter it. It is sufficient in itself to rouse its own powers. Nature has given it—as well as all other minds—enough subjects to judge and elaborate.

Meditation is ample exercise for the man who knows how to explore and use himself. No occupation is at once idler and more fruitful—according to the character of our mind—than entertaining one's own thoughts. Great men make it their lifework. Moreover, Nature has favored us in it: for there is nothing we can keep at so long and easily. It is the business of the gods, says Aristotle; and it creates both their happiness and ours.

With its variety of matter, reading above all awakens my reasoning power. It puts my judgment to work, not my memory. And I would rather forge my mind than furnish it.

CHAPTER XII

Wḩat I find in My Essays

HEN I LATELY RETIRED to my house I resolved, as far as I could, to meddle in nothing, but pass in peace and privacy what little time I had to live. It seemed to me I could not better gratify my mind than by giving it full leisure to dwell in its own thoughts and divert itself with them. And I hoped that with the passage of time, it could do this with greater ease as it became more settled and ripe.

But the contrary was the case. Like a horse broke loose, it gave itself a hundred times more rein. There rose in me a horde of chimeræ and fantastic creatures, one upon the other, without order or relevance. To contemplate more coolly their queerness and ineptitude I began to put them in writing—hoping in time to make my mind ashamed of itself. A mind which has no set goal loses itself. To be everywhere is to be nowhere. No wind serves the man bound for no port.

I never set pen to paper except when an overdose of idleness drives me to it, and never anywhere but at home. My library is situated in a corner of my house; and if anything comes into my head to look up or write there, lest I forget it in walking across the courtyard—for I have no retention at all—I must commit it to the memory of someone else. So my book is built in scraps and intervals, often interrupted by long months of absence.

I have no sergeant to whip my ideas into rank—except chance

itself. Sometimes they come trooping in single file, and sometimes by brigades; and as they come I line them up. I want the reader to see my natural and ordinary gait for the stagger it is.

I have sometimes been urged to write the events of our time, by persons who fancy I view them with an eye less blinded by passion than others, and more particularly because fortune has given me intimate access to the leaders of our various parties. But they do not consider that to purchase even the glory of Sallust I would not spend the pains, and that there is nothing so contrary to my style as continuous narrative.

I am forever cutting myself short for lack of breath. My ability to compose or elucidate anything is worthless. I am more ignorant than a child of the phrases and even the very words to express the commonest things.

This is why I have undertaken to say only what I know how to say, fitting my subject to my powers. Besides, my freedom of speech is so unbridled I would likely publish opinions which both reason and my own better judgment would condemn as indiscreet and unlawful.

Our judgment is a tool of all work. In my *Essays* I try it out on every occasion. If it is a subject I do not understand, even so I essay. I take soundings of the ford; and, if it is too deep for me, I stay on shore. The knowledge our judgment gives us that we can proceed no farther is a virtue on which it prides itself. Sometimes, in an idle and frivolous subject, I see if my judgment can't supply it with body and give it a prop. Again, I exercise it on a worthy theme that has been tossed about by a thousand hands and where it can walk in the paths of others. In this case, its work is to select the best route.

But I have an apish nature. When I used to write verses (I did so only in Latin) they plainly showed the last poet I had read. Therefore I am loathe to write on well-known topics, for fear I'll handle them at another's expense.

I take the first subject chance offers me. They are all equally fertile for my purpose: a fly will serve. I do not intend to treat them exhaustively; for I never see the whole of anything—and neither do they who promise they will show it to us. Everything has a hundred angles and facets: I take up one, perhaps to give it merely a lick, again to lift the skin a bit, and sometimes to pinch it to the bone. I give a stab, not as wide but as deep as I can; and, very often, I like to turn a thing over in an unfamiliar light.

By tossing my ideas about—samples cut from the cloth and pieced together without pattern or promise—I am bound neither to answer for them nor stick to them. I can drop them when I please; and return to my doubt and uncertainty, and to my dominant form which is ignorance.

When I write I gladly do without the company or recollection of books, lest they hinder my style. Also, in truth, because the good authors take the heart out of me. I am of the same mind as the artist who painted cocks most vilely and used to forbid his lads to allow a live cock to enter the workshop. But I can scarcely do without Plutarch. No matter what you treat of, he is always at your elbow holding out to you an inexhaustible store of riches. I am vexed to be so tempted: I hardly ever finger him without stealing a wing or a leg.

It suits me, too, to write at home, in a savage countryside where there is no one to aid or correct me. I hardly know a man hereabouts who understands the Latin of his Paternoster, or as little if not less of French. I myself speak a somewhat different French in Paris than in Montaigne.

I might have done better elsewhere, but my work would have been less my own. And its principal aim and virtue is to be nothing but myself. I readily correct accidental errors, in which I abound, as I speed carelessly on. But the blemishes which are natural and common to me would be a sort of treason to remove.

When someone tells me, or I tell myself, 'You overrun with metaphors—this is of Gascon vintage—that is a dubious phrase (I reject nothing which is current on the streets of France, for the man who would correct usage by grammar is a simpleton)—there's an ignorant opinion—now you go too far—here you fool too much—men will think you mean in earnest what you say in jest'—to all this I reply, 'Do I paint myself to the life? It's enough. I am doing what I proposed. The man who knows me will meet me again in my book, and the man who knows my book will meet it again in me.'

But what annoys me is that my mind usually strikes off its deepest and subtlest thoughts, and those that please me best, when I least expect them and am least prepared—on horse, in bed, or while at meals—but chiefly on horseback, where my brain is most active. And they will suddenly vanish before I can find means to put them down.

When I dream I promise to remember my visions (for I am apt to dream that I dream); but next morning, while I can recall their general tinge—gay, sad, or strange—the harder I try to recapture them the deeper I plunge them in oblivion. I find the same with the ideas that pop accidentally into my head. I retain nothing but a vague image of them—just enough to torment me into a fruitless chase.

Watching the method of a fresco painter I have working for me, I was taken with the desire to imitate him. He selects the best place in the center of a panel to paint his picture, which he finishes with all his craft. The empty space around it he fills in with grotesques, fantastic figures whose only charm is their variety and extravagance.

And what are the essays I scribble, if not grotesque and farfetched creatures, lacking save by chance all order, continuity, and proportion? In this respect I follow my painter nicely. But I fall far short in the better and greater part of his task. I have not the ability even to dare undertake a rich and polished picture executed with the proper art.

Some writers are so ridiculous as to run a mile out of their way for a fine word. For my part, I would rather wrench a sentence to make it fit my thought than go a step from the road to look for the right expression. Words are made to follow and wait upon us. If the French won't come, let the Gascon serve. I want my subject to capture and inflame the imagination of my listener so he will have no time to remember the words. When I see a noble expression, I do not exclaim, *'Tis well said,* but *'Tis well thought.*

Fine minds set off a language not by introducing novelties, but through putting it to more vigorous and varied use by bending it to their own purpose. They do not create words, but enrich their meanings. The rarity of this talent may be seen from the many scribblers about us. They are brave enough not to follow the common highway, but their lack of discretion ruins them. Their writings show nothing but a pitiful delight in new and strange styles which, instead of enhancing, degrade their subjects. Provided they can plume themselves out in a new phrase, they are indifferent to what they say. To take up a new word they discard an old one which often has more vitals and strength. A thousand poets drool prosaically. But the best prose shines with the lustre, vigor, and boldness of poetry, and not without a spark of its fire.

Whenever I take up my pen I owe a sacrifice to the Graces, as Plutarch says of someone, in order to conciliate their favor. For they desert me throughout. Polish and beauty are wanting. When I choose a lively theme, it is to follow my own bent, which is enemy to all grave and ceremonious wisdom; it is to enliven myself and not my style—if I may call that a style which is a formless ungoverned speech, a popular jargon. I speak on paper as I do to the first person I meet. And I see well enough that I sometimes overdo it; and by trying to avoid affectation, I fall into it by a contrary route.

The titles of my essays do not always embrace their content. Often they denote it merely by a sign. It is the careless reader who loses track of the subject, not I. There will always be hid in a corner some word which, however hard to find, will not fail to bring him back.

I wander with indiscrimination and riot. My style and my mind are vagabonds together. You must play the fool a little, if you would not be thought wholly a fool.

I want my subject matter to mark its own divisions: to show in itself where it begins, breaks off, rejoins, and ends, without my interlacing it with stitches and transitions made for dull ears — and without explaining my own explanations. Who doesn't prefer not to be read at all, than read by drowsy inattentive eyes?

If I can't arrest my reader by the weight of what I write, it is something, perhaps, if I can do it by my intricacy. 'Yes, but he will repent afterwards that he ever bothered with you!' True — but still he will have bothered.

The numerous chapters into which I snipped the first part of my book seemed to me to dissolve the attention of my reader before it was aroused. On this account I have lengthened the later ones. The reader who is not willing to give an hour is not willing to give anything.

The stories I borrow I leave to the conscience of those I took them from. My conclusions are my own and depend upon reason, and every reader is free to add his own examples. If he knows of none, let him be wary of concluding that none exist — human experience is strangely rich and varied.

In the subjects I handle, which are our manners and behavior, imaginary examples are as pat as real ones, provided they are within the realm of possibility. Whether they actually occurred in Paris or Rome, to John or Peter, does not matter so long as human beings might have experienced them. I use the shadow as well as the substance of things.

Some authors propose to give an account of only those things that have happened; my purpose, if I can achieve it, is to tell what could happen. Yet in the examples I draw from what I myself have heard, read, said, or done, I have forbidden myself to alter even the most trivial circumstance. My conscience does not falsify so much as a dot: what my ignorance may do, I cannot say.

No doubt I often speak of things which are better handled by masters of the subject, and with more truth. I merely give an essay of my natural faculties, and not of what I have acquired. If you catch me in a mistake, you will not embarrass me. I am not undertaking to be responsible to others in my writings, when I am not responsible for them to myself—or even satisfied with them. The man who is in search of information should fish for it in waters where it swims. There is nothing I profess so little to provide.

I offer reflections of my own, in which I seek to disclose not things—but myself. As for the things, I may know them some future day, or perhaps I knew them once and will again if I can stumble on the passage where I found them.

Let no one, therefore, stress the matter I write, but the turn I give it. In what I borrowed, let them judge if I knew how to choose. I often make others say for me what I cannot say so well myself. I don't count up my borrowings: I weigh them. And they are almost all from such famous authors that they reveal their source, without my explanation.

Sometimes I deliberately omit to mention the author in order to baffle those hasty critics who hurl themselves on everything, but particularly on living authors who write in our common speech—which seems to give everyone the right to criticize and to despise the works themselves as common. I want to see them give Plutarch a poke on my nose, and tear into Seneca when they think they are tearing into me.

I shall indeed be glad to have my feathers plucked by the

hands of sound and clear judgment. For I hold myself responsible if I stumble over my own feet. Many faults escape our own eyes; and weak judgment consists, not in failing to detect them, but in refusing to admit them when pointed out to us.

While I have yielded to the public taste in sprinkling myself with quotations, I do not propose they shall totally drown me. Had I followed my own opinion, I would have spoken only with my own voice. Without pains or learning, I can borrow from the books about me in the room where I write a dozen such patchers and darners, gentlemen whom I hardly bother to glance at. I need no more than the introductory treatise of some German to stuff me with quotations, and head me for a neat reputation by gulling a silly world.

These hasty puddings of banality, by which so many people take a shortcut to knowledge, are of no use except in subjects of the same dough. They serve to show off our learning, but not to instruct us.

I have seen books made of things neither studied nor understood. The author divides the research of its subjects among several of his learned friends, and preens himself on having furnished the plan, and the industry to wrap together this bundle of undigested fodder. Anyhow, the paper and ink are his. This is to buy or borrow a book, not to make one. It is to show the world not that he can write a book, but—lest there be any doubt—that he cannot.

I do the contrary. Among so many things to borrow, I am glad if I can steal something and change and disguise it for some new end, even at the risk of having it said I am ignorant of its true purport. We who love nature and reality think there is greater honor in originality than in learning.

As for the rest, I add to my first impressions, but I never correct them. For my purpose is to study the progress of my ideas, and leave each as it was born. I wish I had begun sooner, so I could have better observed the course they took. Then, too, I believe that if a man thinks he can do better, he should put it in a new book and not adulterate the old. For myself, I fear to lose by the alteration. I have grown older since the first publication of my *Essays* in 1580, but I doubt if I have grown wiser. Finally, anyone who knows my laziness will believe me when I say I would rather write as many more essays again than chain myself down to revising those I've already written.

Their favorable reception has given me more confidence than I expected. Praise is always pleasing, though the common judgment rarely hits the mark. If I am not mistaken, the worst writings of my time have won the greatest applause. Many a man has been a miracle in the world's eye, in whom his wife and page have seen nothing notable. Few men have been admired by their valets. In my country of Gascony, they think it droll to see me in print. The farther off I am read, the more I am esteemed. I have to buy my publishers here in Guienne; elsewhere they buy me.

When I hear anyone dwell on the language of my essays I would rather he held his peace. He is not so much exalting the style as belittling the sense; and the more indirectly it is done, the deeper it stings. Yet I am much deceived if anyone else furnishes stuff more worth pondering—whether, well or badly done, any other writer has poured so much matter on paper, or, at least, spread it as thick. To give fuller measure, I include only the starting points: if I had expanded them I would have multiplied my volume many times over. How many stories I have strewn up and down my pages, which say nothing—but which, if you question them closely, would yield enough to produce an infinity of essays.

Neither my stories nor my quotations are always meant to serve as an example, an authority, or an ornament. Sometimes I do not regard them for the mere use I make of them. They often carry, beyond what I say of them, the seed of a richer and bolder thought. They carry a subtler undertone—both for myself who do not wish to speak more explicitly, and for those who can catch my tune. I have my own reasons, perhaps, to say things by halves, to speak confusedly and awry.

What I find tolerable in my writings are only so in comparison with worse things which I see well enough received. So far from pleasing me, when I review them they disgust me. I have an idea in mind, a certain vague image which shows me, as in a dream, a better line that I can hew to. I don't know how to grasp or exploit it—and even then, the idea is mediocre.

As to my natural parts, of which these are the essays, they bend under the burden. My imagination and judgment grope in the dark. When I go as far as I can, tripping and stumbling, I glimpse ahead more and wider land wrapped in an impenetrable cloud.

When I want to judge someone else, I ask him how far he is pleased with his own work. I want none of these pretty excuses: 'I did it only as a pastime—it didn't take me an hour—I've never looked at it since.' Well then, say I, put it aside, and give me one which is indeed yourself—one you are willing to be measured by.

There should be a law against useless and impertinent scribblers, as against vagrants and idlers. If there were, I and a hundred others would be banished from the kingdom. I do not say this in jest. Scribbling seems to be a symptom of a diseased world. We never wrote so much as since our civil wars began. And when did the Romans so much as on the verge of their decline? Besides, the refinement of our wit makes no one wiser in government. These idle books get born because people don't attend to their proper business, but leap at the chance to divert themselves from it.

But I am less a writer of books than anything else. My business is to shape my life—this is my one trade and calling. The man who has any worth in him should show it in his daily manners and speech, his love affairs and his quarrels, in play, in bed, at table, and in the management of his business and house. The man who writes a good book while sitting in torn breeches should first mend his breeches. Ask a Spartan whether he would rather be a good orator or a good soldier—but don't ask me, for I would rather be a good cook if I didn't already have one. Good God, how I would hate to be thought a pretty fellow with my pen, but an ass at everything else! A servant I employed to write under my dictation imagined he had garnered a rich booty by filching a number of my essays, choosing those which pleased him most. I am consoled to think he will gain no more than I have lost.

If I had chosen to write learnedly, I would have written sooner, when I was nearer to my studies and had more brains and better memory. He who commits his old age to the press is a simpleton if he thinks to squeeze from it anything but dreaming, dotage, and drivel. In aging, the mind grows constipated and thick.

I, however, deliver my learning in thin driblets—but my ignorance in pomp and state. I write of nothing but nothingness itself—not of science but of unlearnedness. And I have chosen the years when my life—which is what I propose to paint—lies all before my eyes.

The rest to come has to do with death. And if I babble when I meet it, as others do, I'll likely give an account of my loquacious departure.

CHAPTER XIII

Why I Paint My Own Portrait

T WAS A MELANCHOLY HUMOR, very much an enemy to my natural disposition and born of the solitude in which I had taken refuge, that first put into my head this notion of writing. And because I found I had nothing else to write about, I presented myself as a subject. When I wrote of anything else I wandered and lost the way.

One day I was at Bar-le-Duc when King Francis II was presented a portrait which King René of Sicily had made of himself. Why, in a like manner, isn't it lawful for every one of us to paint himself with his pen, as René drew himself with a crayon?

If the novelty and strangeness of my design—which are wont to give value to a thing—do not save me, I shall never come off with honor in this foolish attempt. It is the only book of its kind in the world. Yet the subject is so vain and trivial, the best workman could not bring it to esteem; and there is nothing in it worth remark but its extravagancy. Still, it is so fantastic and out of the ordinary that perhaps it will pass.

I have no other aim but to disclose myself. However inconsiderable these essays of myself may be, I will not conceal them any more than my old bald pate, where the painter has set before you not a perfect face, but my own. And tomorrow I shall perhaps have another self, if by chance a new lesson will change me.

I write my book for few men and few years. Considering how

rapidly our language changes—it slips through our fingers every day and since I was born has more than half-transformed itself— I do not fear to use it for a number of private messages which will die with men now living, or which concern such minds as look further into a thing than ordinary.

I do not want men to say of me, as I often hear them say of the dead, 'This is how he lived and thought—that is what he meant—if he could have spoken on his deathbed, he would have said so-and-so and given such-and-such—I knew him better than anyone.' If people are to talk, I want it with truth and justice. I'll gladly come back from the other world to give the lie to anyone who will shape me other than I was, even though to honor me.

If I had not defended with all my might a friend whom I had lost,[1] they would have torn him into a thousand contrary shapes. I know I shall leave no one behind me to do for me what I did for him, nor anyone to whom I can fully confide the painting of my portrait. He alone knew my true face, and he took it with him. That is why I paint myself with such care. And what I can't express, I point at with my finger.

Everyone, says Pliny, has a good curriculum in himself, provided he can spy closely into his own mind. What I offer here is not my teaching, but my study; not a lesson for others, but for myself. If I pass it on, do not take it amiss; for what is useful to me may perhaps serve someone else. For the rest, I do no harm. I make use of nothing but what is mine; and if I play the fool, it is at my own expense. It is a folly that dies with me, and there are no heirs.

We hear of one or two ancients who took this road, though I cannot say if it was in my manner; for I know nothing of them but their names, Since then, no one has trod in their tracks.

---

1. La Boétie.

It is a thorny enterprise, harder than it seems, to pursue the rambling trail of the mind and penetrate its opaque depths—choosing and fixing in your grasp its countless fugitive reflections. It is a new and unusual entertainment, which lures me from the ordinary business of the world, even that which is in most repute.

For many years now, my thoughts have dwelt only on myself. The world looks out and across: I turn my gaze within. I am always meditating on myself, trying and considering. Others, if they stop to think of it, will find that they send their mind abroad; it moves on ahead. As for me, I am forever revolving in myself. If I study something else, it is merely to apply it to, or rather, in myself. And I do not hold it improper if, as others do with less profitable knowledge, I tell what I have learned—though I am little satisfied with my progress. There is no description so difficult as describing one's self.

Custom has ruled all talk of one's self to be vicious, and prohibits it because of the boasting that seems inseparable from it. Instead of giving a child a handkerchief, this is to cut off its nose. I think that condemning wine because some persons get drunk is itself condemnable. These are muzzles for puppies, with which neither the saints whom we hear speak so highly of themselves, nor philosophers, nor divines ever muzzle themselves. And neither will I, who am as little one as the other.

My trade and art is to live my life. The man who forbids me to speak of my experience, feeling, and practice of it might as well forbid an architect to speak of building as he, and not another, knows it.

Perhaps they mean I ought to show myself in action and accomplishments, and not in words. But since my chief business is to paint my thoughts—formless things which cannot be rendered palpable—I have trouble enough to clothe them in the airy robe of the voice. The wisest and most devout men have shunned to put their life in visible deeds. My actions would tell more of my luck than of myself. They would witness their own rôle, and not mine—save by conjecture and guess. They are samples of their own showing.

But I show myself in my entirety: at one view the skeleton, muscles, and veins—here a cough and there a heartbeat, and their elusive effects. It is not my deeds I write—it is I and my essence.

Men fancy that to think of themselves means to be pleased with what they think—that to cultivate the self is to overindulge it. This is true only of those who skim the surface, who look on themselves as a stranger within, who see their real selves in their business, and for whom inner meditation means daydreaming and building castles in Spain.

While we should be prudent in the estimation of what we are, we must, I think, be no less conscientious in giving a report of it, for good or evil. To belittle yourself is not modesty so much as stupidity. If I thought I was altogether good and wise, I'd trumpet it abroad. But to overpraise yourself is not only presumption, but folly. However, the cure for it is not to forbid people to talk of themselves; for that will likewise stop them from thinking of themselves.

And if a man begins to think of himself, he will find nothing to make him proud which doesn't at the same time cast into the scales something to make him humble; and, in the end, the balance can always be tipped by the insignificance of human existence. Because Socrates alone chewed to the heart that precept of his god, 'Know thyself,' he alone has been found worthy of the title of a sage. Whoever knows himself in this fashion, let him boldly speak out.

But someone may tell me: this design to make yourself the subject of your pen is excusable only in a great and famous man whose reputation has whetted our desire to know more about him. A mechanic, I confess, will hardly lift his eyes from his tools to look at an ordinary passerby; whereas, when a prominent personage comes to town, every store and workshop is deserted. Only a man worth imitating, I know, should describe his own character; and it is a pity we have not the diaries of Alexander the Great and other men whose mere statues in bronze and marble we like to contemplate.

The objection is sound, but, so far as I am concerned, it is hardly to the point. In this book I am not casting a statue to set up at the crossroads, or in a public square or church. It is meant for some corner of a library, or to entertain a friend or neighbor who has a mind to renew and deepen his acquaintance with me.

Others have been encouraged to speak of themselves because the subject was rich and worthy—I, on the contrary, because I find it so lean and sterile there can be no suspicion of ostentation. I don't find such goodness in myself that I cannot tell it without blushing. My one relation to the public is that I borrow the public tools of printing; and, as a reward, my pages may perhaps serve in the marketplace to keep a pound of butter from melting in the sun.

And if no one reads me, have I lost my time entertaining myself with pleasant and useful thoughts? Our most delicious pleasures, when enjoyed within themselves, shun the touch of the world's hand or leaving a trace behind. How often has this preoccupation diverted me from troublesome thoughts, and all frivolous thoughts should be accounted troublesome. Nature has given us ample means of diverting ourselves with ourselves, and often invites us to use them, in order that we may learn we owe only a part of us to society—and not the best nor the most.

A man has to comb his hair and brush up before he appears in public. Just so I am forever dressing myself, for I am my own public. Drawing this portrait after my own model, I have often been forced to drape and rearrange myself in order that the pose may offer a truer likeness, with the result that I have created for myself a fresher and brighter complexion than I began with. My book has made me as much as I have made my book. It is of the same stuff as the author, a limb of my body, devoted to its own being and not to the concerns of its reader, as are other books.

What, too, if I read other books a little more attentively, watching to see if I can't steal something to adorn or support my own? For I have not studied in order to make a book; but because I had to make one I somehow studied—if it be studying to scratch and pinch this author and that, by the head or heels, not to form my opinions but to test them.

And how many times, when I am displeased with some action which I cannot, in decency and reason, openly reprove, I unburden myself here—not without the hope of bringing it to the public ear! These rhapsodical lashes lay themselves better on paper than on flesh.

We do not reform the man we hang: we hope to reform others through him. I do the same. My errors are either natural or incorrigible; but the good which virtuous men perform by setting a model before the public, I may do by setting a warning. There may be people of my cast who learn more by avoiding than imitating. The horror I have of cruelty more inclines me to clemency than any example of kindliness. An expert riding master can't improve my seat so well as merely looking at a lawyer or a Venetian in the saddle.

Moreover, the times are appropriate for us to reform backwards: by dissent rather than accord. Since I profit little by the good examples, which are rare, I make use of the bad, which are plentiful enough. I try to become as agreeable as I see others offensive, as constant as others are fickle, as gentle as others are gruff, and as decent as others are unspeakable. But I have set myself an impossible goal.

I find this unsuspected advantage in the publication of my

memoirs. It serves in some sort as a check. Now and then it occurs to me not to betray my own story, not to belie the picture I have drawn. Moreover, I believe I have furnished enough targets so that whoever would attack me can satisfy his malice without shooting in the air. Even if he turns my evil roots into full-grown trees, a free confession disarms slander.

Besides this profit, I am in hopes that if my humors should please some honest man before I die, he will desire to seek my company. I have surrendered him a great deal of territory without battle. All he could learn of me by long years of acquaintance he can now have in three days' reading, and more certain and exact. A droll idea! Things I would not whisper to any individual I tell to the public, and send my best friends to the bookseller to inform themselves of my most intimate thoughts.

If I knew by sure report of someone after my own heart, I would go a long way indeed to seek him out. The sweetness of a companion cannot, in my mind, be bought too dear. Oh, for a friend! How true is the old saying, 'Friendship is sweeter and more necessary than fire or water.'

CHAPTER XIV

About My Physical Makeup

 AM OF SOMEWHAT LESS than medium height, a defect that not only borders on deformity, but carries with it a good deal of inconvenience. The authority of an imposing presence is lacking. Little men, says Aristotle, are pretty, but not handsome. It vexes you, when you are surrounded by your servants, to have a man come up to you and ask, 'Where is Monsieur?'—or that all you receive is the breeze of the hat which is bowed to your secretary or barber. Other beauties belong to women; beauty of stature is the only beauty of men.

I cannot repeat often enough how much I esteem beauty. Not only in the men who serve me, but in beasts, I consider it within two fingers' breadth of goodness. It grieves me that Socrates had; as we are told, an ugly face and body, so little suited to his soul and to a man who was himself such a great lover of beauty. The homeliness which clothed the fair soul of La Boétie was of that superficial sort, a blot on the complexion, which displeases us only at first sight, in an otherwise symmetrical body. A man's looks are, to be sure, small warrant of his nature, yet it is something. I have a favorable aspect—'Did I say, have? No, Chremes, I had' [Terence]—both in itself and as it impresses others, which makes a show quite contrary to that of Socrates.

As for the rest, I am sturdily built and well knit. My face is full, though not fat; my disposition somewhere between jovial and melancholy—moderately sanguine and warm. The best thing about my physical makeup is its suppleness and lack of obstinacy. Some of my leanings are more personal and agreeable than others, but I can be diverted from them with little trouble, and easily follow a contrary course.

My health was vigorous and sprightly until I was well advanced in years, and I was rarely troubled with sickness.

Such I was, for I do not portray myself as I am now when I have entered the avenues of old age, being long past forty. Hereafter I shall be only half a man: every day I steal and leave something of myself behind.

I came into the world with all my senses whole, even perfect. My stomach is still good enough, and my head, and my breath. And they bear up well even in fevers.

My face and eyes always betray the state of my health; any change begins there and usually appears worse than it really is. My friends often wag their heads over me before I know there is anything wrong. My looking glass does not alarm me; for even in youth I had more than once put on a pasty color and look which augured ill, but had no serious consequence. Not finding any bodily ailment, the doctors used to lay it to my mind and some secret trouble gnawing at it, but they were mistaken. My mind was not only carefree, but brimming with joy and contentment, as it commonly is—half by its own nature and half by design.

If I could rule my body as I do my mind, we should get along a little more at our ease. I believe that my temperament has often lifted my body from a slump. The latter, in fact, is frequently depressed; whereas my mind, even if it is not always brisk and gay, is at least tranquil and reposed.

I don't remember that I ever had the itch, yet scratching is one of Nature's sweetest gratifications and right in your hand—but repentance comes too quickly. I scratch myself mostly on the inside of my ears, for they are subject to prickling.

My walk is quick and firm; and I don't know which of the two, my mind or body, I can less easily bring to a halt at a given point. That preacher is indeed my friend who can hold my attention through a sermon. In assemblies where etiquette reigns and everyone wears a starched face, and where I've seen even women keep their eyes fixed, I could never keep some part or other of me from wandering. Even when I am seated, I am not settled. The better to gesticulate I almost always carry a switch, whether on foot or in the saddle. It may be said of me that from my infancy I have had madness or quicksilver in my feet; for they are always fidgeting, no matter where I place them.

As to such indifferent things as clothes, whoever tries to bring them back to their true use—to the mere service and comfort upon which their real grace depends? The most fantastic I can imagine are our flat caps, the long tail of velvet that hangs from our ladies' heads, and that futile bulge we cannot in modesty so much as mention, but which we nevertheless parade in public.

I find fault that people allow themselves to be so much put upon by fashion that, if the styles demand it, they would change their clothes and their opinion of them every month. We had scarcely worn cloth a single year, in compliance with the court, for mourning Henri II, when silk fell in such contempt that to see a man dressed in it wrote him down at once as a burgher. When men wore the busk of their doublet in the center of their chest, they maintained with the soberest reasons in the world that it was in its proper place; and when some years later, fashion dropped it down between the thighs, everyone laughed at the former mode as uncomfortable and ridiculous. And since all the tailors in the world cannot invent enough whim-whams to satisfy our vanity, you may depend upon it that the despised fashion will eventually return.

For myself, although Frenchmen delight in a variety of colors, I seldom dress in anything but plain black or white, in imitation of my father. A perfumed doublet gratifies my own nose at first; but after I have worn it three or four days, it is not I who benefits, but others. I think it superfluous for a gentleman to go about finely dressed in his own home: his house, retinue, and table should answer enough for him.

Whereas I cannot endure to go unbuttoned and unmuffled in winter, the laborers in my neighborhood would feel themselves trussed up in such a costume. Our peasants, like our ancestors long ago, keep their breast and belly bare. Had we really been born with the necessity for wearing breeches and petticoats, you may be sure that Nature would have fortified those parts with a thicker skin, as she has our fingertips and the soles of our feet.

I never cover my legs more warmly in winter than in summer: a simple pair of silk stockings at all seasons. True, in order to relieve my colds I allow myself a warmer headdress, and something more about my belly for my colic. But in a few days my ailments get used to them, and I am as badly off as I was before. From a cap I went to a muffler, from a bonnet to a lined hat; and the quilting inside my doublet is now only an ornament. I've reached the point where nothing will help me unless I add furs and feathers, and a skullcap under my hat—at this rate I will have a fine road to travel.

But I refuse to stir. And if I dared, I would gladly go back to where I began. Thus we destroy ourselves when once we consent to be pestered with precautions. There is never an end to them.

CHAPTER XV

A Jumble of Habits

 HAVE LIVED LONG ENOUGH to give an account of the habits that have brought me this far. If anyone wishes to try them, I have, like his cup-bearer, tasted them first. Here, in a jumble, are some of the details as my memory supplies them. There are none which I do not vary according to circumstance; but I will describe those I have observed hold the deepest and longest sway over me—those I would consider it almost an excess to break.

Without forcing myself I cannot sleep in the daytime, nor eat between meals. I cannot breakfast until a long while after I rise, or go to bed until a good three hours after supper; nor beget children except before I sleep, and never while on my feet.

I cannot tolerate my own sweat; nor quench my thirst with plain water or undiluted wine; nor keep my head bare for any length of time; nor have my hair cut after dinner. I should be as uneasy without gloves as without my shirt, and I must wash when I rise from table or get out of bed. I can't sleep without canopy and curtains to my bed—as if all these things were essential.

I can dine without a tablecloth, but hardly without clean napkins, as the Germans do; for I soil them more than they or the Italians, since I make little use of a spoon or fork. I regret that the royal custom of changing napkins, together with the plates, after every course is not more widespread.

I've allowed myself to prefer certain kinds of drinking glasses, and do not willingly use the ordinary ones, any more than I would drink with others from the same cup. Metal goblets, even gold and silver, are less pleasing to me than the brightness and transparency of glass. I want my eyes to enjoy themselves too.

Several of these niceties I owe to habit. But Nature has given me others. I cannot, for example, eat two full meals a day without overloading my stomach. Yet if I abstain completely from one of them, it fills me with wind, parches my mouth, and upsets my appetite.

I am a great lover of pleasant smells, and by the same token abominate stenches—which I think I can whiff at a greater distance than most men. Of perfumes, the simplest suit me best. You can't imagine how strangely all sorts of odors cling to me. If I but touch my gloves or my handkerchief to my mustaches, which are thick, the smell will linger there all day. They always tell me where I have been.

I wish, the better to judge of it, I could have tasted the cookery served by the King of Tunis to Emperor Charles V: the meats were so stuffed with odoriferous herbs that one peacock and two pheasants cost one hundred ducats; and when the carver cut them, not only the dining hall and apartment but the streets round about were laden with the fragrance. When travelling, my chief concern in choosing my lodgings is to avoid thick and stinking air; and those beautiful cities, Venice and Paris, lose much of the kindness I have for them, the one by the offensive smell of her marshes, and the other by that of her mud.

So, too, I suffer from long exposure to night air. Of late years, in military marches which often last through the night, my stomach begins to trouble me after five or six hours, together with violent headaches, so that I always vomit before dawn. When the others go to breakfast, I go to sleep, and afterwards I am as brisk as ever.

Both kings and philosophers go to stool, and ladies too. They, for their part, must maintain discretion; but as a simple private individual, I enjoy a natural dispensation. Besides, a soldier and a Gascon is allowed a little latitude of speech. So I will say of this action that a man should set for it a fixed hour in the evening, and force himself by habit to stick to it, as I have done. He should not chain himself, as has been my wont in my declining years, to the convenience of any one place or seat, nor make it troublesome by long and dilatory sitting. Where, but in foul offices, are cleanliness and despatch more necessary? Of all the actions of nature, this is the one I am most unwilling to be interrupted. I have seen many soldiers troubled by the irregularity of their bowels; but mine and I never fail to keep their appointment, which is immediately upon leaping out of bed—unless illness or importunate business interferes.

I am slow and late at everything: rising, going to bed, and meals. Seven in the morning is early for me, and where I have sway I never dine before eleven, nor sup till after six.

Formerly I attributed the fevers and other ailments that beset me to the heaviness caused by my prolonged sleeping, and I always repent going to sleep again after I once wake up. Plato thinks that excessive sleeping is worse than drunkenness.

I like to sleep on a hard bed, alone, even without my wife— like royalty—and rather well covered. My bed is never warmed; but since I have grown old, I am given, if needs be, an extra cover for my stomach and feet. People found fault with the great Scipio because he was a big sleeper: in my opinion, the real reason was that he annoyed them by furnishing them nothing to be annoyed at.

Sleep has consumed much of my life, and even at my present age I sleep eight or nine hours at a stretch. I am weaning myself from it, and to my benefit. The change is hard at first, but after three days it is over with.

I see few men who can do with less sleep when they have to, who exercise more constantly than I, or to whom a spell of hard work is less fatiguing. My body is capable of sustained, though not heavy or sudden, exertion. Of late I avoid all violent exercises and such that make me sweat: my limbs grow tired before they are warmed up. When I am not with a switch, I am accustomed to carry a cane, even to the point of elegance and leaning on it with an affected weakness. My friends have warned me that this hobby may one day turn into a necessity. If so, I shall be the first in my family to have the gout.

I can remain on my feet all day long, and I never tire of walking. But on the highways I have always preferred the saddle: afoot I splash myself with mud to the buttocks, and in the streets little fellows like myself are liable to be elbowed and jostled aside. Once I am on horseback I do not willingly dismount, for whether well or sick I find myself most at ease in the saddle. Pliny says it is excellent for the stomach and the joints. I would not have been the worst as a courier, which is suitable for a man of my build, short and well knit. But I am quit of the business, as it is too fatiguing to keep at for long.

Whether lying or sitting I like to stretch myself out—my legs as high as my seat or higher.

My friends think I could do something at letter writing; and I am willing to confess I should have preferred to publish my notions in that form, if I had someone to write to and sustain my interest—as I once had. I have, however, a naturally comic and familiar style, like my speech, unsuitable for public display. In formal polite letters I am wholly at sea.

I always write my letters posthaste—so precipitously that although my handwriting is intolerably wretched, I must use my own pen, for I can find no one able to keep up with me. I never copy them over, and have accustomed my eminent correspondents who know me to put up with my erasures, my words written one over the other, and my paper without margin or fold. Those I work hardest over turn out the worst—when I begin to drag, it is a sign I am not there. I never plan my letters: the first word leads to the second.

Just as I would rather write two letters than fold and seal one—I always let another tend to that—so, when the real business of my letter is done, I would gladly give someone else the task of adding those strings of rhetoric, proffers of service, and well-wishes we tag on the end. I wish some new custom would likewise relieve us from inscribing that parade of titles and qualities at the beginning, which for fear of bungling I often omit—especially to financiers and men of the law. In these fields there are so many newfangled titles, offices, and distinctions which, since they have been dearly bought, would greatly offend the recipient, if confused or forgotten.

I have no complaint against my imagination. Few unruly thoughts have broken my sleep, except those of desire which have not discomforted me. I seldom dream; and when I do, it is of fantastic things commonly pleasant or absurd, rather than sad. I maintain that our dreams are the faithful interpreters of our inclinations, but it takes skill to disentangle and understand them. My dreams are always gentle, without agitating my body or moving me to speech.

At table I rarely choose a dish, but fall to the nearest one at hand, and I am reluctant to move on to another. A crowding of dishes and courses annoys me as any other crowding. I am easily satisfied with a small variety. I like salt in my meat, yet I prefer unsalted bread, and my baker never serves up any other at my table, contrary to the custom of the region.

Sitting long at table both exasperates and harms me, perhaps because since a child I accustomed myself to keep eating as long as I sat, for lack of something better to do. Therefore, in my own house, though our meals are of the shortest, I usually come to the table a little after the others—as Augustus did, but I do not imitate him in rising before the rest. On the contrary, I love to dally a long while after the meal is over and hear the company talk, provided I don't have to join in, for it is just as tiring and bad for me to talk on a full stomach as it is pleasant and beneficial to argue vociferously before I sit down.

It is easy for the people who look after me to keep me from eating what they think is harmful, for I never wish or ask for anything I don't see. But once a dish is in sight, I can't be talked out of it. When I diet, therefore, I must eat apart, for if I go to the table I forget my resolutions. When I ask the cook to change the preparation of a dish, all my people know what it means: I am tired of it and won't touch it.

I like my meat cooked as little as possible, and high even to the point of smelling. Nothing annoys me but toughness: in everything else I am as patient or indifferent as any man I know. Contrary to the common taste, I often find fish to be too fresh and firm—though not because of my teeth, which were always sound and which age is only now beginning to threaten. I learned from childhood to rub them with a napkin before and after meals and in the morning.

I am not very fond of salads and fruits, except melons. My father hated and I love every sort of gravy. Overeating bothers me, but as to the kinds of food, I know of nothing that I am certain will disagree with me. We all have varying and inexplicable appetites; for example, at one time I found radishes gratifying, later nauseous, and now they are grateful again to my stomach. So, too, I am forever switching between white wine and claret.

I am a great lover of fish—to my mind its taste is more delicate than that of meat and I believe it more digestible—so my Fridays and Lents are feast days. Just as I make it a point of conscience not to eat meat on fast days, so my taste is conscientious about eating fish and flesh together: the difference seems too great.

From my youth up I have been used to skipping a meal occasionally, either to whet my appetite or keep me alert for some business on hand. For both my mind and body are cruelly dulled by repletion. Above all, I hate the coupling of so healthy and lively a goddess as Venus with that belching little Bacchus, swollen with the fumes of his own liquor.

Sometimes, too, I do without a meal for lack of agreeable company. I say, with Epicurus, that a man should consider less what he eats than with whom. No sauce is so pleasant to me and no dish so gratifying as good company.

I find it better to dine at noon, and my digestion goes easier when I am awake than asleep. I am seldom thirsty, and commonly drink only from the thirst that comes with eating, and rather along in the meal.

For a man of ordinary build, I drink pretty well. In summer and at a good meal I don't exceed the limits of Augustus, who drank but three fills; still, in order not to offend Democritus who maintained that four was unlucky, I slide on, if needs be, to five—about a pint and a half in all. Small glasses are my favorites, and I like to drain them, which others think is poor manners.

I mix my wine with a third or a half part of water. At home I follow the custom of my father, prescribed him by his physician, and have the wine I am to drink mixed in the buttery two or three hours before it is served. The custom of the country is the most becoming to follow: I should as much dislike to see a German mix water with his wine as see a Frenchman drink it straight.

Drunkenness seems to me a brutish vice. Certain vices have, if a man may say so, something generous in them: knowledge, valor, prudence, or skill. But this is wholly sodden. The grossest nation in the world today is the one that esteems drunkenness: the Germans drink any sort of wine with delight—their business is not to taste it, but to pour it down. Yet to drink in the French fashion—at but two meals a day and then very moderately—is to be too sparing with the favors of the god. I think we grow more abstemious every day. As I recall it, the lunches, snacks, and evening bites were more frequent in my father's house when I was a boy. Not that we are growing better: no, we are more given to Venus than our fathers were, and these are two sports that go poorly together.

I am afraid of heavy air, and fly from smoke as from the plague. The first repairs I undertook in my house were the chimneys and toilets, the common and unbearable nuisances of old buildings. I count among the worst hardships of a military campaign the dust which buries you the whole day in the heat of summer. Yet my breathing is free and easy, and my colds usually vanish without a cough or any injury to my lungs.

The rigors of summer are more my enemy than those of winter. Besides the discomfort of the heat, which is harder to combat than cold, and besides the effect of the sun on my head, all brilliant light bothers my eyes. I am no longer able to eat while facing a blazing fire.

It is indecent, besides injurious to the health and to the pleasure itself of eating, to gobble up the food as I do. In my haste I often bite my tongue and even my fingers. I lose, too, the leisure to talk, which is the best seasoning for food, provided it is timely, merry, and not long-winded.

There is a jealousy between our pleasures. They cross and impede one another. Alcibiades, a savant in the art of providing good cheer, banished music from meals, lest it should disturb the talk. To dine your friends well requires no little skill and gives no mean pleasure. The greatest generals and philosophers scorned neither the knowledge nor the practice of good eating. I can remember three dinners which fortune rendered sovereignly sweet to me, when I was in my prime. My present state no longer permits me this enjoyment; for each guest supplies the best savor and grace of it from out of his own temper and appetite.

Being made of common clay I hate men who would have us despise the culture of the body: I think it as unjust to loathe natural pleasures as to be infatuated with them. A man should neither pursue nor flee them: he should receive them.

I who boast so minutely of embracing the comforts of life find, when I examine them closely, nothing but wind. Well, what of it? We are wind throughout. And wiser than we, the wind loves to bluster and veer, contenting itself with its own nature and giving no thought to a stability and solidity that does not belong to it.

Some men, says Aristotle, despise physical pleasure because they are stupid; but I know of some who do it because they are ambitious. Why don't they swear off breathing. And why enjoy the daylight which costs them nothing? Let them try to sustain themselves on Mars, Pallas, and Mercury instead of Venus, Ceres, and Bacchus, and see what happens. Are they the sort of people who try to square the circle while perched on their wives?

When I dance, I dance; when I sleep, I sleep; when I stroll in an orchard, sometimes my thoughts wander to other things, but again they return to my walk, the orchard, the sweetness of solitude, and to myself.

CHAPTER XVI

I Have a Thousand Humors

OT ONLY THE WINDS of chance move me as they list, but I am constantly moving and disordering myself. No one who watches himself will often find himself in the same posture. My soul assumes a different profile according to the pose I give it. If I speak diversely of myself, it is because I regard myself diversely. Truly, man is a creature marvellously vain, fickle, and undulant.

I contain in some fashion every contradiction, as the occasion provides. Bashful, insolent, chaste, lustful, talkative, silent, clumsy, fastidious, witty, stupid, morose, gay, false, true, wise, foolish, liberal, greedy, prodigal: I see myself somewhat all of this as I turn myself around—and so will everyone if he does the like. I can therefore describe nothing of myself in a simple, absolute, or single word. 'I distinguish' is the most universal device of my logic.

When I am fasting I am quite another man than after a meal. If health and sunny weather shine on me, I am a good fellow; if a corn troubles my toe, I am sullen, out of sorts, and inaccessible.

The same pace of my horse seems to me now a joggle and again a glide; the same road shorter one trip and longer another; and the same shape more pleasing today and less tomorrow. At one moment I am for doing everything; and at another, for doing nothing. What is a pastime for me now will be drudgery later on. I have in me a thousand rash and chance humors. I am gloomy, I am choleric, I am tormented, I am blithe.

When I take up a book I will discover a passage to strike my very soul. Let me light on it another time; and turn and twist and tumble it as I may, it remains a shapeless unrecognizable botch. Even in my own writings I cannot always recapture the sense of my thought. I don't know what I wanted to say; and having lost the original and probably better meaning, I work myself into a sweat to give it a new one.

I do nothing but come and go. My judgment does not always steer ahead; it floats and drifts 'like a small bark caught in a great and windy sea' [Catullus]. Many times I have undertaken to maintain an opinion contrary to my own, as I am fond of doing for the sport and exercise of it; and my mind applies itself so convincingly to the new belief that I abandon the old. As I tip myself, so I am drawn; and I am carried away by my own weight.

I have scarcely any memory, and do not think there is another in the world so imperfect as mine. My other faculties are average and ordinary, but in this I think myself rare and singular, and entitled to some fame.

If anyone wants to propound something to me, he must do it piecemeal; for I am not able to hold or consider more than one point at a time. I can't receive a commission without jotting it down in my notebook. I am forced to call my servants by their occupation or birthplace, for names are hard for me to retain. I can tell, indeed, if a name has three syllables, or a harsh sound, or if it begins or ends with a certain letter—but that is all. If I live long enough, I shall no doubt forget my own. More than once I have forgotten a password which I myself gave out or received three hours before; and where I have hidden my purse. I help myself lose what I have carefully locked up. I do not study books, but turn them over: the author, place, words, and other circumstances vanish. I am so good at forgetting that I forget my own compositions as well, and often quote myself without knowing it.

If I have a long or important speech to make, I am reduced to the miserable necessity of getting it by heart—I whom it takes three hours to learn three verses. Besides, in your own work the liberty you have to alter the words and order makes them harder to remember. The more I mistrust my memory, the worse it behaves: it serves me best by chance and at its own hour. If I venture to digress ever so little from a subject I am lost, which is the reason that, in talking, I keep strictly to what I have to say. Yet being tied to what I have to say loosens me from it. And the preparation arouses more expectation than it can satisfy. A man often strips to his shirt to jump no farther than he would have done in his gown.

In my part of the country, when they want to say a man has no sense, they say he has no memory; and if I complain of my defect they reprove me for calling myself a fool—which makes matters worse for me. But they do me wrong. Experience shows, on the contrary, that a powerful memory usually goes with a weak judgment.

They also wrong me—for I am as perfect in nothing as I am in friendship—when they question my affection because of my poor memory. 'He has forgotten,' they said, 'this request or that promise—he no longer remembers his friends.' True, I am liable to forget many things, but never obligations. It is enough that I feel the misery of it without branding me with malice or ingratitude, both so contrary to my nature.

However, I derive comforts from my infirmity. It is an evil which has saved me from one much worse—namely, ambition. Lack of memory is intolerable in those engaged in public affairs. Then, too, it has rendered me less talkative, for a man usually has a greater stock of memories than ideas. If mine had been faithful, I would long ago have deafened my friends with my babble. This would have been a pity; for I notice that several of my intimates, whose memory supplies a full view of a thing, begin their story so far back and crowd it with so many irrelevant details that they ruin it. My forgetfulness likewise keeps me from nursing my injuries. And, again, the places I revisit and the books I reread still smile on me with the bloom of novelty.

Besides the defect in my memory, I have others which contribute no little to my ignorance. I have a backward and torpid mind; the least cloud stops its progress. I have never, for example, found a riddle easy enough for me to solve. In chess, cards, checkers, and the like, I understand no more than the rudiments. My grasp is tardy and muddled; though when I do grasp something, I see it clearly and closely for the time I retain it.

My talk is always worse when I am master of my tongue. The occasion, the company, even the rise and fall of my voice, draws me out more than when I deliberately measure my words. The things I say are therefore better than those I write—if there must be a choice when both are worthless.

Deliberating, even in the most trivial things, is a burden for me. I find it harder to endure the tumblings and tossings of doubt and deliberation than to stiffen myself to take what comes after the die is cast. Few passions ever break my sleep; but deliberations always do.

When I travel I prefer to avoid slippery and steep roads; and I stick to the valley, no matter how muddy and floundering, and seek my safety where I know I can sink no lower. So, too, I like downright misfortunes which do not torment and tease me with hopes of betterment.

In events I behave like a man; but in my preparation for them, like a child. The fear of a fall is worse for me than the fall itself. The game is not worth the candle. The lowest rung is the firmest: there you need only yourself for support.

I am most sensitive to the suggestive power of the imagination. Everyone is moved by it, but some are thrown off their feet. On me it has a piercing effect, and my art is not to resist but dodge it.

I would live only with healthy and cheerful people. The mere sight of suffering affects me with physical pain. The sensations of another often induce the same in me. A man who continually coughs irritates my throat and lungs. I am less willing to visit a sick person who is near and dear to me than one to whom I am more indifferent. For the diseases I am concerned over I catch and root in me; and I don't wonder that the imagination brings fevers and death to those who give it full play.

Simon Thomas was a great physician when I was a youth. I happened to meet him once, at Toulouse, in the home of a rich old consumptive. He told his patient it would benefit him to have me frequently about. By gazing on my fresh complexion and dwelling with his imagination on my health and vigor, the patient might find his condition improved. But M. Thomas forgot to add that mine might be worsened.

Whoever I look at with attention leaves some impression on me: a silly countenance, a disagreeable grimace, or an affected way of speaking—vices most of all, because they naturally stick to me and can hardly be shaken off. I swear chiefly by imitation. My own oath is merely 'By God!'—the simplest and most direct. I am so apt, without knowing it, to take on these superficial impressions that if I have 'Your Majesty' or 'Your Highness' in my mouth for three days together, out they come instead of 'Your Excellency' or 'Your Lordship' for a week after. And a trick of speech that is meant for foolery today, I'll repeat tomorrow in all seriousness. Yet the gift for playing the mimic to amuse or impress people is no more in me than in a log.

My virtue is more innocence than virtue; or, better said, it is the product of chance. If I had been born with a more lawless nature, I would have made poor work of it. For I have never observed that I possessed any firmness to resist a passion if it was the least violent. I do not know how to quarrel and struggle with myself, and I can little thank myself that I am free from many vices. It is owing more to fortune than reason that I hold most of them in horror.

Both by nature and judgment I mortally hate cruelty as the worst of vices. I cannot see a chicken wrung by the neck without suffering a pang, and I cannot endure the cry of a hare caught by my hounds, though I am passionately fond of riding to the chase. I seldom take a beast alive that I do not release it.

I am strongly moved by the afflictions of others; and if I knew how to weep I would readily do it for company's sake. Nothing tempts me to tears but the tears of others: and feigned ones as well as real.

No man living is freer from sadness than I, who neither like it in myself nor admire it in others. Yet the world is pleased to honor it, and say it is a mark of wisdom, virtue, and conscience. A silly and ugly mark! The Italians do well to use the same word for sadness [la tristezza] as for malignity: for it is a passion as harmful as it is cowardly and base—and always useless.

I am not melancholic, though much given to revery. My imagination has always been concerned with death, even in my most wanton days. Once, while gaming and in the company of ladies, I was suspected of being preoccupied with some ill-digested jealousy or with my player's luck. But in truth I was meditating on never mind what friend. Only a few days before, as he was returning from just such a party, his head filled like mine with nonsense, women, and merriment, he had been surprised by fever and death—which for all I knew hung about my own head. I am eternally brooding over my own thoughts, yet I wrinkle my brow no more than the next man.

My soul naturally abhors lying and hates the very thought of it. I have an inward shame and biting remorse if a lie escapes my lips, as it sometimes does if an occasion surprises me and gives me no chance for second thought. A man must not always tell everything: that would be folly. But everything he says should be what he thinks; otherwise, it is knavery. Lying is a cowardly vice, which one of the ancients portrays in the most odious colors when he says, 'it is to show a contempt for God, yet a fear of men.'

I am nice, even to superstition, in keeping my promises; and, therefore, on all occasions I take care to make them vague or conditional. The knot of integrity binds me tighter than any constraint of society. You will not throttle me as easily with a notary as with my own word. In a bond, my faith owes nothing, for it was credited with nothing. For their security, let my creditors look to the collateral they have taken instead of taking me. I would much rather break prison or the laws themselves than my own word. If an action has not some flash of liberty in it, it has neither grace nor honor. I know some men who will sooner give than restore, lend than pay, and will do the least good to those who have the most claim on them. I don't go so far, but pretty near it.

When I find myself beset by a fault which displeases me both because it is bad in itself and because it annoys me, I try to correct it, but I can never uproot it. As a result I undervalue what I am and have, and overvalue what is not my own and what I lack. Foreign ways, governments, and languages insinuate themselves in my esteem. I am well aware that Latin appeals to me above its true worth, as it does to children or unlettered people. I always prize my neighbor's house or horse above my own, not because they are better, but because they are not mine. The self-assurance and confidence of others always amaze me.

Taking one thing with another, I fancy that men as often praise me without reason, as condemn me. It seems to me that they have given me, from childhood, a place in rank and honor above rather than below my due. I should find myself more at ease in a country where titles and rank were either better regulated or altogether despised. In our society, as soon as a dispute over precedence concerned with where you are to sit or walk exceeds three retorts, politeness ends. The better to avoid such annoying disputes I never stickle at giving or taking a place out of turn. No man ever desired to precede me without my yielding at once.

In fine, the only thing I esteem in myself is something no one thinks he lacks: which is good sense. There never was a porter or chit of a girl who didn't believe they had sense enough for their business. I believe that the source and nursing mother of most false opinions, both in public and private affairs, is the exaggerated opinion a man has of himself. For my part, I think it would be hard to find a man who has a meaner opinion of me than I have. I look upon myself as ordinary in every respect, except in the fact that I look upon myself as ordinary.

The simple peasants are worthy people; and so are the philosophers—or whatever the present age calls them—strong and clear natures enriched with a great store of useful knowledge. The mongrels like myself and a great many more, who have disdained the ignorance of the one and can't achieve the knowledge of the other—who sit between two stools—are dangerous, useless, and a nuisance: it is they who trouble the world. Therefore I seek as best I can to return to the first and natural condition, from which I have fruitlessly.tried to depart.

CHAPTER XVII

French Knight and Roman Citizen

E WHO LEFT ME my house foretold that I would likely ruin it, in view of my vagabond humor. But he was mistaken. Here I am as well off as when I first took charge of it, if not a little better—though still without the perquisites of office or benefice.

If Fortune has not done me any violent injury, neither has she granted me any untoward favor. All the gifts she lavished on my house were there a hundred years and more before my time.

She has, it is true, allowed me certain airy trifles, honorary and titular, and without substance. These she has not so much granted as offered me—to a man who, God knows, is utterly material and takes as current coin nothing but realities, and downright palpable. I am almost prepared to confess that I think avarice better than ambition, health than learning, riches than nobility, and disgrace less to be avoided than pain.

Yet a man cannot discover his needs by consulting his desires. Not only in the enjoyment itself, but in our fancy and wish for it, we cannot agree on what is required to satisfy us. You wish an example?

When I was young I wanted, above all things, the order of Saint Michael. It was then the highest honor among the French nobility, and very rare.

Fortune pleasantly gratified my longing. On the twenty-eighth of October, 1571, upon command of the King and following the letter which His Majesty sent me, I was made Knight of the Order of Saint Michael at the hands of Gaston de la Foix, Marquis de Trans. But Fortune spared me the trouble of being raised to its height; instead, she lowered and cheapened the honor down to my shoulders—and below.

On the twenty-ninth of November, 1577, Henri de Bourbon, King of Navarre—without my knowledge and during my absence—sent me letters patent of Gentleman of His Chamber.

Again—I cannot visit the ruins and tomb of that great and mighty city of Rome, without admiration and reverence. We are bidden to care for the dead, and I have been brought up from my childhood with these dead.

I knew the affairs of Rome before I knew those of my own house. I knew the Capitol and its layout before I knew the Louvre, and the Tiber before the Seine. The lives and fortunes of Lucullus, Metullus, and Scipio ran more in my head than those of my countrymen. They are dead. But so is my father, and no less. He is as separated from life and from me in eighteen years as they in sixteen hundred. Yet I do not cease to cherish his memory and embrace his love and companionship in a perfect and very living union.

I speak most tenderly of my friends when they can no longer know it. I have started a hundred quarrels in defence of Pompey and Brutus. This friendship still persists between us: for our hold even on contemporary things is only through the imagination. Finding myself of no use in our present age, I have slipped back to that other. And I am so infatuated with ancient Rome that her free, just, and flourishing prime (I love her neither at her birth nor in her old age) impassions me.

I cannot, therefore, revisit the site of her streets and houses, and those ruins deep as the Antipodes, without losing myself in revery. Is it by nature or through some trick of the fancy that the sight of places we know to have been frequented by famous men moves us even more than to hear tell of their deeds or to read their works? I delight in dwelling on their face, bearing, and clothes. I turn those great names on my tongue and make them ring in my ears. I could wish to see them talk, walk, and eat.

Moreover, the Rome we have today deserves our love. It is the one universal city, the metropolis of Christian nations. Spaniard and Frenchman, both are at home there. Even her ruins are glorious, and in her tomb she retains the mark and image of empire.

Among the empty favors of Fortune none, therefore, pleases so much this silly fancy of mine—which indeed feeds on it—as the official patent of Roman citizenship conferred on me when I was last there—a thing glorious in seals and gilt lettering, and granted with gracious liberality.

I set all my five senses to work in order to obtain it, if only out of respect for its former dignity. I had some difficulties in the matter, but overcame them at last, without having recourse to any favor and without even the knowledge of any Frenchman.

The authority of the Pope was invoked through his major-domo, Philippo Musotti, who had taken a singular liking to me and exerted himself to the utmost in my behalf. The letters of patent were granted me on the third of the ides of March, 1581; and I received the official document on the fifth of April, couched in the same complimentary language that was addressed on the like occasion to Jacomo Buoncompagnone, Duke of Sero, the Pope's son.

A vain title, but I was delighted to get it; and I would have been glad to see the way it is worded even before I possessed it.

'Wherefore, the most illustrious Michel de Montaigne, Knight of the Order of St. Michael and Gentleman of the Chamber in ordinary to the Most Christian King, being by the rank and distinction of his family and by his personal qualities highly worthy to be admitted to the rights of Roman citizenship, it has pleased the Senate and People of Rome that the most illustrious Michel de Montaigne, adorned with every species of merit, and very dear to this noble people, shall be inscribed as a Roman citizen, himself and his posterity, and admitted to enjoy all its honors and advantages . . . this Senatus-Consultus to be deposited among the archives of the Capitol and sealed with the common seal of this city. *Anno ab urbe condita* CXC.CCC.XXXI'—this to satisfy such as are sick with the same curiosity as mine.

Never having been a citizen of any city, I was pleased to be created one of the noblest that ever was or ever will be.

If other men would look deep enough into themselves they will discover, as I do, a full store of inanity and foppery. I can no more get rid of it than get rid of myself. We are all steeped in it; but those who are not aware of it have the advantage—or perhaps they haven't.

It was a paradoxical commandment given us in the days of old by the god of Delphos: 'Examine yourself; know yourself; remain in yourself. All is vanity for you, within and without; but less of it if confined to within. Excepting you, O man, everything studies chiefly itself, and limits its labors and desires to its needs. There is nothing so vain and destitute as you who embrace the universe: you are the searcher without knowledge, the magistrate without authority, and, when all is said, the fool of the farce.'

CHAPTER XVIII

𝔐y 𝔇iversions

OME NATURES ARE RETIRING and turned inward. I am essentially communicative, outward, and on view, born for society and friendship. The solitude I love for myself and preach to others means a withdrawal of my desires and concerns, not my behavior: it is more to shun business than men. To tell the truth, local solitude gives me greater room and sets me at large. When I am alone I am more willing to throw myself into affairs of state—and of the universe.

At home, surrounded by a large family and in a much frequented house, I see people enough, but rarely those with whom I delight to converse. The men whose society I covet are those we call genuine and talented, and the very thought of them makes me disrelish the rest. Rightly understood, they are of a most unusual type and owe their character almost entirely to Nature.

We come together simply to meet and talk and give our minds free play, with no further fruit. All subjects are alike to us; if weight and depth are lacking, it is no matter—there is still charm and point. A ripe and steady judgment tinges it all, and mingled with it are kindliness, freedom, gaiety, and fellowship. Our minds disclose what we have of power and beauty not only in discussing the politics of kings, but quite as much in intimate chat. I understand my men even in their smiles and silences, and perhaps learn more about them at the dinner table than in the council room. Hippamarchus said he knew a good wrestler simply by seeing him walk down the street.

If Learning chooses to share in our talk, she is not thrust aside, provided she does not put on her usual magisterial, overbearing, and impatient airs, but shows herself amenable and willing to listen. Our purpose is to pass away the time. When we want to be preached to and lectured, we will seek out Learning at her throne. Let her stoop to us for the nonce if she pleases; but useful and desirable though she is, I take it that, if needs be, we can do our business without her. A naturally good mind can please everyone by its own strength. And art is nothing but the control and record of the works of such minds.

In my opinion, the most fruitful and natural play of the mind is conversation. I find it sweeter than any other action in life; and if I were forced to choose, I think I would rather lose my sight than my hearing and voice. The study of books is a drowsy and feeble exercise which does not warm you up.

If I converse with a strong mind and a rude jouster, who presses me hard and digs me right and left, his ideas touch off my own. Jealousy, emulation, and contention stimulate and raise me something above myself. Agreement is absolutely boring in conversation. And it can't be said how much we lose and degenerate by continual intercourse with poor and sickly minds. No contagion spreads as that does—I know only too well from experience how much it is worth a yard.

I love to hold forth and dispute, but only for my own pleasure. To do it as a spectacle, to impress some notable onlookers with your parade of wit and power of gabble is, I find, a business most unbecoming a man of honor.

I enter into discussion with my mind free and easy, for ideas do not readily penetrate its soil or take root in it. No assertion astonishes me, no belief offends mine, however contrary; and there is no idea so frivolous and extravagant that I do not find it a perfectly natural and appropriate product of the human intelligence. People like ourselves, who do not credit our judgment with the power of making absolute decisions, are always ready to give an adverse opinion calm and ready hearing, even if we are not convinced.

When nothing is to be said on the other side of the balance, I gladly let one scale hover among old wives' tales. I am willing to forgive myself if I prefer Thursday to Friday, or to sit twelfth rather than thirteenth at table, or rather give my valet the left foot first when he comes to dress me.

I suffer myself to be roughly handled by my friends—'You are a ninny, you don't know what you are talking about!' I love robust talk among gallant men, and the words speedy as the thought. I want strong and manly familiarity, a friendship that bites and scratches like love: it is neither vigorous nor noble if it is polite, artificial, shy of the shock, and soft footed.

When anyone contradicts me, he arouses my attention, not my anger. I leap toward my antagonist as toward a teacher. The cause of truth is presumably our common cause—and what will he answer? Has anger already warped his judgment and confusion usurped his reason? It would be rather useful to bet on the outcome, and have a material loss mark our defeats in order to remember them better—to have my valet tell me, 'Monsieur, your ignorance and obstinacy cost you a hundred crowns twenty times last year.'

But it is hard to bring the men of our time to this point of view. They lack the courage to correct you because they haven't the courage to be corrected themselves, and they are forever dissimulating before one another. I am much prouder of the victory I gain over myself when I force myself to yield to another man's superior reason than when I triumph over a weaker head.

I am indifferent as to whether I win or lose. I can contentedly argue the whole day through, provided the discussion is conducted in an orderly fashion. I do not demand forcefulness or subtlety so much as order—the order which we see every day in the wranglings of shepherds and shopboys, but never among ourselves. If they digress, it is considered bad manners—though we do it constantly. Their tumult and impatience never throw them off the track; the argument still keeps its course. If they anticipate and do not wait for the other fellow, at least they understand one another.

Anyone answers suitably enough for me, if he only directs his answer to what I say. But when he begins to wander and loses the point and himself, I call him to order with hot and hasty words and I fall into a headstrong, malicious, domineering strain, of which I am afterwards ashamed. But it is impossible to deal fairly with a fool: it ruins my judgment as well as disturbs my conscience.

But this is to take things other than they are? Perhaps I do; and I therefore blame my impatience, and find it as vicious in a man who is right as in one who is wrong. Besides, there is no greater or more enduring folly than to become angry at the twaddle of the world. How many ridiculous things, even in my own opinion, do I say every day? And how many more, God knows, in the opinion of others? We are not annoyed upon meeting a hunchback, and why then are we enraged at a malformed mind? In fine, we must live among the living and let the water flow under the bridge without care, or, at least, without anxiety.

Every apt word is not to be accepted at its face value. Most men are rich in borrowed words, and many say a good thing without knowing it. In the heat of debate, I have sometimes launched sallies that carried me further than I hoped or planned: I paid them out only in number, but they were pocketed by weight.

Then, these general statements that I see so common signify nothing. This is to greet a crowd with one sweeping salute;

whereas, if you really knew your men, you would bow to them individually and mention them by name.

Every day I hear fools talk sense; but let us examine where they got it and how far they understand it. You lend them a hand, but to what avail? They snatch up your explanation: 'That is just what I was about to say—it was precisely my thought—if I didn't express it so, it was for lack of language.' Play them along! Cunning must be used to correct this proud stupidity; it would be inhuman and unjust to relieve men who stand in no need of it and are worse for it. I love to let them sink deeper into the mire—so deep that, if it is at all possible, they will at last realize their error.

What vexes me most in folly is that it pleases itself more than reason can ever reasonably do for itself. Moreover, this arrogance of speech and complacent smirk give fools the better of it in the opinion of the audience. Is there anything more cocksure, disdainful, and solemn than an ass?

As to repartee, which mirth and familiarity introduce among friends, my natural gaiety makes me apt enough at it. I contribute to it more licence than wit, and have more luck than skill. But I am perfect as a butt. I can take a retort that is not only sharp but personal, and remain unhurt. If I have no immediate answer, I don't fight for time by tediously pursuing the point; but I let it pass, and lower my flag for the moment. A merchant can't always gain. Most men change their voice or looks when their wit fails them, or by an unseasonable outburst of anger lose their revenge and betray their own incompetence. In this game we often pluck the secret strings of our imperfections which, were we in sober earnest, we could not touch without offence; and thus we can profitably give one another a hint of our shortcomings.

There are other sports, practical jokes, rude and indiscreet after the French manner, that I mortally hate. My own skin is thin and tender. And I have seen two of our princes of the blood buried in such affairs. In play, it is unhandsome to fall out and fight.

Few conversations absorb me, without a special effort on my part. Felicity and charm of speech, it is true, attract me as gravity and profundity do not; but when they are absent, I am apt to drowse and lend only the rind of my attention. It often happens that in casual conversation, when we chatter only for the sake of chattering, I make silly remarks and stupid replies unworthy of a child; or ruder and clumsier still, I lapse into obdurate silence.

I have a pensive turn that withdraws me into myself and, together with it, a monumental and childish ignorance of many ordinary things. As a result, five or six tales can be told of me as ridiculous as of any man.

My difficult nature has therefore rendered me rather particular in my association with men. I have to sift my company, and am unfit for general society. Yet we live and deal with the generality of men; and if their talk bores us and if we disdain to adapt ourselves to plain mortals, who are often as much to the point as the most refined of us, we ought to cease meddling with both our own business and that of others. All business, public or private, has to do with just such people; and all intelligence is unintelligent if it cannot accommodate itself to the unintelligence of others.

Isn't it a silly whim of mine to stand off from a thousand men to whom fortune has joined my lot, and who are indispensable to me, in order to cling to one or two altogether remote from my circle—or, rather, to a vain ideal I can never realize? My gentle and easygoing manners have doubtless saved me from enmity, and made me unhated if not beloved; but the iciness of my talk has, reasonably enough, lost me the goodwill of many who may be excused if they have misinterpreted it.

I am capable, indeed, of forming and keeping rare, exquisite friendships. I throw myself so heartily into them I hardly ever fail to stick—as I have happily proved. But in common friendship I am somewhat aloof and sterile: for my gait is not natural unless I am going full speed. Besides, my taste was spoiled by the one perfect friendship fortune gave me in my youth. And then, too, I have difficulty in speaking by halves, as we must do in these prudent friendships; for we dare not talk of the world today without falsehood or danger.

Yet I am fully aware that a man who, like myself, makes his goal the conveniences of life (I mean the essential conveniences) ought to shun as the plague these fastidious humors and niceties. I am all for the man who can speak with his neighbor about his buildings, hunts, and squabbles, or delight in chatting with a carpenter and gardener. I envy those who can be familiar and merry with the least of their servants, and talk among their own attendants. It is neither human nor just to set store by these chance prerogatives of class; and the society which least encourages the difference between master and man seems to me the most equitable.

But, in my opinion, to play the perfect fool is to put on learned airs before the ignorant, to speak with unrelenting elegance and proffer everything you have to say 'on the tip of a fork.' The learned readily succumb to this temptation. They are forever parading their pedantry and spilling their books in all directions.

They have filled the boudoirs and ears of our ladies to such good purpose that, even if the women do not know what it is all about, they make a fine show of it; and when they talk on the commonest subjects, they use nothing but newfangled learned words. If the well bred among them would be persuaded by me, they would be content to shine by their own light. The fact is, they do not sufficiently know themselves. The world has nothing fairer. What more do they want than to be loved and honored?— and for that they already have and know only too much.

In their society the mind has not so much to enjoy itself with, as in the companionship of men; but the bodily senses, which share to a larger degree in it, bring it near, though in my opinion not quite, to the level of the other.

These two kinds of intercourse are dependent on chance and on other than ourselves. The one is annoying for its rarity, the other withers with age; so neither could be sufficient for the business of my life. Intercourse with books, which is the third, is much more certain and in our own control. The first two have every other advantage; but this is within hand's reach, and when you reach your hand it is always there.

These, then, are my three favorite diversions.

I formerly loved cards and dice, but have long since abandoned them, for only one reason—that no matter what a good face I wore in my losses, I could not avoid an inner rankle. In a like manner, I run from melancholic and sour-natured men as from the plague-stricken; and I never meddle in matters which arouse my concern, unless duty compels me.

I hate and avoid chess, a silly, puerile game, because it is not game and play enough. It is too grave and serious, and I would be ashamed to give it the attention that could be put to much better use.

I have just come from playing a game with my family, at seeing who could think of the most names and things which apply equally to two extremes. Women of high rank, for example, are called Dames; those of intermediate rank are Demoiselles; but the lowest sort of women, like the highest, are known as Dames. A king and a tradesman are both entitled Sire, but no one of a rank between them. The canopy over our dinner tables is permitted only in the houses of princes and in taverns. Distaste and violent desire both provoke the same weakness in the jousts of Venus. Extremes of fear and courage will equally relax the bowels. Infancy and senility meet in a common imbecility.

These are frivolous subtleties from which some men expect

applause. It is strong evidence of a weak judgment when men delight in a thing for being novel or difficult, despite its uselessness. I am mightily pleased with the humor of a prince that was presented with a man who could throw a grain of millet through the eye of a needle. When the prince was asked to give the man something as a reward for such a remarkable performance, he pleasantly—and in my opinion rightly—delivered him a bushel of millet so he could never run out of practice.

CHAPTER XIX

My Children

N JUNE 28, 1570, there was born to me and Françoise de la Chassaigne a daughter, whom my mother and M. de la Chassaigne, my wife's father, christened Toinette. She was the first child of our marriage, and died two months later. On September 9, 1571, about two o'clock in the afternoon, my wife gave birth, at Montaigne, to Léonor, second fruit of our marriage and my only child, whom my uncle, the Seigneur de Gaviac, and my sister Léonor baptized.

I once jestingly said of a certain person that he had evaded divine justice because, when three of his grown-up children died in one day presumably as a severe punishment, he took it as if it were a special favor from heaven. I do not follow these unnatural humors, though I have lost two or three babes at nurse, if not without grief, at least without repining—yet there is hardly any accident which pierces nearer to the quick.[1]

The generality and more solid sort of men look upon an abundance of children as a great blessing. I and some others think it is as great a benefit to be without them. As for that strong bond

---

1. In July, 1573, was born my third daughter, Anne, who lived only seven weeks; in December, 1574, a fourth girl, who died about three months later; in May, 1577, the fifth child—a girl—who died within a month; and in February, 1583, another girl, baptized Marie, who lived but a few days.

which, they say, attaches us to the future by reason of having children, I am—as it is—too much tied to the world and to life. It is enough to be in the power of Fortune by the necessity of my own existence, without enlarging her jurisdiction over me. Children, moreover, are among those things which are not to be overmuch desired in these days especially, when it is hard to make decent men of them.

I have very little relish for the inclinations which arise in us without the aid and sanction of our reason; and I cannot share that love of dandling newborn babes that have nothing as yet in their form, movements, or mind to make them lovable, and I do not willingly tolerate their being nursed where I am about.

True and reasonable love ought to spring and grow from the knowledge our children unfold us of themselves. Commonly we behave otherwise, and find ourselves more taken with the games, romping, and nonsense of our children than we do, afterwards, with their maturer actions—as though we loved them for our amusement, like monkeys and not like men. Some parents are as liberal in buying toys for their children as later they are stingy in putting themselves to the least expense when the children turn into men.

Worse, it looks as if jealousy at seeing them enter and enjoy the world, when we are about to leave it, makes us more niggardly. It vexes us to see them tread on our heels as though to urge us to be gone. If we feel this way—for, in truth, they cannot live save at the expense of our purse and life—we have no business to become fathers.

For my part, I think it cruelty and injustice not to let them share our company and possessions; and not to curtail our expenses in order to provide for theirs, since that is the consequence of our begetting them.

Yet a father is miserable indeed who has no hold on the affection of his children save through their need of his aid—if that can be called affection. A father must make himself worthy to be respected for his virtue and wisdom, and loved for his kindness and gentle manner. Even as the ashes of a precious thing have their value, no old age can be so broken down and musty in a man that, if he has brought them up aright, it will not be revered by his children.

I condemn all violence in the education of a young soul that is meant for honor and liberty. There is I know not what of servility in rigor and constraint; and I believe that what you cannot accomplish by reason, prudence, and skill, you will never do by force. I was brought up in that manner, and I used it with Léonor, my only daughter. Up to the age of five or more she had never been corrected for her childish faults (her mother's indulgence readily agreeing with mine), except by words and those very gentle. Even though my method would not succeed, I should lay the blame elsewhere; for I know it to be natural and just. I would have pursued it even more scrupulously toward boys, as destined to less subjection. I should have made it my business to fill their hearts with frankness and freedom. I have never observed that whipping does anything to children but make them either cowardly or stubborn.

The late Maréchal de Montluc told me how it broke his heart that he had never allowed himself to be familiar with his son — who died at Madeira, a youth of great promise. By keeping up a stern paternal air, he said, he lost his chance to know his son and let his own love be known. 'That poor boy,' he said to me, 'only saw in me a grim and distant countenance, and he is gone in the belief that I knew how neither to love nor esteem him. For whom, then, have I kept back this great love I have in my soul? Was it not he who should have had all the pleasure and gratitude of it?'

I find this plaint well grounded; for experience has taught me only too dearly that, in the loss of our friends, there is no consolation so sweet as the knowledge that we had a perfect and complete understanding with them, and had withheld from them nothing that lay close to our heart. O my friend! am I better off or worse for feeling that this was so with us? Surely I am better off. I am consoled and honored by my grief. Is it not a pious and pleasing service in my life to be forever upon his funerals?

I open myself to my family as much as I can, and gladly let them know what I think and feel of them, as I do everyone. I make haste to present and introduce myself to them.

A father worn out with years and infirmities wrongs himself to be still at raking wealth together. He is old enough, if he is wise, to think of disrobing and going to bed. Not to his very undershirt, I concede: that much he may keep, and a good warm dressing gown besides. But the remainder should go to his children, where, in the natural order of things, it belongs.

I am now at an age when such things should be attended to. I would give them the enjoyment of my house and goods, but keep the power to take them back, if their behavior made me change my mind. I have always held it must be a great satisfaction to an aging father to see his children begin to take over his affairs.

If my moroseness and infirmities annoyed them or their friends, I would live apart in some retired corner of the house—not the handsomest, but the most comfortable. I would try by pleasant conversation to create in my children a warm and genuine friendship for me, which in well-bred children is not hard to do.

Never would anyone allow himself to be more fully governed by another than I, if I had anyone to whom I could entrust myself. One of my wishes at this time would be to have a son-in-law who knew how to fondle my old age and rock it to sleep—into whose hands I might deposit, in complete sovereignty, the management and use of all my goods, provided he was truly a friend. But we live in a world where loyalty from one's own children is unknown.

On Sunday, May 27, 1590, Léonor, my only child, married François de la Tour in the presence of Bertrand, his father, my wife and myself, in our home. And on Saturday, June 23, at the break of day—the heat being extreme—my daughter left our house and set off for her new home. In 1591—March 31st—her first child, a girl, was born, and my wife christened her Françoise.

When we come to die, the most judicious disposal of our estate is, in my opinion, to distribute it according to the custom of the country. My destiny has been kind in not giving me any temptation to do otherwise. I see many men who play with their wills as with apples and switches, as though to reward or punish every action of their heirs. That child is the lucky one who happens to be in a position to oil their final departure. It is the last deed, not the best or the most frequent, that counts. Perhaps they might have done me an injustice by dispossessing me of my rightful heritage because, in truth, I was the dullest, the slowest, and the most unwilling at my tasks, not only of my brothers, but of all the boys in the province.

Fortune has likewise aided me in this: since my main profession was to live at ease, and rather idly than busily, she has deprived me of the necessity of growing rich in order to provide for a multitude of children. If there is not enough for one, where I had so plentifully enough, let it be at her risk. Her imprudence would then hardly be deserving that I should wish her any more.

Loving our children and calling them our second selves because we have begotten them, leads us, I think, to consider another sort of procreation whose offspring should no less recommend itself to our love. The works our soul engenders, the issue of our understanding, heart, and abilities, spring from nobler parts than our body, and are more truly our own. We are both father and mother in this act of generation.

They cost us a great deal more; and, if they have any good in them, bring us more honor. For the worth that lies in the children of our body is much more theirs than ours; but in these, all the beauty, charm, and value is our own. It is they who represent and resemble us most. Plato adds that these are immortal children who immortalize their fathers. There are few lovers of poetry who would not be prouder to be the father of the Æneid than of the handsomest youth in Rome.

I hardly know whether I had not rather beget a very beautiful child through intercourse with the Muse than by lying with my wife. To the present one, such as it is, what I have given I gave absolutely and irrevocably, as men do to their human children. It may indeed know many things I have forgotten. If I am wiser than my book, it is richer than I.

CHAPTER XX

Notable Men of My Day

HE LONG ATTENTION I have given to the consideration of myself has trained me to be a passable judge of others. I can often distinguish the qualities of my friends better than they can themselves. I have astonished some of them by the aptness of my descriptions, and so warned them against themselves. Having accustomed myself from boyhood to observe my own life in the mirror of others, I let few things escape me in their traits, looks, and talk.

I discover their inner inclinations by their outward behavior. I do not try to classify their endless variety of disparate and disconnected actions into any system of chapters and heads; I see no further than experience shows me, and give my opinion in unrelated detail as something that cannot be swept into one general term. I leave it to artists to marshal the infinite facets of human nature into an ordered whole, and know not whether they can succeed. For myself, it is hard even to designate any single action by a dominant quality—so ambiguous and motley they appear.

It was thought a rare thing in Perseus, King of Macedon, 'that his mind was so vagabond and his manner of living so diverse, neither he nor anyone else knew what kind of a man he was.' I think this can be said of nearly every one of us.

I hate all tyranny, whether in word or deed. I am quite ready to resist being imposed upon by those idle circumstances with which the senses deceive our judgment. And, keeping a sharp eye on our extraordinary men, I find that for the most part they are like any other. Perhaps, indeed, we underestimate them because they try to do more than they can, and so expose themselves.

There ought to be more strength in the bearer than weight in the burden; and the man who sinks under his load reveals the weakness of his shoulders and gives us his measure. This is why we see more weaklings among the learned than elsewhere. Knowledge is a thing of great weight, and they faint under it: it can serve none but strong natures, and these are rare. Our savants would have made excellent householders, merchants, or artisans; instead, they ruin and make fools of themselves.

Neither is it enough for those who govern and rule us, who have the whole world in their hands, to possess an average mind and be able to do what you and I can do. They are much beneath us if they are not far above us: having promised more, they must do more.

Yet silence in these grandees is not only appropriate to their majesty, but often proves of remarkable advantage. The satrap Megabysus once visited the atelier of the painter Apelles; and, after standing a long while without saying a word, he at last began to talk of the paintings. Whereupon Apelles gave him this sharp rebuke: 'While you were silent, your gold neckchain and pomp made you out to be a great thing; but now that we have heard you speak, there is not a boy in my workshop who does not despise you.' In my time, how many asses have procured the reputation for judgment and ability by keeping their mouths coldly and firmly shut.

It takes no more than to see a man raised to high office, and though we knew him three days before as of little account, the idea of grandeur begins to work on our opinion, and we persuade ourselves that since he has increased his retinue and standing he has also increased his merit. And if by chance he falls from his position and again becomes one of the crowd, everyone asks with astonishment how he ever came to climb so high. 'Is this the man?' they say. 'Did he know no more when he held the reins? Are our princes satisfied with so little as that? Truly, we are in fine hands.' I've seen this happen often enough.

I have known plenty of men with fine qualities, either of mind, heart, skill, conscience, language, knowledge, or the like. But a great man, taking him all for all, who has the whole of these qualities together, or one of them in such excellence we must admire and compare him with those we honor in times past, my fortune has never privileged me to meet.

The most notable men, as I have judged them by outward appearance (for to judge them according to my own method, I must penetrate them much deeper), were, for military conduct, the Duke of Guise, truly one of the first men of his age, who was killed in the chamber of the King at Orleans; and the late Marshal Strozzi. For men of ability and more than common virtue, Olivier and L'Hospital, chancellors of France.

The lives of the Duke of Alva, who died recently, and of our Constable Montmorency had many rare resemblances of fortune; but the beauty and glory of the death of the latter, in the full sight of Paris and his King, upon their service and against his nearest kin, at the head of a victorious army and suddenly stricken in his extreme old age, merits, I think, to be recorded among the remarkable events of our time. As likewise the constant goodness, gentle manners, and unfailing friendliness of M. de la Noue amid all the injustice of partisan strife (the true school of treachery, inhumanity, and brigandage), in which he upheld throughout the reputation of a great and skilled warrior.

Other virtues have had little or no repute in this age, but valor has become general through our civil wars. In this we have souls brave even to perfection, and to such number that choice is impossible.

I have always foreseen whither fortune would carry Henri IV; and he may remember that even when I had to confess it as a sin to my curé, I could not help looking with pleasure on his success. Popular opinion always flows in tides; and if the current once sets in his favor, it will follow him, by its own impetus, to the end. In conducting such affairs, arms and force have been made perfect by clemency and generosity—excellent baits to lure men, especially toward the just and lawful side. A great conqueror of the past boasted he gave his enemies as much reason to love him as his friends.

What I have done for the predecessors of His Majesty I will do for him, and more willingly. I am as rich as I could wish to be; but when I have emptied my purse in his service at Paris, I will be bold enough to say so, and he will find me a cheaper bargain than the least of his officers.

I do not think that for able and graceful horsemanship any nation surpasses the French. A good horseman, as we call him, is judged more by his dash than his skill. Of all I have ever seen, the master of that art—who had the steadiest seat and the best method for breaking in horses—was M. de Carnavalet, who served our King Henri II.

Poetry, too, in my opinion, has flourished in this age of ours. We have had an abundance of good workmen at the craft: D'Aurat, Beza, Buchanan, L'Hospital, Montdoré, Turnebus. As to the French poets, I believe they have raised their art to the highest pitch it can ever achieve; and in the fields where Ronsard and Du Bellay excel, I find them little inferior to the perfection of the ancients.

Innumerable minds have been destroyed by their own force and suppleness. What a fall through his own power of flight has overtaken Torquato Tasso, one of the most judicious and ingenious of the Italian poets, and closer than any of them to the pure air of antiquity! Did he not owe his blindness to his own brilliant light, the loss of his mind to his own vastitude of reason, and to this diligent and strenuous search for knowledge his ultimate achievement of imbecility? I felt even more chagrin than compassion to see him at Ferrara in such a pitiable state, surviving himself, oblivious to both himself and his works, which without his knowledge and yet before his very eyes were published uncorrected and chaotic.

Adrian Turnebus never made any other profession than that of learning, at which, in my opinion, he was the greatest man we have seen in a thousand years. He knew more and knew it better than any other man of our time or long before. Yet he had in him nothing whatever of the pedant, except the wearing of the gown and some external mannerisms that could not be ironed away into the smoothness of a courtier—in themselves of no consequence. I hate your people who are less tolerant of a poorly tailored cloak than of a poorly fashioned mind, and who judge a man by his etiquette or his boots.

Within the gown of Turnebus was the most finished soul on earth. Many times I have deliberately led him to talk on things far removed from his studies. And I found he had so clear an insight, so quick a grasp, and so solid a judgment, you would have thought he had employed his entire life in military affairs or politics of state. These are handsome and vigorous natures who can keep their footing despite their miseducation.

How I wish that, while I live, Justus Lipsius, who is the greatest scholar still among us—a polished and judicious mind, true cousin-german to my Turnebus—would have the will, the health, and enough leisure to gather into one work all the opinions of ancient philosophy on human life and its conduct; the controversies that arose, together with the development and fortunes of the various schools; and how the founders and followers applied their precepts on memorable and telling occasions: the whole done with all the detail and impartiality our knowledge permits. What a handsome and useful work it would be!

I give—and I think with reason—the palm to Jacques Amyot over all our French writers, not only for the purity and simplicity of his language, in which he surpasses all others; not only for his persistence in his vast undertaking and for the profundity of his scholarship; but, above all, because I am deeply obligated to him for having the judgment to choose such a worthy and appropriate work as Plutarch to present to our century. We ignoramuses would have been lost if this book had not raised us out of the quagmire. Thanks to him, we now dare to speak and write. The ladies can give lectures on Plutarch to the schoolmasters, and he is become our breviary. If the good old man is still alive, I would recommend him Xenophon to do as much by; it is an easier task and more suitable to his years.

I have taken pleasure in making known in many places the hopes I have of Marie de Gournay le Jars, my adopted daughter, whom truly I love with more than a paternal love and treasure in my retreat and solitude as one of the best parts of my own being. I am no longer interested in anything in the world but her. If youth is any forecast, she will one day be capable of great things: among others, the perfect practice of that sacred friendship which, up till now, we have not read any of her sex has achieved. The sincerity and fidelity of her manners are already enough for the purpose.

She more than abounds in affection for me. Indeed, in that respect nothing more could be wished, save that her anxiety for my approaching end—I was fifty-five when she first met me—might abate its torments.

Very worthy of consideration is the opinion she formed of my first *Essays*—though a woman, young, a child of these times, and living in isolation—as well as the notable ardor with which she longed to know me and already loved me, merely from the impression she had of me long before we met.

This is all of uncommon preeminence that has so far come to my knowledge.

CHAPTER XXI

A Man from the New World

I HAVE LONG HAD A MAN in my house who lived for ten or twelve years in that other world discovered in our century—in the part where Villegaignon landed and called Antarctic France.[1] The discovery of this illimitable country deserves consideration: we can't be sure that in the future another may not be found, since so many wiser men than we were mistaken in this.

Testimony from antiquity which some would apply to this new world is in Aristotle; at least, if that little book *On Unheard-of Marvels* be his. But Aristotle's account no more agrees with our newfound lands than other of the ancients.

This man of mine is a plain, ignorant fellow, and therefore more likely to tell the truth. Though your knowing sort see more and see it better, they are always interpreting what they see; and in order to give weight and credibility to their interpretation, they cannot keep from somewhat stretching the story. They never describe a thing as it is, but rather as they make it out to be, or as they would have it appear to you; and to bolster their reputation as men of judgment, they don't mind helping out the business with a good measure of their own invention.

But in our case, we have a man so simple he has neither the power to give the color of truth to a lie, nor any purpose in lying.

1. Brazil, where the French landed in 1555.

Besides, my man brought me, at different times, merchants and sailors whom he met on the voyage. I shall therefore be satisfied with what he told me, and not ask what the cosmographers say of the matter.

We need topographers to give us a specific account of the places they have visited; but because they enjoy the advantage over us of having seen Palestine, they want the privilege of telling us what is new in all the rest of the world. I would like everyone to write what he knows, so much and no more. A man may have some special knowledge of a river or a fountain, who in other things knows no more than we. Yet to retail this penny's worth of information, he will write a book on the whole of physics.

I find, from all I can gather, that there is nothing barbaric in this newly discovered nation, except that everyone calls barbarism anything not in use in his own country—there is always the perfect religion, the perfect government, the perfect everything. This nation are savages in the same sense that fruits are wild which nature produces and develops by her own processes. Whereas, in truth, we ought to call those wild which we have changed the nature of and diverted by our artifice.

They live in a pleasant country and so temperate, as I am informed, that one rarely hears of a sick person. Moreover, my witnesses tell me they never saw a native palsied, blear-eyed, toothless, or broken with age.

It is a nation with no kind of commerce; no knowledge of letters or numbers; no name of magistrate or political superiority; no wealth, poverty, or need of servants; no contracts, inheritances, or divisions of property, for there is no property, no occupations save idleness, and no respect of kindred beyond the common rights of man to man; no clothing, agriculture, or metal; no use of wine or wheat. The very words which signify falsehood, treachery, dissimulation, avarice, envy, slander, forgiveness, are never heard of.

Their country lies along the coast and stretches about one hundred leagues inland to vast and lofty mountains. They have an abundance of fish and flesh totally unlike our own, which they prepare by the simplest sort of cooking. The first man to bring a horse to the country had visited there several times before; nevertheless, they were so terrified at seeing him mounted, they killed him with their arrows before they had a chance to recognize him.

Their buildings are very long, and able to house two or three hundred persons. They are covered with the bark of large trees; the roof slopes from the ridgepole to the ground and serves for walls, as with some of our barns. They have wood so hard they can fashion it into swords, and grills for cooking their food. Their beds are woven of cotton and slung from the roof, like those on our ships. Each has a bed to himself, and the wives lie apart from their husbands.

They rise with the sun, and eat at once their only meal for the day. They do not drink while they eat, but at frequent intervals during the day, and sometimes large amounts. Their beverage is made from a certain root; it is like our claret in color, and is drunk warm. It will keep only two or three days; it has a sharp taste, is not at all heady, but wholesome for the stomach, agreeable to drink when once you are used to it, though laxative at first. Instead of bread, they use a certain white substance like preserved coriander. I have tasted it, and found it sweet but insipid.

The young men go hunting wild beasts with bow and arrow. Meanwhile, part of the women busy themselves warming the drink, which is their chief duty. Before they eat in the morning, one or another of the old men preaches to the whole barnful of people, while walking to and fro from one end to the other, and repeating the same sentence until he has completed his round. Valor against the enemy and love toward their wives are the only themes of his discourse; and as a token of their obligation they never fail to end with the refrain that it is their wives 'who keep their drink warm and seasoned.'

A collection may be seen in many places—among others, in my own house—of their beds, ropes, wooden swords, wooden armlets (with which they cover their wrists when fighting), and the great canes, hollowed at one end, by the sound of which they keep time in their dances. They shave all over and much closer than we, although they have only wood or stone for razors.

They believe in the immortality of the soul, and have some sort of priests and prophets, who rarely mingle with the people, but live in the mountains. When they descend among them, several villages assemble and feast their arrival—that is to say, several families, for each house makes up a village, and they lie about a French league apart. The prophet exhorts them to virtue and duty; but all their ethics are bound up in these two articles: bravery in war and affection in marriage. He also foretells events to come; but if his predictions prove wrong, he is cut to a thousand pieces—if they catch him.

They wage war against the nations who live beyond the mountains. Everyone brings home, as a trophy, the head of an enemy he has killed, and fastens it at the door of his lodge. After they have taken a prisoner, they treat him well, feed him with every sort of delicacy, and then kill him with the thrust of a sword. Then they roast him, eat him, and send a morsel or two to their absent friends. This is not done for need of food, but as an extreme measure of revenge.

I am not sorry that we denounce the barbarity of such acts; my sorrow is that, in justly condemning them, we remain blind to our own. I think it is more barbarous to eat a man while he is still alive than after he is dead: to tear and torture a living, feeling body on the rack, to roast it piecemeal, to fling it to be mangled and devoured by dogs and swine. And this is not something we have read, but all of us have seen with fresh memories. And these were not the acts of revenge between inveterate enemies, but were inflicted between neighbors and fellow citizens, and, what is worse, in the name of piety and religion.

We may indeed call these new peoples barbarous, if we judge them by the rule of reason. But not if we judge them by ourselves, who outstrip them in every sort of barbarity. There is no judgment disordered enough to excuse treachery, disloyalty, tyranny, and cruelty, which are our daily vices.

Their wars are altogether noble and generous, and have whatever excuse and beauty this human disease can provide. They fight only for the sake of valor. Their battles are never for the conquest of land, since nature gives them an abundance for their needs, and they are still in that happy state of desiring only what their necessities require. All they ask of their prisoners, and seek to elicit with the direst threats, is a word of surrender, a proof of their own power to terrify him. If rightly understood, the only true victory is 'the victory which forces the foe in his own mind to acknowledge himself conquered' [Claudian].

Yet these prisoners, so far from showing the slightest weakness, always keep up a bold face and beg their captors to bring them to the test. I have a song composed by one of them, in which he bids his enemies come and dine off him and welcome, since they will be eating the flesh of their own fathers and grandfathers on whom he has feasted in his day.

'These muscles, meat, and veins,' runs the song, 'are your own. Poor fools, you little think that the substance of your fathers' limbs is still walking about. Taste it well, and you will find in it the flavor of your own flesh!'

It is certain that to the last gasp they never cease defying their foes. In truth, either these men are savages in comparison with us; or we are, in comparison with them. For there is a wondrous difference between their character and ours.

Besides this war song, I have another, a love song which begins as follows:

'Stay, adder, stay, that my sister may fashion after your hues a rich girdle which I shall give to my beloved: and thus forever will your motley beauty be preferred above all other serpents!'

This first stanza is likewise the refrain of the song. Now I am enough at home in poetry to claim, not only there is nothing barbaric in this fancy, but it is entirely in the strain of Anacreontic verse. Indeed, their language is soft, pleasant to hear, and it somewhat resembles Greek in its terminations.

Three of these people—not foreseeing how dear their knowledge of our corruptions will one day cost their happiness and repose—came to Rouen at the time the late King Charles IX was there. Unhappy men, to allow themselves to be so deluded by the desire for novelty and to leave the serenity of their own skies in order to gaze at ours! The effect of this commerce will be their ruin, which I suppose is well under way. I much fear we have already hastened it by our contagion, and sold them our ideas and arts at a terrible price.

The new world discovered by the Spanish was in its infancy, and we have neither whipped it and brought it beneath our own discipline by the superiority of our valor and natural advantages; nor have we enticed it by our justice and goodness, or subdued it by our magnanimity.

Much of the negotiations the Spanish had with them show they were nothing behind us in natural clarity of mind. The astonishing magnificence of the cities of Cusco and Mexico—among other things, the beauty of their manufacture in jewels, feathers, tissues, and painting—gave ample proof they were little behind us in industry. But of devotion, lawfulness, righteousness, generosity, loyalty, and plain dealing, it served us only too well that we had less than they. For they lost, sold, and betrayed themselves by their virtues.

Why did not such a noble conquest as that of Mexico and Peru fall to Alexander or the ancient Romans, and these many peoples come into hands that might have smoothed their rough edges and nourished the seeds of their arts? What reparation it would have been to them, and general good to the whole world, if our first examples and behavior in those parts had created a fraternal bond and society between them and us! How easy it would have been to have benefitted minds so fresh and so hungry to learn!

But no, we took advantage of their ignorance and inexperience to lure them into treachery, luxury, and avarice, and led them by our example into every species of inhumanity and cruelty. Who has ever demanded so high a price for the benefits of merchandise and traffic—so many cities laid to the ground, so many nations extinguished, so many millions put to the sword, and the richest and fairest portion of the world overwhelmed for a parcel of pearls and pepper? Mechanical victories! Never did ambition, never did national hatred impel men against one another in such horrible slaughter and miserable calamities.

But let us return to my cannibals.

The King talked with them at length, and they were shown our ways, our pomps, and the sights of a great city. Then they were asked what they most marvelled at of all they had seen.

They answered, three things—I am annoyed that I have forgotten the third, but two I remember. They said, in the first place, they thought it very strange that so many tall bearded men, strong and well armed, who were about the King (I suppose they meant the Swiss guards) should submit to obeying a lad, and that they didn't choose one of themselves to take command. Secondly—you must understand that in their way of speaking, men are called 'halves' of one another—they noticed that among us were men gorged with all sorts of comforts, while their halves went begging at their doors, reduced to skin and bones by hunger and poverty; they thought it curious that these destitute halves submitted to such injustice, and didn't seize the others by the throat and burn down their houses.

I spoke for quite a while with one of them. But my interpreter followed me so imperfectly, and through stupidity so little understood what I was getting at, I learned nothing of account.

I asked him what advantages he received from his high rank among his people—for he was a captain, and our sailors called him a king. He told me, he marched at their head in war. How many men did he lead? He indicated a stretch of ground, as though to signify as many as could march in it—which might be four or five thousand. Outside of war, I asked, did his authority expire? He said, it was still his, and that when he visited the villages under his command, a path was cleared for him through the underbrush of the forests, so he might walk at ease.

Not so bad, all this—but, bah! they don't wear breeches.

CHAPTER XXII

𝔐y 𝔈mblem: 'What Do I Know?'

 ONCE TRIED TO JUSTIFY a common practice among our people, one that was taken as absolute authority for leagues around us. Not content to base it on the force of law and example, as men usually do, I investigated its origin. And I discovered the foundation to be so dubious that I who had set out to confirm it was ready to abandon it.

Most abuses in the world arise from the fear, instilled in us, to confess our ignorance, and from the way we have been taught to accept everything we can't refute. I am prepared to hate even probable things as soon as someone tries to impose them on me as infallible. I love words which soften and temper the rashness of our assertions—'perhaps—somehow—it is said—it seems to me' and the like. Whoever wishes to be cured of ignorance must first avow his own.

Wonder is the foundation of all philosophy, research the means, and ignorance the end. But there is one sort of ignorance, strong and noble, which yields nothing to knowledge in honor and courage—an ignorance which requires as much knowledge to attain as knowledge does itself. The ignorance which knows, judges, and condemns itself as such is not altogether ignorant.

Here our language betrays our weakness and defects—as does everything we have. The cause of most of our quarrels is grammatical. Skeptical thinkers, I observe, cannot express their general idea in any known language: it would need a new one for the purpose. When they say 'I doubt' or 'I do not know,' they are immediately caught by the throat and made to confess that at least they are certain they doubt, and that they know they do not know. Their intention is therefore better stated in the form of a question, 'What do I know?' And it is this question, together with a pair of evenly balanced scales, which I use as my emblem.

Two days ago I saw a child carried about by its father, aunt, and uncle, in order to get money by displaying its freakishness. It could walk and prattle like other children; but below the breast was joined to it the headless body of another child, which had life and sensibility in its limbs. Such freaks, which are contrary to our ordinary experience, we call 'contrary to nature.' 'Natural' means for us whatever we can understand: anything beyond that we deem monstrous and disordered—it is the measure of our ignorance. But nothing, no matter what it may be, is contrary to nature. We should learn to quell our astonishment at these curiosities by recognizing the universality of natural order.

I see men ordinarily more eager to discover a reason for things than to find out whether the things are so. They drop the things themselves and hurry off to investigate the causes. A silly business. They usually begin by saying, 'How did such a thing happen?' Whereas they ought to be asking, 'But did it happen?' I find that most often we should conclude, 'It never did.'

I am frequently tempted to make this answer; but I do not dare, for then I am told that I evade the question because I haven't intelligence enough to grapple with it. So I must entertain the thing for company's sake, and go batting about subjects and tales I do not believe a word of. Besides, it is a trifle rude and contentious to give a direct lie to something stated as a fact. For in telling things hard to believe, most people will swear they saw it with their own eyes, or refer to witnesses whose authority stops us from flat contradiction.

In this way we learn the causes and operations of a thousand things that never existed, and the world scuffles over a thousand questions both sides of which are false. We are not only slack in defending ourselves from deception, but we lay ourselves open and seek to be fooled. We love to entangle ourselves in humbug as something appropriate to our character.

I find people poring over almanacs for omens and forecasts, and pointing to their authority if something falls out pat. For my part, I would prefer to govern my affairs by a throw of dice. Though it would hardly be possible for these forecasts not to hit upon the truth once in a while, I never think better of them for that. Besides, nobody counts up the false prognostications.

A man of Samothrace once showed Diagoras the Atheist votive tablets and paintings given to a temple by men saved from shipwreck. 'Look,' said the man, 'you who think the gods are indifferent to us—what do you say to all those people spared by divine favor?' 'I say this,' answered Diagoras, 'that if we had the tablets and paintings of those who were drowned, we would see a great many more.

Miracles arise from our ignorance of nature, not from nature itself. Our judgment is blinded by our habits. There is nothing that Custom cannot impose upon our beliefs: she is empress of the world. Is there any notion so bizarre that habit has not implanted it in some spot on the globe? I do believe that no absurd idea can enter the human imagination without being put into practice somewhere, and once acted upon, justified by our reason. For human reason is a tincture brewed from equal parts of opinion and habit—both infinite in variety and matter.

I have seen the birth of many miracles in my time. The first man who sets about to tell the tale finds, from the objections he meets, where the worst holes are, and proceeds to caulk them up with a bit of false stuffing. Moreover, we make it a point of conscience not to return what has been lent us without adding a trifle from our own pocket by way of interest. So the original error of a private individual becomes a part of the public fund of error, and this in turn breeds further private error. And the whole fabric grows from hand to hand, with the result that the witness furthest removed from the event knows more about it than the nearest, and the last one to hear is better persuaded of its truth than the first.

There is nothing men more readily give themselves to than pushing their own beliefs. When ordinary means fail, they add commandment, violence, fire, and sword. It is a misfortune that, as things are, the best touchstone of truth is the multitude of its believers, in a crowd where fools so far outnumber the wise. For my part, what I would not believe from the lips of one man, I would not believe from a hundred and one.

Up till now, all these miracles and uncanny doings somehow never show themselves in my presence. I have never seen a greater miracle or monster than myself. Usually we become habituated to strange things through time and contact with them; but the more I am with myself, the more my deformity astonishes me, and the more I know of myself, the less I understand.

Riding the other day through a village about two leagues from my house, I found the place still hot with the rumor of a miracle that had lately failed to come off. A young fellow, a stupid silly girl, and one other, hid themselves at night under the church altar and began announcing threats of Judgment Day. The poor devils are now in prison and likely to pay for our common folly. We see through this well enough, when the trick is revealed; but in other cases that are beyond our ken, I am of the opinion we ought to suspend our judgment. Let us have some form of sentence which says, 'The court understand nothing of the matter'—even more freely than the judges of the Areopagus who, finding themselves baffled by a case, ordered the litigants to come back again in a hundred years.

The witches in my neighborhood run the risk of their lives upon the report of every new author who wants to give substance to their dreams. To apply the examples in Holy Writ to contemporary events, when we understand neither the causes nor the means, takes a different sort of brain from mine. God, certainly, ought to be believed; but not someone or other among us who is astounded at his own tale—and he must be astounded unless he is out of his mind.

I am slow-witted and lean to the solid and probable. I know very well that some people become furious at this, and forbid me to doubt upon pain of abominable punishment—a new method of persuasion! Thank God, I am not to be cuffed into my beliefs. Let them rage against those who deny their opinion. I only say it is unwarranted and hard to believe. The man who tries to establish his argument by bluster and command shows the weakness of his proofs. To kill men, we need a clear and shining light. Our life is too real and essential to use it as a guarantee for these fantastic and supernatural doings.

I say it is enough to believe a man, whatever claims he may offer, simply as a human being. I have had my ears dinned with a thousand tales, as 'Three persons saw him one day in the far East, the next day in the far West—at this hour, that place, and clothed in such a garb.' I would not believe it if I saw it myself. How much more likely it is that two men should lie than that one man should fly with the wind halfway round the world in twelve hours? How much more natural that our imagination should take wings than our flesh and bones ride a broomstick up the chimney? We have enough delusions of our own and within us not to bother with those outside.

Some years ago, when I was travelling through the territory of a sovereign prince, he did me the favor—to lessen my incredulity—to let me see ten or twelve prisoners of this kind, among them an old hag, a real witch in hideousness and deformity, who had quite a reputation in her profession. I saw proofs and free confessions, and some sort of insensible mark on the miserable old creature. I examined and talked with her and the others as long as I wished, and gave the soundest attention to what they said; and I am not the man to be carried away by preconceived ideas. In the end, and in all conscience, I should have prescribed hellebore rather than hemlock—'it was madness rather than malice' [Livy].

As to the arguments and objections made to me by worthy men, there and elsewhere, I have met none that convinced me, and that did not admit of a more likely solution. It is true, the proofs and reasons that are based on experience and fact I cannot unravel; nor have they any end by which one can begin to untie them. So I cut them, as Alexander did the Gordian knot. After all, it is setting a very high price on one's conjectures to burn a man alive for them.

What I believe today, I believe with all my powers; but how often it has happened to me, not once but a thousand times, to believe something else and deny my former beliefs with the same powers and conviction! Isn't it foolish of me to allow myself to deceive myself again and again? And it is always the last belief that is certain and infallible, and warrants the risk of goods, honor, life, and salvation.

No, whatever is preached us, whatever we learn, we must remember that it is man who gives and man who receives, a mortal hand that offers and a mortal hand that takes.

CHAPTER XXIII
Professors and the Sciences

S A BOY I WAS OFTEN ANNOYED to see professors brought in as the fools of our Italian comedies. Since my education was placed in their hands I was naturally concerned for their honor and reputation. I tried to excuse them by the disparity which exists between ordinary men and those of rare and excellent minds. But I wasted my ingenuity, for I found that the most gallant men despised them worst. Our good du Bellay, for example, said: 'But above all I hate pedantic learning.' It was the same in ancient times. Plutarch tells us that Scholar and Greek were terms of contempt among the Romans.

I still don't understand how it happens that minds enriched with the knowledge of a great many things should remain so dull. A young lady, a princess of the highest rank in France, once said to me, in speaking of a certain professor, that no doubt his own mind must have been squeezed and crowded out in order to make room for the minds of so many others.

We labor only to stuff our memory, and leave the conscience and understanding empty. We can say, 'Cicero says thus—these are the opinions of Plato—here are the very words of Aristotle.' A parrot could do as much. But we, what do we ourselves say?

If I try to fortify myself against the fear of death, it must be at the expense of Seneca. If I am looking for consolation, I borrow it from Cicero. Yet I might have found it in myself, if I had been trained to use my own head. I dislike this begged and dependent understanding. For though we can become learned through another man's knowledge, we can never be wise except by our own wisdom.

I know a man who, when I ask him what he knows, fetches me a book to show me. He cannot so much as tell me he has piles in his behind until he first looks up in his dictionary the meaning of piles and behind. We take other men's opinions and knowledge into storage, and then—that is all. Whereas we should make them our own.

What shall we do with people who will admit no evidence unless it is in print—who will not believe a man unless he is between the covers of a book? We merely dignify our twaddle when we commit it to the press. It is more impressive to say, 'I read such a thing' than merely 'I heard it.' But I no more disbelieve a man's mouth than his pen. I look on the present as no less credible than the past; and I would as soon quote my neighbor as Aulus Gellius or Macrobius, and what I have seen as readily as what they have written. Just as virtue is not more virtuous for having flourished longer, so I hold a truth is no wiser for being older.

I often say, it is folly to run after remote and learned examples. Present examples are no less fertile than those from the days of Homer or Plato. As if we were any better off by borrowing our proofs from the publishing houses of Vascosan or Plantin than from our village street! If we say we want the weight of great authority, we defeat, I believe, our own purpose. The greatest authority, especially on the subject of human behavior, is to be found in the commonest and most ordinary actions, if we can only see them aright.

These professors of ours claim, of all men, to be useful to society. Yet they do not fashion the material we confide to their care into something better, as do carpenters and masons. They spoil it, and make us pay for it to boot. They are marvellously at home in Galen, but not at all in the disease of the patient. They deafen you with a long rigmarole of legal points, but understand nothing of the case in hand. They have a theory for everything, but somehow always let the other fellow have the trouble of putting it into practice.

I have watched a friend of mine, in my own house, serve up a jargon of high-sounding nonsense in reply to one of these learned gentlemen who happened to be arguing with us. He strung together far-fetched phrases without head or tail—merely slipping in a word now and then that bore on the subject—and kept the man in play for the whole afternoon. The fool never once suspected that his arguments were not seriously answered; yet he was a man of letters and reputation, and wore a handsome cap and gown.

If you look closely into these gentlemen, who are pestering the whole world, you will find that they understand neither others nor themselves. When we see a shoemaker out at the toes, we say no wonder—for usually no one is worse shod than they. In a like manner, experience usually shows us a physician worse medicined, a clergyman less reformed, and—always—a scholar less knowing than other men.

I have seen in my time a hundred artisans, a hundred field laborers, wiser and happier than university rectors—and men whom I would much rather resemble. Learning has its place, I think, among the necessities of life, as have heroism, beauty, and riches; but more remote and more by our opinion of it than by its own nature. Whoever values us for our behavior will find more excellent men among the ignorant than among the learned, and excellent in every sort of virtue.

Hear us poor calamitous animals boast! 'There is nothing,' says Cicero, 'so sweet as the pursuit of learning, by which nature—the heavens, earth, and seas—is revealed to us. It equips us with the means to live well and happy.' Yet, in sober fact, a thousand little village housewives have lived a steadier, pleasanter, and more tranquil life than he.

Now who would not distrust the sciences, considering the use we make of them? There is more to-do about interpreting interpretations than interpreting the facts themselves. There are more books about books than about anything else. We do nothing but make commentaries on one another. Commentators swarm everywhere, but authors are scarce.

Is there any more confusion in the scoldings of fishwives than in the disputes of scientists and professors? I would rather that a son of mine learned in a tavern how to speak, than in a college to blather. Take a doctor of philosophy and talk with him. Why doesn't he impress us with his excellence? Why doesn't he delight the ladies and ignoramuses like ourselves with marvelling at the firmness of his reason and the beauty of his logic? Why can't he persuade us? And failing to do so, why must a man who has his advantages of knowledge and skill bring mockery, scolding, and anger into his arguments? Strip him of his cap, gown, and Latin, and shut off his stream of Aristotle, and you will find him like any jack and man of us—or worse.

I love and honor learning as much as they who have it. But in such as I speak of, and their number can't be counted, I hate it worse than stupidity itself. In the hands of some men, knowledge is a sceptre: in the others, a bauble.

Philosophy is nothing but sophisticated poetry. Plato himself is only a rambling poet. Just as women use false teeth when their real ones drop out, and in place of a natural complexion lay on a manufactured one, and round out their figures with cotton stuffing—so the law uses legal fictions to bolster up its justice, and science pays us with hypotheses, which it confesses are pure invention. These epicycles with which astronomy moves the stars are merely the best devices it can contrive.

It was the stars and the heavens which were in motion for three thousand years. Or so everyone believed until Cleanthes the Samian (or, according to Theophrastus, Nicetus of Syracuse) decided to maintain that it was not the stars but the earth which moved. Now, in our time, Copernicus has so firmly established this doctrine that it serves everything we can observe astronomically. What shall we conclude from this, except that it is hardly worthwhile to heat ourselves up over one or the other? Who knows but what in a thousand years from now a third opinion will not supplant them both?

One of these reformers and novelty touters in physics recently told me that all of the ancients were notoriously mistaken in the nature of the movement of the winds. After I had listened for some while to his arguments, which were very plausible, I said, 'Well—what then? Did the seamen who sailed according to the theory of Theophrastus head westward when they steered to the east?' 'No,' he answered, 'but that was pure luck—no matter which way they went they were mistaken.' I then replied that I preferred to follow the rudders of fact than the winds of theory.

They often clash. I am told that in geometry, which claims the highest degree of certainty among the sciences, there have been found inescapable demonstrations which run directly counter to experience. Jacques Peletier, for example, told me in my own house that he had discovered two lines which constantly approach one another, but which he verified could never meet, even if prolonged to infinity.

A thousand years ago, Ptolemy, who was a noted scientist, established the bounds of the earth; and all the ancient geographers felt they had taken the measure of it, except perhaps for some remote islands that might have escaped their knowledge. It would have been skepticism then to have doubted the findings of geography. It became heresy to believe in the existence of the Antipodes. And, behold, in our age an illimitable expanse of *terra firma* is discovered—not an island, not a country, but a part nearly as great as the whole we knew before. And now the geographers do not fail to assure us that all is found, all has been seen. But the question remains whether it is not foolish to trust these modern people any more than the ancients, and whether the world is not, still, quite another thing from what we judge it to be.

Before the principles of Aristotle received reputation, other principles contented human reason as these do now. Yet what privilege, what letters patent, have these that our human invention should stop with them? They are no less likely to be thrown out of doors than their predecessors.

When anyone presses me with a new theory I ought to consider that if I can't refute it, another may. For to believe everything you can't refute is very simpleminded. If we did this, the beliefs of ordinary people, and we are all ordinary, would be whirling about like a weathercock.

If we observe that one art and one belief flourished at one period, and another in another, that each age bends mankind to this or that bias, that the minds of men are now gay and now bare like our fields, what becomes of all the fine superiority with which we flatter ourselves? Since we see that one wise man may be mistaken, and likewise a hundred wise men, and even a hundred nations, nay, even human nature itself—as we have seen it err through many centuries in many things—what assurance have we that we are not mistaken here and now?

But it is not only the heavens which science has equipped with ropes, engines, and wheels. It has forged for this poor little human body no less an array of retrogradations, trepidations, accessions, recessions, and aberrations. To fit the movements they see in man, into how many parts, orders, and storeys have they divided the structure of the mind? They make of it an imaginary thing. They paw, rip, place, displace, piece, and stuff it to their hearts' content, yet to this day they have not grasped it. Not only in reality, but even in theory, they cannot master it so that some sound or cadence does not elude their architecture, enormous as it is and plastered with a thousand false and fantastic patches.

How long is it that medicine has been practiced in the world? Yet it is said that the newcomer Paracelsus has overthrown all of the old rules, and maintains they were only fit to kill men with. That much I believe he can prove without any trouble. But I would not think it wise to risk my life on his new experiments.

We cry 'miracle' at the invention of artillery and printing. But other men, at the other end of the world in China, employed them a thousand years ago. There is nothing rare and singular in nature: it is only in our knowledge of it, which is a wretched ground on which to base our conclusions. It is as silly of us to conclude, as we do nowadays, that the world is entering its dotage and ruin, because we ourselves are weak and degenerate, as it was silly of the poet Lucretius to think the world was in the spring of its childhood because, in his day, men were vigorous, arts flourished, and inventions abounded.

I am delighted with the Milesian girl who noticed that Thales was always observing the arch of heaven, and therefore put something in his path to stumble over, in order to remind him that it will be time enough to think of things in the clouds after he has seen what lies before his feet. These people who are always riding the epicycle of Mercury, who roam the distant heavens, give me a worse pain than the dentist. For in my study, which is man, I find an overwhelming variety of opinions and labyrinth of difficulties, even in the schools of wisdom itself. Since they cannot agree on their knowledge of themselves, nor give an account of the springs of their own being which they themselves govern and use, you may judge how little I am to believe them about the rise and fall of the Nile.

It is the lot of man to have the knowledge of what lies in our own hands as remote from us as the clouds and stars. No philosopher knows what his neighbor does, or what he does himself: no one knows what either of them are—whether they are animals or men.

Our disputes are verbal. I ask, What is nature, pleasure, or circle? The question is words and I am paid back in the same coin. A stone is a body. But we pursue the question and ask, 'What is a body?' 'Substance,' we are told. 'And substance—what is that?' The game may be kept up until the dictionary is exhausted. Worse, we often exchange one word for another more obscure. I know what Man is better than I know Rational, Mortal, or Animal. To satisfy one doubt, we are given three.

Thus the world is filled with falsehood and patter—an accepted and conventional jargon. The reason we seldom doubt of things is that we do not try to examine the most ordinary experiences. We do not dig to the roots, but are content to argue about the twigs. We do not ask if a thing is so, but only if it is said to be so. The god of scholastic science is Aristotle; it is irreligious to question his ordinances: his doctrine is supreme law. Yet, perchance, it is as false as any other. I do not know why I should not accept Plato instead of Aristotle, or the atoms of Epicurus, or the numbers of Pythagoras.

The liberty of these ancient minds produced various schools. But now men all travel the same road. We receive our sciences by civil authority and decree, so that every school has the same pattern and curriculum. We no longer note what the coin weighs and is really worth—the alloy is not disputed—we only ask if it will pass. We take medicine as seriously as geometry. Hocus-pocus, witchcraft, magic, talking with the dead, astrology, fortune-telling—all passes without contradiction.

Can you trust in philosophy, can you boast of having found the plum in the pudding, when you hear the noisy wrangling of so many philosophic brains? Don't let them tell us, 'It is true because you feel and see it to be true.' First they must tell me whether I really feel what I think I feel. And if I do, they must tell me why and how and exactly what I feel. They must, for example, tell me the cause and operation of heat and cold, the nature of the thing that creates it and the thing that feels it—or let them give over their claims.

Theophrastus said that human reason, guided by the experience of the senses, might ascertain the causes of things in some degree. This is a plausible opinion and supported by well-ordered minds.

Where one man fails in an experiment, another succeeds. What is unknown in one age is clarified in the next. The arts and sciences are not cast from a mold: they are shaped and polished little by little, here a dab and there a pat—as bears leisurely lick their cubs into shape. What my powers cannot solve I still persist in sounding and trying out. By kneading and working over the new material, turning and warming it, I make it more supple and easier to handle for the man who will take it up after me. And he will do as much for a third. This is why I should not despair of difficulties or of my own incapacity—for it is only my own.

But the rub lies in curbing the mind. In science, extremes are as vicious as in morals. I find that in the pursuit of knowledge man grasps at more than he can hold. He cuts out for himself more work than he needs to do. What if it turns out that Science, in trying to arm us against the discomforts of life, has made us more keenly aware of them than she has provided us against them? For my part I would rather believe that men have treated knowledge as a game and a toy. It is not good to be too subtle and cunning. Remember the Tuscan proverb: 'If you draw the thread too fine, you will break it.'

CHAPTER XXIV

Over the Ears in Law

S A YOUNG MAN I was plunged over the ears in law—magistrate of the king in the Cour du Parlement of Bordeaux and, before that, magistrate in the Gour des Aides of Périgueux. ¶There is nothing more subject to mutation than the laws. Since I was born I have seen those of our neighbors, the English, changed three or four times, not only in civil matters but, what is worse, in religious. I am more concerned and mortified at this, because they are a nation with whom our part of the country formerly had a long and familiar acquaintance.

Here, among us, I have known a capital offence to become lawful; and we who hold a different opinion of it run the chance, if the fortunes of war go against us, of being strung up for high treason.

Men amuse me when they try to give certainty to our laws by saying that some of them are perpetual and unchangeable—which they call 'natural laws.' Some men reckon them at three or four, others at more or less—a sign that the number is as doubtful as the rest of the matter. But we are indeed unfortunate that there is not one of these picked natural laws which is not denounced and disowned by not one nation, but several. The Spartans esteemed cleverness in thievery. One people or another have sanctioned the murder of infants or fathers, community of wives, traffic in robbery, and all manner of licentious pleasures.

It is credible that natural laws exist for us as for other creatures. But they are lost to us, thanks to our fine human reason which has insinuated itself into governing, shuffling, and confounding the face of things into the image of its own futility and fickleness.

It is a pity that there is not a closer relation between the laws we do have and our capacity to obey them. To set a mark we can seldom hit is not an honest game.

There is no man so good who, if he were to submit all his thoughts and actions to the law, would not deserve hanging ten times in his life. And he would be the very man it were unjust to punish and a shame to kill. On the other hand, many a man who has broken no law is so far from being virtuous that our philosophy would look with composure on his being soundly whipped.

Is a man wrong for not doing what he cannot do? To whom do we prescribe the laws which we expect no one will obey? We take good care not to be righteous according to the laws of God, and we make it impossible for us to be righteous according to our own.

I often notice that we propose rules of conduct which neither the lawmakers nor the public ever hope or, what is worse, ever wish to observe. From the same sheet of paper on which a judge writes his sentence against an adulterer, he tears off a piece to scribble a love note to his colleague's wife. There are judges who will condemn men to death for a crime which they do not themselves think is so much as a misdemeanor.

At best this two-facedness, this doing one thing and saying another, may pass with authors who treat of things outside of us, but not with me who must write about myself. I must move my pen as I do my feet. The life of a public servant, I admit, must have some relation to other men's lives. In a man dedicated to public office, who takes part in the government of men, the virtue of a Cato is, if not unvirtuous, at least useless and out of place. Maybe I am wrong in being disgusted with the world I frequent.

Certainly I would be wrong if I complained at its being disgusted with me, since I am utterly so with it.

How does it happen that our ordinary language, which works nicely in other matters, becomes involved and unintelligible in wills and contracts? Unless it is that the princes of this art, by applying themselves with peculiar attention to raking up solemn words and devising artful phrases, and weighing every syllable and plucking over every seam, have so confounded and obfuscated themselves in an endless number of clauses and points that the result baffles rule, order, and understanding. By sowing and retailing questionable details they create for themselves a splendid harvest of suits and disputes. And, as far as I can make out, experience shows that a multitude of interpretations dissipates and destroys the truth.

The Baron of Caupene and I hold in common the right of appointment to a benefice of large extent, called Lahontan, at the foot of our mountains. The inhabitants of this nook lived a life apart, with clothes, manners, and fashions of their own, and governed themselves solely by the force of custom. They managed so happily that from time out of mind no neighboring judge was ever put to the trouble of looking into their affairs.

Then, so I am told, one of these people became fired with a noble ambition. For the honor of the family he resolved to have 'Counsellor-at-Law' tacked to the name of his son. So Pierre or Jean was sent to some nearby town to learn how to write, and in due course he became a village lawyer. Now that he was a 'Monsieur,' the fellow began to sneer at the old ways. Presently, when someone cut off the horn of a goat belonging to one of his cronies, he advised him to bring suit before a royal magistrate in the vicinity. One thing led to another, and in the end he had corrupted the whole place.

I am little pleased with the opinion that a multiplicity of laws curbs the authority of the judges. The man responsible for it cannot be aware that there is as much latitude and liberty in the interpretation of laws as in the making of them. We have more laws in France than in all the rest of the world put together; yet so much is left to the opinion and decision of our judges that never was their liberty more unshackled.

What have our legislators gained by culling out one hundred thousand individual actions and pasting a law to each of them? Add one hundred thousand more, and still human behavior will never fit any one of them exactly, and there will always remain circumstances at the mercy of interpretation and opinion.

The most desirable laws are the simplest, the most general, and the least likely to be invoked. I am of the further opinion that none at all would be better than our present prodigious number. What danger would there be if the wisest heads decided each controversy as it arose and on its own merits? King Ferdinand wisely provided that no lawyers could join in the new colonies sent to America, lest lawsuits should get a footing in the new world: he agreed with Plato that 'lawyers and doctors are the pest of a country.'

What can be more outrageous than to see a nation like ours where, by lawful custom, the office of judge is bought and sold, where judgments are paid for cash down, and where justice may legally be denied a man who cannot pay! A country, moreover, where justice becomes such a profitable article of merchandise, as it is with us, that at the side of church, nobility, and commons has arisen a fourth estate of lawyers, who manage the laws and hold sovereign power over men's lives and fortunes. The result is, we have two codes of law: one of honor and one of the law-courts. And they frequently collide.

In some of our courts the magistrates, upon being admitted to office, are examined only as to their learning. Other courts, however, add to this a test of their understanding, by asking their judgment on some cases in law. I think the latter proceed with better method; for, though both are necessary, judgment can indeed make a shift without knowledge, but knowledge is helpless without judgment. Would to God that, for the sake of justice, our gentlemen of the robe were as well furnished with understanding and conscience as they are stuffed with knowledge!

I have heard tell of a judge who, when he read a sharp conflict of opinion between Bartolus and Aldus or other points bristling with contradictions, used to write in the margin of his book: 'Question for a friend.' That is to say, in such a disputed case the truth was so obscured, he might well favor whichever party he pleased. He needed only a little more wit and discernment to write in the margin of all cases, 'Question for a friend.' The lawyers and judges in our time find enough things aslant in every case to justify their taking any side that suits them.

In a field of learning so illimitable as law, which depends for its authority on multitudinous opinions, and the subject of which is itself so obscure, an endless confusion of decisions must result. One court decides differently from another, and on occasion differs from itself. And then there is that remarkable blemish in our justice which, as we frequently see, allows a case to be dragged from judge to judge, and court to court. I am reminded of Chrysippus who said, 'A philosopher will turn a dozen somersaults, yes, and without his breeches, for the sake of a dozen olives.'

A chief magistrate once bragged in my presence that he had packed two hundred and some passages from out-of-the-way sources into one of his decisions. In tooting this abroad, he robbed himself of whatever glory he might have won by it. A fatuous and absurd boast, as I see it, for such an exploit and such a person!

I have often been angered to see our judges shamelessly make use of fraud and false hopes of pardon in order to trick a criminal into confessing his crime. This is a malicious justice; and it violates itself, I think, as much as any wrongdoer.

The use of torture is a dangerous device, and seems to me more a trial of endurance than of truth. The man who can withstand the pain conceals the truth, but so does the man who cannot. For why should pain force me to confess the truth rather than a falsehood? And, on the contrary, if an innocent man has the courage to withstand these torments, why shouldn't a guilty one have the same courage—with life and liberty as his reward? The ground for this device lies, I think, in the power of conscience. It is considered that conscience will aid the rack in making the guilty confess, and strengthen the innocent to bear its torments.

But, when all is said, it is, in plain truth, a dubious and dangerous method. What will a man not say to escape such horrible pain? The result is, a man whom the judge has racked in order not to put him to death if he is innocent, dies both innocent and racked. How can torture help out our ignorance? Are you not unjust who, in order to avoid killing a man without cause, do worse than kill him? Thousands upon thousands have lost their lives through false confessions. 'But it is,' we are told, 'the least evil that human frailty can contrive.' Nevertheless, it is altogether inhuman and, in my opinion, altogether useless.

Our law cannot expect that a man who will not be deterred from crime by the fear of being hanged or beheaded, will be any more awed at the thought of being punished by burning pincers, slow fire, or the wheel. I do not so much pity the dead—and should rather envy them; but I deeply pity the dying. I cannot look with a steady eye on even the reasonable executions of justice.

Even in justice itself, anything that exceeds simple death seems to me sheer cruelty. This holds especially true for us who are Christians and who ought to have regard for the souls of men, and dismiss them in a calm and composed frame, which cannot be when we have rent them with unbearable torments.

If we intend that our severity shall impress the public, I advise that we exercise it on the bodies of the criminals after they are dead. To see them deprived of burial, or quartered and hung, works almost as much upon the imagination of the crowd as pain inflicted upon the living.

In Rome, I happened to be passing by when they were executing Catena, a notorious robber. He was strangled to death without the slightest emotion on the part of the spectators. But when they came to cut his body in quarters, every blow of the hangman was followed by a doleful cry from the people, as though everyone present had lent his feelings to the miserable carcass. These inhuman excesses should be inflicted on the bark, and not the living core.

I live in a time when we abound in incredible examples of this vice of cruelty—as a result of our civil wars. Nothing in history is more extreme than we bear proof to every day. Before I saw it with my own eyes, I could hardly believe that men can be so savage as, for the sole pleasure of killing, to hack and lop off the limbs of their fellows, and sharpen their wits to invent strange torments and new forms of death—all this without hatred or profit, but simply to enjoy the pleasant spectacle of anguished gestures and lamentable groans and cries. For this is the utmost limit to which cruelty can attain: 'that a man should kill a man, without anger or fright, but merely for the spectacle' [Seneca].

How often I have done myself a manifest injustice to avoid the risk of having our judges do me a worse one; and that, after interminable vexations and vile and foul practices more hateful to me than fire and rack! If we are wise, we will boast and rejoice like the boy I once heard telling, with innocence and in high glee, that his mother had lost her lawsuit—as if it were a cough, a fever, or something equally annoying to keep.

Even the favors which fortune might have given me through my kinship or friendliness with those in high office I have scrupulously avoided using, either to the disadvantage of others or the unmerited advancement of myself. In fine, I have made such a good day's work of it (thanks to luck, I may say) that I am still a virgin at lawsuits. And this, despite the fact that I have often been tempted by having very just and promising grounds.

I am virgin of quarrels too. Soon I shall have passed a long life without having given or received an offence of any moment, and without ever hearing myself called a worse name than my own— a rare grace of heaven!

I am so slow to offend that I cannot do it even in behalf of reason itself. When occasion has demanded that I sentence criminals, I have rather chosen to fail in justice. 'I would prefer men not to sin, but I have not the heart to condemn them for it' [Livy].

Most men exasperate themselves to punishment out of horror at the crime; but it is precisely this which cools me off. The horror of one man killing another makes me fear the horror of killing him: the hideousness of his cruelty makes me abhor any imitation of it.

It may be said of me, who am but a two-spot in the deck, what was said of Charillus, King of Sparta: 'He cannot be a good man, for he is not bad to the wicked.' Just as in lawful actions I am loathe to proceed against a man if it will be to his hurt, so, too, I am not so conscientious to refrain from an unlawful action if it is in behalf of someone who consents to it.

Since the laws of ethics which govern the duty of the individual within himself are so hard to teach and observe, it is no wonder that our public laws are even more so. Do but consider this justice which rules over us: it is the true testimony to human frailty, filled as it is with error and contradiction.

Some peasants have just come to me in great haste, to tell me they left in one of my woods a man stricken with a hundred blows. He was still breathing, and begged a drop of water for pity's sake, and help to raise him from the ground. But they told me they dared not go near him, but ran off, lest the officers of justice should catch them there, and, as it happens to those found near a murdered body, they should be called into question—to their utter ruin, having neither friends nor money to defend their innocence. What could I say to them? It is certain that this act of humanity could have plunged them into trouble.

How many innocent persons have we known to be punished—and without fault of the judge! And how many more that we do not know of? This happened in my time: certain men were condemned to die; the sentence was concluded upon, but not pronounced. At the last moment the judges learned that other men had unquestionably committed the crime. Whereat they proceeded to ponder the novelty of the situation: the fact that once the death sentence was passed, the judges had no power to revoke it; and what effect the reversal of judgment might have on precedent. So the poor devils were sacrificed to the formalities of justice. And how many sentences have I seen more criminal than the crimes they punished!

There is no remedy. I am at one with Alcibiades: I will never, if I can help it, put myself into the hands of a man who shall determine my head, and where my honor and life shall depend more on the skill and diligence of my lawyer than on my own innocence.

No judge, thank God! has ever yet spoken a word to me in his office as judge, on any account whatever—my own or that of another, civil or criminal. No prison has ever yet received me, even as a visitor. Imagination renders the very outside of a jail odious to me.

I so love freedom that if someone forbade me access to the remotest corner of the Indies I should feel myself a little hemmed in. While I can find earth or air in any part of the globe, I shall never live where I must keep in hiding. If the authorities under whom I live should so much as wag a finger at me, I would immediately go in search of others, no matter where. All my little prudence in these civil wars of ours is employed in keeping me free to come and go as I will.

Now our laws maintain their credit not because they are just, but because they are laws. This is the mystic foundation of their authority—which is their good luck. For they are often made by fools, and more often by men who because they hate equality deny equity, and always by men—that is to say, futile and irresolute creatures. Whoever obeys them because he thinks they are just does not obey them as he ought. And our French laws, by their disorder and botchery, lend a generous hand to the corruption manifest in their execution.

True justice, natural and universal, is quite another thing from this national justice which is tied to the necessities of our government, whose laws not only permit but often instigate wickedness. 'There are crimes authorized by the decrees of the Senate and the votes of the people,' says Seneca. I use the ordinary language which makes a distinction between useful things and righteous things; and in my way of speaking, there are not only useful but necessary actions which are knavish and filthy.

CHAPTER XXV

My Religion

 HAVE KNOWN, in my time, some men's writings criticized for being purely human and philosophical with no tinge of theology. Yet it might be said, on the contrary and with some show of reason, that since divine doctrine is queen and regent of all science, she better keeps her throne apart. Perhaps it is a greater fault that doctors of divinity write too humanly than that humanists write too untheologically.

The human way of speaking is on a much lower plane and ought not use the majesty of sacred eloquence. Anyone who wishes should talk of Fortune, Destiny, Luck, the Gods, and similar notions, according to his whim. For myself, I throw out merely human ideas, and merely my own, to be considered as such and not as sanctioned by Heaven or beyond human dispute. They are matters of opinion, not faith—things which I discuss as a layman, though always in a reverent manner. Indeed, an edict ordering everyone but doctors of divinity to be extremely reserved in writing about religion might be rather useful, to make perhaps me, along with the rest, stop my prating.

We should either wholly and absolutely submit ourselves to the authority of our ecclesiastic laws, or throw off our obedience in its entirety. It is not for us to determine which and how much of them we should obey. I can say that I once tried it out, and took the liberty to omit or neglect certain rules of our church, which seemed to me rather futile and strange. But after discussing them with learned men, I found they were established on solid grounds, and nothing but ignorance or stupidity would make us respect them any less than the others.

Why don't we ever stop to consider the contradictions we find in our own judgment—the many things which yesterday were articles of faith and which today appear to us as fables? Pride and curiosity are the scourges of the mind: the latter prompts us to stick our nose into everything, and the former forbids us to leave anything doubtful or undecided.

I don't know if I am right or wrong, but since we have received a certain prayer from the mouth of God, I have always believed we should use it oftener than we do. I wish that Christians would always use the Lord's Prayer—if not alone, at least together with whatever other—at sitting to and leaving the table, at going to bed and rising from it, at all occasions when prayer is in order. It is the only prayer I use at all times, and I remember no other as perfectly.

We must have our souls pure and clean at the moment, at least, we pray to God; otherwise, we ourselves give Him the rods with which to chastise us. This makes me slow to applaud the men whom I see frequently on their knees, if their actions do not give me some evidence of their improvement. A man who mingles religious devotion with an abominable life is worse than the man who is true to himself and dissolute in religion as in everything else.

Generally we pray by custom and for fashion's sake, or rather go through the words and motions of prayer. We seem to use our prayers as a kind of gibberish—like those who employ holy words in sorceries and magic and as if we thought the benefit from them depended on the texture, sound, and flow of the words, or on our keeping a solemn face. And I am scandalized to see a man cross himself thrice at Benediction and at Grace, and give over the rest of the day to acts of malice, greed, or injustice. I am the more outraged because it is a sign I have in great veneration and use, and I make it even when I yawn.

Marguerite of Navarre tells us of a young prince who, though she does not name him, is easily identified. In order to keep his assignations with a lawyer's wife, in Paris, he had to pass through a church; and coming or going, he never failed to stop and pray. I leave you to judge the subject of his prayers—there are very few men who dare publish to the world the prayers they make to Almighty God—but Marguerite gives his case as an instance of remarkable piety. However, this is not the only proof we have that women are hardly fit to treat of theology.

What shall we say of men who devote their lives to profiting by what they believe are mortal sins? How many trades and callings we countenance, yet knowing that their very essence is vicious!

A man voluntarily confessed to me that he had all his life professed and practiced a religion which he felt was damnable and contrary to the beliefs of his heart—and did it merely to keep his reputation and the honors of public office. How could his courage suffer such a confession! And what can such a man think of divine justice?

It seemed to me fantastic that in recent years every intelligent man who professed the Catholic faith was accused of hypocrisy. Whatever he might say to the contrary, his opponents held him to be a Protestant at heart. What wretched disease is this which rivets a man so firmly to his own belief he becomes incapable of conceiving that other men may believe otherwise? Or that he fancies other men would risk eternal salvation for the sake of the fortunes of this world? He may believe me when I say that if anything could have tempted my youth, it would have been the very ambition to share the risks and dangers of this new enterprise.

Amusing people those! who think they have rendered the

Holy Scripture fit for public consumption by translating it into the common tongue. Do they think the meaning of it lies obvious in the words? It is a book too serious and venerable to be glanced at and fingered casually, to be tumbled about a drawing room or kitchen. Reading it ought to be a premeditated and attentive act, preceded by a *sursum corda* and accompanied by a grave and composed mind. It is a book not for everyone to study, but only for those dedicated to the task and called of God. The ignorant and wicked merely grow worse by reading it. Shall I venture to add that by coming so near to understanding a little of it, they are wider of the mark than they were before?

Those people who of late years have created an almost purely meditative and immaterial ritual need not wonder if some of us think that religion would melt away and vanish between their fingers if it were not maintained by some exterior mark and instrument. For the senses are our first and proper judges. The use of incense in our churches, widespread among all religions, is intended to cheer us by exciting and purifying the senses, in order to render us more susceptible to meditation. The music in the somber vastitude of our churches moves and ravishes me. A wise man ought to withdraw his soul from the crowd, and give it liberty within himself and the power to judge freely of things. But in externals, he should follow and conform to accepted usage.

Frankly speaking, it seems to me great presumption and conceit to set one's own ideas in such high esteem as to overthrow the public peace in order to establish them. Is it wise housekeeping to introduce the inevitable miseries and dreadful corruptions of civil war, to encourage known and certain evils, for the sake of doubtful and debatable errors of opinion? I have observed that, in Germany, Luther has left as many disputes concerning his own beliefs as he himself raised concerning the Bible—and more.

The Roman Senate dared evade the issue when it came to a

religious dispute between the people and the government. 'These things,' it said, 'are not for us but for the gods to decide—therefore let them safeguard their own sacred affairs.'

It was this commonplace which supported me in my own position. It checked me, even in the exuberance of my youth, from trying to load my shoulders with the weight of such responsibility. It seemed to me most unjust to set about trying to subject public and established customs to private individual notions. The mind of an individual has authority only over itself.

God knows in our present quarrel—where there are a hundred important articles of faith at stake—how few men can truly claim to have weighed and understood the grounds on either side! The number of them, if there is any number, is so small that in themselves they would cause no disturbance. As for the others, under what banner do they march? They are like a poor and ill-applied medicine. The poisons they would purge, they only stir more actively in motion: the dose is too feeble to clean us out, but strong enough to weaken us. We are left with the poisons in us, and have gained nothing but additional cramps and gripes.

The true field and subject of imposture are these things which are unknown to us. Not being amenable to ordinary reasoning, we have no way of disputing them. Therefore we most firmly believe the things we know least, and no people are more self-confident than those who gull us with fables: such as our alchemists, astrologers, fortune-tellers, and physicians. If I dared I would willingly add to the list a pack of people who undertake to interpret and superintend the designs of God Himself. Even though the discordance of events tosses them from pillar to post, from east to west, they persist at sticking to their game and with the same crayon draw black and white.

We must not mock God. Yet the best of us are not so much afraid to offend Him as to offend our neighbors, kinsmen, or rulers. We owe more love to God than to ourselves and we know

Him less well—yet we speak of Him to our hearts' content. Man fashions a thousand pleasant social relations between himself and God: isn't he His fellow townsman?

All this is manifest evidence that we accept our religion after our own fashion, by our own hands, and in the same way that other religions are accepted. Either we follow the custom of our country; or we revere the antiquity of our religion, or the authority of those who maintain it; or we are terrified by its threats against unbelievers; or we are allured by its promises. We are Christians by the same token we are Frenchmen or Germans.

Yet what kind of faith is this which cowardice and faint heart plant and establish in us? A neat faith, which believes only because it lacks the courage to disbelieve! Some men persuade the world that they believe what at heart they disbelieve. Others, and by far the greater number, persuade themselves that they believe—not knowing what it means really to believe. Miserable, senseless creatures who strive to be worse than they are.

The best witness of human ignorance in divine matters is the god Apollo, who gave men to understand that their religion was a thing of their own contrivance and that 'every man's true worship was the one he found customary wherever he happened to be.' What kind of righteousness is this which I see in repute today and denounced tomorrow, and which the crossing of a river turns into unrighteousness? What kind of truth is this which is true on one side of a mountain and false on the other?

Plato believes it smacks of impiety to inquire too closely into the nature of God, the universe, and the first causes of things. We are quick to say Almighty Power, Truth, Justice: these are words that portend a great thing, but what the thing is we can neither see nor conceive. We say, God loves—God fears—God waxes angry. But these or similar emotions cannot exist in God in any form akin to the emotions of men, and we cannot imagine what they are like in Him. It is for God alone to know Himself and interpret His works. When He does this in mortal language, it is only an approximation, a stooping and bending to us who crawl on the earth.

For the moment let us consider man alone, with no aid but himself, and no arms but his own weapons. Let us see what he can seize and compass with this goodly equipment. Who has persuaded him that this marvellous march of the vault of heaven, that the eternal light of these lamps rolling in majesty over his head, that the awful tides of this cosmic sea, were established and kept in motion through untold ages for his convenience and use? Can one imagine anything so ridiculous as this miserable and puny creature, who is not so much as the master of himself but is the butt of all things, and yet who dares to call himself emperor of the universe? And this privilege which he claims for himself of being the single creature in this vast fabric to appreciate its beauty and parts, the sole who can render thanks to its builder and do the bookkeeping of infinity—who, I wonder, signed and sealed him this privilege? Let him show us the letter of appointment to this high and noble office.

A goose, too, may say: 'Every part of creation is concerned with my welfare. The earth serves me to waddle upon, the sun to light me—I am the darling of nature. Doesn't man feed, house, and wait on me?—It is for me he sows and grinds. If he eats me, he eats his fellowmen as well, and I eat the worms which in turn eat him.'

Of all human and ancient opinions concerning religion, that one seems to me most likely and reasonable which recognizes in God an incomprehensible power, the origin and preserver of all things—a power that receives and takes in good part the honor and reverence man pays to Him, under whatever form, name, or manner it may be. Of all the cults Saint Paul found in Athens, the most pardonable seemed to him the one dedicated to the 'Unknown God.'

The hand of His government lies upon all things with like hand, like measure, and like force. Our human interests have no part and place in it. Our movements and measures concern it not.

Worship of God is expressed by physical words and actions, for it is man who believes and prays. I cannot be persuaded that the sight of our crucifixes, pictures of the Passion, and the ornaments and ceremonies of our churches, that the chants accommodated to our thoughts and the stimulation of our senses do not warm the souls of the people with a religious passion most beneficial in its effect.

But it would be a pity to fool ourselves with our own silliness and inventions. 'Men fear what they have themselves devised' [Lucan], like children who are frightened by the face of a playfellow which they have, with their own hands, smeared and blackened. It is a far cry from honoring the God who made us, to honor a god whom we have made.

Knowing my own shifting nature I have, by good fortune, cultivated in me a certain stedfast belief, which has hardly changed from its first original form. Since I am incapable of choosing for myself, I have stayed in the place where God has put me—in no other way could I prevent myself from perpetually rolling. Thus, by the grace of God, I have kept myself whole, without anxiety or trouble of conscience, in the very midst of the many sects and divisions our century has produced.

CHAPTER XXVI

Gravel and the Doctors

 HAVE AGED since I began this book, and it has not been without some acquisition. The years have been so generous as to familiarize me with the stone in the bladder. Though if they had to present me with one of those gifts they reserve for the old, I wish they had chosen something more welcome. For there is no disease which, all my life, I have held in greater horror.

I often thought that I was going too far—that in such a long journey I must at length run into a grave mishap. I have felt and frequently said to myself: 'It is time to quit. Let us cut this life where it is still alive and healthy, as a surgeon amputates a limb. Nature demands huge interest from the man who does not pay the principal on the dot.'

Yet I was so far from ready to depart that within eighteen months after I had become afflicted, I had already learned to put up with the disease. I was already making terms with the stone, and finding something in it to console and hearten me. So easily are men inured to their miserable condition that there is nothing they will not accept, provided they may continue to exist.

I am not so sensitive to purely mental suffering as most men. This is partly the result of deliberation, for the world judges dreadful and worse than death many things which appear indifferent to me. But partly, too, because I am of a naturally sluggish and callous disposition, which I regard as one of the best traits of my character. However, I feel downright physical pain most vividly.

Yet I was more afraid of it than I find I had reason to be. Once again I discover that our mind, as we generally employ it, is more liable to make us trouble than give us security.

I am at grips with one of the worst diseases—painful, dreadful, and incurable. Yet even the pain itself, I find, is not so intolerable as to plunge a man of understanding into frenzy or despair. At least I have one advantage over the stone. It will gradually reconcile me to what I have always been loath to accept—the inevitable end. The more it presses and importunes me, the less I will fear to die.

As for the rest, I have found that the counsel to keep a stiff upper lip in the face of suffering is pure show. Why should philosophy, which is concerned with the essential things of life, occupy itself with these externals? Let us leave that to actors and elocutionists who put such great weight on gestures. Philosophy should not hesitate to permit our giving voice to pain, even if it does no good. It should allow the sighs, sobs, palpitations, and pallor which nature renders involuntary, provided our courage is undaunted. What does it matter if we wring our hands, so long as we do not wring our thoughts?

In such extremities, it is no great matter if we screw up our face. If the body finds relief in complaining, let it complain. If agitation gives it ease, let it toss and tumble at will. If the disease seems to evaporate (as some doctors think it helps women in childbirth) in loud outcries—or if they only divert us from its torments—let it roar at the top of its lungs. We have enough to do in dealing with the disease itself, without bothering over these superfluities.

In my own case I have come off a little better. I do not need to roar—merely groaning does the work. Not that I try to hold myself back; but either the pains are not excessive for me, or I have more than ordinary patience. When I am in the depths of torment, I try myself out; and I have always found I could talk, think, and give as coherent a reply as at any time—but not so steadily, due to the interruption of the pains.

When my visitors think I am stricken worst and hesitate to trouble me with talk, I often essay my strength and set on foot a conversation as remote as possible from my ailment. I can do anything by fits and starts—but it must not be for long. What a pity I am not gifted like that man in Cicero who, dreaming he was lying with a wench, awoke to find he had discharged his stone in the sheets! My own pains have strangely blighted my taste for wenching.

During the intervals between attacks, when my vessels are merely sore and weak, I quickly recover my usual frame of mind. For I have always trained myself to take alarm at nothing but what is immediate and palpable.

Yet I have been rather roughly handled for a beginner. The stone caught me suddenly and unawares, dropping me at one swoop from an easy and pleasant life into the most dolorous that one can imagine. It attacked me at the outset more sharply than it does most men. The spells come so fast I am scarcely ever at ease. Yet up till now I have kept my head; and, if I can continue to hold my mind steady, I will be better off than thousands of others who suffer from no ills or fevers except those created by their own mental instability.

It may be that I inherited my hatred for doctoring, but in any case I have strengthened it by arguments and reasons. In the first place, the experience of others makes me fearful of it. No one, I see, falls sick so often and takes so long to recover as those who are enthralled by the rules of medicine. Their very health is weakened and injured by their diets and precautions. Doctors are not satisfied to deal with the sick; but they are forever meddling with the well, in order that no one shall escape from under their thumbs. I have been sick often enough to learn that I can endure my disease (and I have had a taste of all sorts) and get rid of it as nicely as anyone else, and without adding to it the vileness of their prescriptions.

My mode of living is the same in sickness as in health: the same bed, hours, food, and drink. I add nothing to them but moderation according to the state of my appetite. My health consists of maintaining my habitual course. I find that illness puts me off on one side; if I followed the doctors, they would put me off on the other—so that between nature and art I would be completely unseated.

I firmly believe that I cannot be harmed by things to which I have been long accustomed, and I lay great weight on my inclinations and desires. I do not like to cure one disease by another, and I hate remedies which are more troublesome than the disease itself. To be afflicted by colic and to be afflicted by abstaining from oysters are two evils in the place of one. Since we must run a chance one way or the other, let it be in the direction of our pleasures.

A gentleman in my neighborhood, who is terribly beset by the gout, was ordered to give up all salted meats. And he used to reply that in the height of the attacks he needed something to rage and swear at. By cursing now a Bologna sausage and again a smoked tongue he found great relief from his pains.

My appetite regulates itself according to the condition of my stomach. Wine is hurtful to sick people, and it is the first thing my palate disrelishes—and most invincibly. Whatever I take against my liking harms me, and nothing hurts me that I eat with appetite. I have never received harm from any action that was very agreeable to me, and accordingly I have made all my medical theories yield to my pleasures. Indeed, when I am sick I am often sorry I do not have some longing that would give me pleasure to satisfy.

You will always find in medicine an authority to endorse your whims. If your doctor does not approve of your drinking this kind of wine or eating that sort of food, do not worry over it. I'll find you another who will be of a different opinion.

Experience has taught me that we do most damage to ourselves by impatience. We ought to give free passage to our diseases, and I find they linger less if I let them alone. They yield more readily to courtesy than curses. Let us allow Nature to have a bit her own way: she understands her business better than we. 'But such-a-one died?' Yes, and so will you—if not of this disease, then of another.

I have permitted colds, gouty defluxions, headaches, palpitations of the heart, and other accidents to grow old in me and die—just when I was prepared to nourish and keep them. If someone offers you a pleasant remedy, take it—it is so much to the good. But we must patiently suffer the laws of our condition.

Let us, in God's name, follow the general course of nature. If we do, it will carry us along. If we don't, it will drag us anyway—ourselves, our rage for cures, and our medicines all together. Order a purge for your brain—it will do you more good than one for your belly.

Doctors have a clever way of turning everything to their advantage. Whenever nature, luck, or anything else benefits our health, they lay it to their medicine. When things go badly they disown all responsibility and throw the blame on their patient. 'He lay with his arms uncovered—the rattle of a coach worsened him—somebody left the window open—he slept on his left side—he has the wrong mental outlook.'

Or else they make our turn for ill serve their own business. They try to tell us that without their treatment things would have been still worse. When they have plunged a man from a chill into a recurrent fever, they say that if it were not for them it would have been a continual fever. They run no risks of failing in their trade, for they convert even their losses into profits.

In antiquity and since then, there have been countless changes in medicine—for the most part sweeping and entire. In our times, for example, we have those introduced by Paracelsus, Fiorvanti, and Argentier. They have altered not only the prescriptions, but, I am told, the whole body and rules of the art, accusing all their predecessors of ignorance and imposition. At this rate you may imagine the plight of the poor patient.

How often we see one physician impute the death of a patient to the medicine of another physician! Yet how, God knows, shall a doctor discover the true symptoms of a disease when each is capable of an endless variety? How many controversies have raged between them on the significance of the urine? For my part, I would prefer to trust a physician who has himself suffered from the malady he would treat. The others describe diseases as our town criers do a dog or horse—such color, height, and ears. But bring the beast to him, and he can't recognize it.

In my own sickness I have never found three doctors of the same opinion. Aperients, I am advised, are proper for a man afflicted with the stone—by dilating the vessels they help discharge the viscous matter out of which the gravel is formed. Again, aperients are dangerous, because, by dilating the vessels, they help the formative matter to reach the kidneys which naturally seize and retain it.

It is good, they say, to urinate frequently, for this prevents the gravel from settling in the bladder and coagulating into a stone. But frequent urinations are bad, because the deposits cannot be voided without grave violence to the tissues. It is good to have frequent intercourse with women, for that opens the passages; and it is bad, because it inflames, tires, and weakens the kidneys. Hot baths are good because they relax the parts, and they are bad because they help bake and harden the gravel. Because the doctors were afraid of stopping a dysentery lest they put the patient in a fever, they killed me a friend who was worth more than the whole pack of them together.

Thus they juggle and prate at our expense. They can't furnish me one argument that I'll not find a contrary of equal force. So let them not rail against those who, gripped by a disease, allow themselves to be gently guided by their own appetites and the promptings of nature, and trust to common luck.

Moreover, writers on medicine claim that every drug has something harmful in it. And if, even at best, they must do us some hurt, what of those which are misapplied. And is not the danger increased when the prescriptions are compounded by still a third hand, to the mercy of whose skill and fidelity we must abandon our lives?

In short, I honor physicians not for their services, but for themselves. I have known many a good man among them, and most worthy of affection. I do not attack them, but their art. Nor do I blame them for taking advantage of our folly, for most men do as much. Many professions, both of greater and lesser dignity, live on gulling the public.

When I am sick, I send for them if they are near at hand, merely to have their company; and I pay them as others do. I give them leave to order me to keep myself warm, for I like to do it anyway. I let them recommend leeks or lettuce for my soup, put me on white wine or claret, or anything else that is indifferent to my taste and habits.

I know right well that I am not coddling them in this, for to them bitterness and strangeness is the very essence of a remedy. A neighbor of mine takes wine as an effective medicine for fever. Why? Because he abominates it.

Yet how many doctors do we see who, like myself, despise taking medicine, who live on a liberal diet and quite contrary to the rules they prescribe for their patients? What is this but sheer abuse of our simplicity!

It is fear of pain and death, impatience at being ill, and reckless search for cures, which blind us. It is pure cowardice that makes us so gullible. Yet most men do not so much believe in doctors as submit and consent to them. I hear them complain as much as I, but they finally yield and say, 'What then should I do?'

Just the other day I was talking with some men afflicted like myself, and one of them told me of a pill compounded of a hundred and more ingredients. It put us in excellent humor and cheered us mightily; for what stone could withstand a battery of that charge? But now I hear from those who tried it out that not a grain of gravel so much as stirred before the blast.

And when all is over and a cure effected, how can a man know whether it was not because the disease had run its normal course, or because he had eaten or drunk something quite by chance, or because his grandmother had prayed for him?

I should not be so bold in my handling of the mysteries of medicine if I did not have encouragement from medical authorities themselves. If Pliny or Celsus ever falls into your hands, you will find that they speak of the art much more roughly than I. Pliny twits the doctors in this: when they are at the end of their rope, they have a neat device for saving themselves. They order their patients, whom they have tortured with drugs and diets in vain, to visit a shrine or go to a watering place. But there is still a third recourse—which saves their face, and takes us off their hands and out of range for complaint. They send us travelling in foreign lands.

I do not promise that I will not be such a fool one day as to commit my life (and death) into their hands. But if fear and impatience thus get the better of me, it will be a symptom that the fever has reached my brain.

I can't expect a miracle—I pay with the stone my dues to old age, and I needn't hope for a better bargain. Everywhere I meet men who are tormented with it, and I am honored by the fellowship. That few have it with less pain and many with the additional torture of daily drugs, I owe to my good fortune. They pay a thousand crowns to their physician in order to void a little gravel, which I often do by the favor of nature.

When I am in company, even the common decencies are not disturbed by it. I can hold my water ten hours or more, or as long as any healthy man. In fact, my disease often says to me, 'Look how late I have come! I have attacked only that part of you which is already sterile and lost. Think of the pleasure you get when people say, What a patient self-controlled man! I am often as long-lived as you. You will not die because you have the stone, but because you are alive.'

And when I void a stone, what is sweeter than the speedy change from excessive pain to the beautiful light of health! Is there anything in the pain that outweighs the pleasure of this sudden improvement? In other diseases, a man is a year recuperating. And before they have unwrapped your muffler, removed your cap, allowed you to walk outdoors, take a taste of wine, lie with your wife, eat a melon, it is a thousand to one you will have relapsed into some new illness. The stone has this advantage: it carries itself off at a stroke.

Since I have come down with it I find, too, that I am freer of other ailments. Moreover it generally plays its own game by itself, and leaves me free to play mine. All I need is the courage to do so, and have indeed gone ten hours on horseback during its greatest fury. Finally, it leaves me little to guess at and go consulting over with the doctors. My feelings tell me plainly enough what and where it is.

Thus I try to beguile my imagination, and rock it to sleep. If I find it is worse tomorrow, I will provide new devices. Of late, for example, I discover that the least movement forces me to void blood. But what of it? I still ride after my hounds with the ardor and pride of youth. After all, it costs me little more than an uneasiness and heaviness in the afflicted region; and evacuating by degrees a substance which is devouring my life, I rid myself of a troublesome excrescence and not without some natural pleasure.

I judge of my condition only by what I actually feel, and not by my fears and reasoning. Would you like to know how much I gain? Look at those who behave otherwise.

CHAPTER XXVII

The Enemy at My Gate

ERHAPS THE EASE with which my house can be attacked is one of the reasons why it has escaped the violence of our civil wars. Defence invites enterprise, and defiance provokes assault. I have crippled the designs of the soldiery by shearing the exploit of all danger and glory, which commonly serves them for a pretext: bravery takes the place of honor when justice is dead.

I made the conquest of my house cowardly and base. It is closed to no one who knocks. My gate has no other guard but the porter, with his old-fashioned ceremony, who is there not to protect my door but to open it with more politeness and courtesy. I have no other sentinels but the stars.

A gentleman would play the fool to make a show of defence unless his defences were perfect A breach in one wall is a breach everywhere. Our fathers did not think they were building frontier strongholds. And the means of attacking—I mean without battery or army—and surprising our houses surpass every day, by more and more, our means of defending them. Men's wits are everywhere sharpened in that direction: everyone has a stake in invasion, only the rich in defence.

Mine was strong enough for the days when the house was built. I have added nothing to it in that respect, for fear that its very strength would turn against me—apart from the consideration that in interludes of peace it would have to be dismantled.

Again, there would be the chance of not being able to recover it. And the risks of holding it are enormous; for in civil war, your own footman may be on the other side. And when religion serves as the cloak for the war, even your relatives may, with an appearance of justice, become unreliable.

And suppose you fail? Instead of pitying you, the chances are that your friends will busy themselves blaming you for ignorance of your business and lack of foresight and vigilance.

The fact that so many fortified houses are destroyed and mine still stands, makes me suspect that they were lost because they were guarded.

Let who will, if God pleases, throw himself against me; but so far as in me lies, I will not, by defence, invite his attack. This is my retreat to give me peace from the wars. I have tried to withdraw this corner from the public fury, as I have another corner for my soul. Our war may change its face as it will, our parties mask and multiply; but for my part, I will not budge.

With armed houses on every side, I alone that I know of in all France trust mine purely and simply to the protection of Heaven. I have not so much as removed a silver spoon or a title deed. I will neither tremble nor escape by halves. If plain gratitude can win me divine favor, it will abide with me to the end. If not, I have lasted long enough to make my survival remarkable and worthy of record. How long? It is a good thirty years.

I was writing this about the time when a great load of our civil troubles lay for several months with all their weight upon me. On the one side, I had the enemy at my gate. On the other were the freebooters, who are worse than enemies, for 'they fight not with arms but with crimes.' I tasted at one stroke every kind of military violence.

O monstrous war! Other wars are directed against outsiders, this against ourselves—destroying us with our own poison. It comes to crush sedition, and of itself creates it. It proposes to punish disobedience, and is itself an example of it. Employed for the defence of law and order, it rebels against its own law and order. Where are we indeed, when our medicine carries the disease?

My people suffered not only immediate damage, but future loss. The living were made to suffer, but so were the yet unborn. They were stripped—and I too—of hope, and ravished of all they had laid up in store for long years to come.

Whoever will ask our troopers their experiences in this civil war will find an endurance and resolution among our common people altogether worthy of comparison with the Spartans.

I know of simple peasants who allowed the soles of their feet to be broiled over a gridiron, their fingertips crushed with the trigger of a pistol, and their bloodied eyes squeezed out of their heads by twisted cords, before they would so much as consent to a ransom.

I saw one peasant left for dead stark naked in a ditch, his neck black and swollen—the halter still about it with which they had dragged him all night at the tail of a horse, his body pierced with a hundred dagger thrusts, given not to kill but to torture and terrify him. Yet he had endured it all, even to the point of being rendered unconscious, resolved, as he himself told me, to die a thousand deaths—as indeed he had—before he would pay a penny. Yet he was one of the richest in the countryside.

And how many men have been seen who allowed themselves to be burned and roasted for opinions taken on trust from others — opinions they could neither give an account of, nor understand.

Besides this violence, I ran the mischances that moderation brings in such maladies. I was robbed on all sides. To the Ghibelline I was a Guelf, and to the Guelf a Ghibelline. The location of my house—planted as I am in the very mine and center of the new religion—and my friendliness with the neighbors gave me one face; my life and actions another. I was deprived of the intimate confidences of other men and the tie of interest and religion which held them together; and I had for my share the danger of living among people to whom all things were lawful.

No formal accusations were laid against me: only mute suspicions which ran from hand to hand, and which are never wanting in such confused times, any more than there is a lack of envious and empty heads. I usually lend color to such injurious rumors that fortune sows against me by the way I have of refusing to justify, excuse, or explain myself. For I hold it would compromise my conscience to plead in its behalf. In fact, rather than denying an aspersion, I improve on it by an ironic and mocking confession—that is, unless I sit absolutely silent, as though the thing were not worth an answer.

Those who look on such behavior as too haughty have little kindness for me—I mean the great folks who think independence is a grave fault and who are harsh to all justice that knows and feels itself. I have often knocked my head against this pillar.

In such circumstances, an ambitious or avaricious man would have hanged himself. I have no love of gain, yet the losses that come to me by way of theft or violence touch my heart almost as they would a miser. The offence strikes me deeper than the loss.

A thousand mischiefs fell upon me in single file, which I could have borne more cheerfully if they had come in a rush. Taking everything into consideration, I do not know a man of our party who pays as dear as I do for the defence of our laws, both *cessant gain* and *emergent loss,* as the lawyers say. Many who make a brave show of their zeal and constancy do less, by any just measure, than I. My house has stood open and free to all comers, and has won a merited popularity. So it would be a hard matter to insult me justly on my own dung heap.

Yet I find it a remarkable masterpiece that it is still virgin from plunder and blood, despite the long storm that has swept our neighborhood. It is possible, I might say, for a man of my disposition to withstand any one uniform and continuous threat; but the invasions now on one side and then on the other, the changes and vicissitudes of fortune all around me, have so exasperated the temper of the country that I am time and again faced with invincible dangers.

My brother—the Sieur de la Brousse—and I were one day travelling together, and met a gentleman of reassuring appearance. He was of the opposing faction, though I did not recognize it at the time, for he pretended otherwise. But when we passed any loyal troops or entered a town that held for the King, the man looked so desperate and half dead I at length discovered it to be the alarms of conscience. The poor fellow seemed to fear we could see his heart through all the crosses stitched on his cassock.

The mischief of this sort of war is that the cards are so shuffled your enemies can't be distinguished by any mark of language, clothes, or manners, and it is hard to avoid confusing them with your friends. This used to make me afraid to meet any of our own troops in a place where I was not known, lest I be compelled to tell my name or have something worse befall me. This happened to me once, when through just such a misunderstanding I lost both horses and men. Among them my page, an Italian lad whom I had brought up with great care and affection, was miserably slain—and a youth of great promise extinguished.

At Mussidan, not far from my house, I heard those who were driven out by our troops complain of treachery. During an armistice and while both factions were negotiating, they were attacked by surprise and cut to pieces. In another age this might, perhaps, have had some color of foul play. But today the practice of arms is quite another story. Until a treaty is signed and sealed, it will not do to have the slightest confidence in your enemy. Even after, the victor will have it hard enough to keep his word.

Yet it has often happened to me that simply as the result of my manner, persons who did not know me have given me their confidence and trust.

A certain neighbor planned to seize by surprise my house and myself. His scheme was, to arrive at my gate unattended, and beg admittance as though rather pressed.

I knew him by name, and had tolerable reasons for trusting him both as neighbor and a distant relative. So I ordered the gate opened to him, as I do to everyone.

I found him in a sad state of alarm, his horse panting and all in a foam. He proceeded to beguile me with this fairy tale: He had encountered, about half a league away, an enemy of his, whom I likewise knew and had heard of their quarrel. Taken by surprise and finding his forces too weak, he had fled to my gate for refuge. He was desperately worried (he said) about his men, whom he held for either captured or dead.

I innocently did my best to comfort, reassure, and refresh him. Soon after, four or five of his soldiers appeared in the same state of terror, and begged to enter. And then more, and still more, to the number of twenty-five or thirty, well mounted and armed, all claiming they had the enemy at their heels.

This mystery began to arouse my suspicion. I knew how much my house might be envied, and I recalled several similar affairs among my acquaintances.

But I decided there was nothing to be gained, once having begun courteously, unless I went through with it. I would spoil everything, I thought, if I suddenly changed my behavior. So I acted in the most natural and simple way, as I always do, and invited them all to come in.

I naturally take men as I find them, without mistrust, and gladly throw myself headlong into the arms of Fortune—whom I have hitherto found a greater friend to my affairs than I am myself. When I am in danger, I don't think so much about how I shall escape as how little it matters: if it should be the end, what of it?

The last batch of soldiers remained mounted in my courtyard. My neighbor, who was with me in my hall, would not allow his horse to be stabled, saying he would withdraw once he had news of all his men. He saw that he was master of the situation, and nothing remained but to put his plan in action.

But, as he has told me several times since—for he makes no bones about repeating the tale—my frankness and open countenance tore the treachery from his hands.

He remounted his horse; and his retainers, who had their eyes on him waiting for the signal, were astonished to see him ride off, and leave the prey untouched.

Another time, I was relying on a truce just proclaimed by the armies, and took a journey through a ticklish stretch of country. My departure was no sooner winded about than three or four parties of horse started out from different points to capture me.

One of them overtook me on the third day. I was attacked by fifteen or twenty horsemen, who were followed by a swarm of troopers.

I was captured and led into the thick of a neighboring wood. There I was unhorsed and robbed. My trunks were ransacked, my strongbox seized, and my horse and equipment divided among the new possessors.

We were a long time in the thicket arguing the amount of my ransom. For they rated me so high it was clear they did not know who I was. They likewise began hotly debating over my life. Altogether, there were circumstances enough to show me my danger.

I kept insisting on my rights under the truce; and was willing to grant them the spoils they had taken, which were not to be despised, but no further ransom.

After two or three hours, they had me mounted on a nag which was not likely to escape; I was placed under the special guard of fifteen or twenty musketeers; my men were divided among the others; and we were ordered to be led off as prisoners, each in a different direction.

I had not proceeded more than three or four musketshots from the thicket, when they suddenly and unexpectedly changed their minds. I saw their leader approach me with more kindly words. They began to search among the troops for my scattered goods, and did what they could to recover and restore them to me—even to my cashbox. But the best gift they made me was my liberty.

To this day I do not exactly know the reason for this sudden and almost miraculous change of mind. For it was a planned and deliberated enterprise, right enough for the times; and at the first dash I had told them my name and where I was going. The apparent leader, who removed his mask and gave me his name, told me over and over that I owed my release to my face and the frankness and freedom of my speech, which, he assured me, made me undeserving of such mistreatment. And he made me promise I would do the like for him in return.

It is just possible that the divine bounty made use of this silly characteristic of mine in order to save me. I do know that as a result of the warning given me by my assailants, I was spared the next day from worse ambushes. Of the leaders, one is still walking about to tell the tale; the other was killed not long ago.

On July 10, 1588, I was taken prisoner by the captains and the people of Paris. I had just returned from Rouen where I had left His Majesty; and I was lodging in the Faubourg St. Germain, ill with a sort of gout which had seized me three days before. It was at the time when M. de Guise had assumed command and chased the King from the city.

Between three and four in the afternoon I was led on my horse to the Bastille. And I was told that my arrest had been made at the request of the Duke of Elbeuf, as a reprisal for the imprisonment of his relative, a Norman gentleman whom the King held prisoner in Rouen.

The Queen Mother, hearing the noise of the people and being informed of my arrest by M. Pinard, a secretary of state, solicited the Duke of Guise, who happened to be in council with her. By great insistence she prevailed on him to have me released. The Provost of the Merchants and M. de Villeroy, another secretary of state, also made great and unwonted efforts in my behalf.

The upshot was that about eight o'clock the same evening a steward of Her Majesty brought the order to M. Clerc, at that time Captain of the Bastille; and I was set at liberty. It was the first prison I ever knew.

I escape, but it grieves me to think it is more by luck and a little by my own prudence, rather than by justice. As matters stand I live more than half by the favor of others, which is a bitter obligation. I do not like to owe my safety either to the liberality and goodwill of princes who consent to be pleased with my attitude toward law and freedom, or to the pleasant manners of my predecessors and myself.

For what if I were a different sort of man? If my behavior and the frankness of my speech happen to please my neighbors or my relatives, it is cruel that they are in a position to pay their debt by letting me live—that they should be able to say, 'We'll pardon him for holding divine service in the chapel of his house, although we have laid waste all the churches round about; and we'll allow him his life and property because in time of need he shelters our wives and cattle.'

I believe that a man should live by right and authority, and not by way of favor or reward. If a man must owe something, it ought to be by a better title than that to which the necessities of this miserable war reduce me; and it ought not to be so huge that it means my very existence. It overwhelms me.

A thousand times I have gone to bed in my own house feeling

I would be betrayed or murdered before morning, and bargaining with fortune that it be done without terror or lingering. And after my paternoster I would exclaim, with Virgil, 'Shall godless soldiers these newploughed fields possess!'

But what can I do? It is the place where I was born, and the greater part of my ancestors: they have given it their name and love. Thankfully, we harden ourselves to whatever custom forces on us. In the misery that has overtaken our country, it is a blessing of nature that habit can numb our senses.

Civil wars are worse than others in this respect: we must stand sentinel in front of our own doorway. It is a terrible extremity to be threatened in one's own house and domestic retreat. And the district where I live is always the first and the last battlefield. Peace never shines on it with her full face.

I began considering to whom, among my friends, I might commit my helpless and decrepit old age. And turning my eyes about me, I found myself stripped to the shirt. To fall plumb down from such a height, it ought to be in the arms of a strong and solid friendship: but they are rare, if any there be. Finally, I saw that the safest thing to do was to trust in myself.

Everyone runs elsewhere or to the future, because no one has caught up to himself. For a long while I had preached to myself to stick to my own business, yet I was always cocking an eye to one side. A bow, a look, a kind word from a great person would tempt me—yet God knows how seldom they are these days and what little they mean. When persuasions were offered me to draw me into the marketplace, I refused as though I were half willing to consent. Now for such a spirit, blows are required; and I am content that they were.

Let us thank fortune we are not born in an effeminate, idle, and effete age. Some who could not have achieved it otherwise will be famous by their misfortunes.

I seldom read in history the turmoils of other days without the regret that I was not there, the better to examine them. And today my curiosity gives me a certain pleasure in seeing with my own eyes the notable spectacle of our public death.

Since I can't hinder or prevent it, I am content to be present, and learn from it what I can.

CHAPTER XXVIII

These Troubled Times

HEN THE VINES in my village are nipped by the frost, our priest concludes that the wrath of God has fallen on the whole human race, and that the cannibals have already got the pip. On seeing the havoc of our civil wars we all of us cry out that the machinery of the universe is cracking, and that the Day of Judgment is at our throat. We do not stop to consider that the world has seen worse times, and that even at the present moment people are enjoying themselves in a thousand corners of the globe.

For my part, I often wonder that in view of the widespread licence and impunity, there is so little mischief done. But the man who feels the hail coming down on his head thinks the entire hemisphere is swept by the storm. We all unconsciously commit this error.

Yet whoever will set before himself, as in a painting, the great image of Mother Nature in her full majesty; who will read in her aspect the universal and ceaseless variety that is there; who recognizes himself in it, and not only himself but a whole kingdom, as the merest dot of a hairline brush: that man alone will judge things in their true proportions.

The corruption of our age is made up of the individual contributions of each of us. Those who are influential enough to do so contribute injustice, cruelty, avarice, and tyranny. The weaker sort—of which I am one—contribute folly, futilities, and idleness. Yet it would seem that when most people are doing ill, to do as good as nothing is commendable. At least I am comforted that I shall be one of the last to be called to account; and, while the major offenders are being dragged over the coals, I'll have time to mend my ways. For, in my opinion, it would be unreasonable to punish misdemeanors while crimes are rampant.

Yet it was not long ago—when neither law, justice, nor magistrates performed their office any more than now—I saw a man, whose name and memory I esteem, publish I don't know what paltry proposals to reform our clothes, cookery, and legal etiquette. These are crumbs thrown to a starving people, as much as to show they are not entirely forgotten.

They do the same who set themselves to prohibiting dancing, gambling, and indecent speech among a people lost in all sorts of truly execrable vice. When we are stricken with a high fever, it is no time to comb and prink our hair.

But our judgments are become as sick as our morals. I see most of the wits of our day set themselves up as clever fellows by blackening the glory of the brave and noble exploits of times gone by, giving them a base interpretation and contriving for them fatuous causes and idle motives. Magnificent subtlety! It does not occur to them that if you will cite me the greatest and most unblemished action, I can plausibly fit it out with fifty knavish incentives. God knows, if you stretch any one of our purposes far enough, what a diversity of intentions it will cover. As a matter of fact, our clever gentlemen are not so much slanderers as bunglers at their filthy trade.

Behold the horrible impudence with which we toss divine arguments to and fro, and how irreligiously we reject and adopt them again as fortune changes our allegiance in these intestine storms. This solemn question: 'Whether it is lawful for a subject to rebel against his prince in defence of his own religion'—recall in whose mouths, a year ago, the affirmative was the buttress of one faction, and the negative of the other. Remark now how both parties have changed sides in the matter, and tell me if their arms make any less noise and rattle for the change. We burn people alive for saying that truth must be made to bear the yoke of our necessity, and how much worse does France than merely say it!

Let us confess the truth: if you should pick out from the army, even the King's own, the men who were fighting out of purely religious conviction or to protect the laws of their country or to render loyal service to their prince, you would not be able to muster from all of them put together enough to make up a single company.

It is evident to me that there is no enmity like the Christian. Our zeal does marvels when it seconds our bent for hatred, cruelty, greed, and rebellion. But when it comes to kindness and moderation, our religion will neither fly nor walk: it is not there, unless carried along almost miraculously by some unusual quirk. Our religion was made for uprooting sins; instead, it hides them, nurses them, and incites them.

What makes our civil broils so mortal is that, unlike our fathers who had some scale in their vengeance, we begin with the last resort. At the outset we cry nothing but, 'Kill, kill!' Is this anything else but cowardice?

There are many in our times who wish that these burning passions might expend themselves in a war against our neighboring nations, lest the fever raging in our body politic bring us to total ruin. While, in truth, a foreign war is less destructive than a civil, I cannot believe that God will favor such an iniquitous design as to quarrel with our neighbors in order to appease our own ills.

In so sick a time as this, the man who boasts that he is employing a true and sincere virtue in the world's service either does not know what virtue is—and very likely, for our brains are grown as rotten as our hearts—or, if he does know, boasts without warrant. Let him say what he will, he does a thousand things against his conscience.

The most honorable mark of goodness, in necessities such as these, is to confess honestly our own faults as well as those of others; to struggle against our impulse towards evil; to yield, if we must, reluctantly; and to hope and desire to be better.

I observe that everyone tries to defend his own side, but even the best of them with dissimulation and lies: the man who would tell the truth about his party must write scathingly and be a bold man indeed. The most just faction is at best but a member of a decayed and worm-eaten body. Even so, it is by comparison the soundest member; for civic virtues must be measured according to time and place.

We may regret better days, but we cannot flee from the present. We may wish other men in authority, but we must nevertheless obey those we have.

So long as some reflection of the ancient and established laws of this monarchy shines in any corner of the land, there I shall plant myself. If it unfortunately comes to pass that they contradict and thwart one another and give birth to two parties of doubtful choice, my choice will be to escape and slip away from the storm. Meanwhile, Nature and the fortunes of war may lend me their hand.

The general and just cause attracts me, but with due moderation and lack of heat. Anger and hatred are beyond the bounds of justice. A man who knows his cause is just cannot act unjustly without doing an injustice to his cause, and himself degenerating into a rebel against justice.

It is this which enables me to walk everywhere with my head up and my face and heart open. To tell the truth—and I am not afraid to confess it—I would as readily, in case of need, burn one candle to Saint Michael and another to the dragon. I am willing to follow the right side to the fire—but not, if I can help myself, into it. If needs be, let Montaigne fall in the public ruin. But if there is no need, I will thank fortune it is saved; and so far as duty gives me rope, I'll call it my duty to save it.

For a man to vacillate and stand aside, to keep his affections unmoved and impartial, while his country is racked and torn, is neither handsome nor honest. It is a kind of treason; for, in our domestic affairs, everyone must necessarily take sides. Though for a man to sit still who has not been ordered into the fray I hold more excusable in civil than in foreign wars—even if I do not excuse myself on this ground.

Yet even those who engage in the struggle may behave with such temper and decency that they may come out of it untarnished. I know some among us whose manners are so gentle, obliging, and just, and who conduct themselves so finely in the present wars, that they will, beyond all doubt, stand like a rock, no matter what outcome Heaven has decreed for us.

We are not to call duty—as we do every day—the bitter hate born of our private interests and passions; nor courage, a treacherous and malignant behavior; nor zeal, a lust for evil. It is not the cause which incites such men, it is their ambitions. They flock to war not because it is just, but because it is war. Yet a man may very well act justly and loyally towards his opponents and bear them a decent, if not the same, affection. He should swim in troubled waters without fishing in them.

In these troubled times, my own interest has not blinded me to the praiseworthy qualities of our adversaries, nor to the reproaches that can justly be made against those of our own party. Others worship everything on their side: I do not so much as excuse most things on mine. A good work never had worse grace in my eyes for being opposed to me. Except for the heart of the question, I have always maintained my poise and sanity; and I am pleased with myself for it.

Those who carry their hatred and wrath beyond the limits of

the dispute, as most men do, show they are not concerned in the cause for the common good, but for their own private advantage. I would like to see the advantage fall on my side; but, if it does-n't, I'll not tear myself to pieces with rage.

I am a mortal enemy to this way of judging: 'He admires the Duke of Guise, therefore he belongs to the League—he marvels at the energy of Henri of Navarre, obviously he is a Huguenot—he finds this or that fault with the morals of the King, conse-quently he is a rebel at heart.' I'll not grant the right of a magis-trate to condemn a book because it ranked a heretic among the best poets of France.

What! Shall we not dare say of a thief that he has a handsome leg. Because a woman is a strumpet, does it follow that her breath stinks? They want all of us, for party reasons and in party opin-ions, to be either blind or blockheads, and that our judgment should serve not the facts but our desires. I am inclined toward the other extreme, so much I fear being misled by my desires. To which I might add that I always have a lively distrust of my hopes.

In my time I have seen marvels in the prodigious ease with which people allow themselves to be led by the nose, and made to believe and hope whatever their leaders please. And this despite a thousand blunders, one on top of the other, and a thou-sand illusions punctured. I observed it mainly in the first of our civil factions; but the other, which has sprung up since, in imi-tating it has surpassed it. I am satisfied, therefore, that credulity is inseparable from popular errors. A man is no member of a movement if he dares to breast the wave, if he does not roll in with the tide. As for me, I should have to hate too many people.

The better and comparatively saner party in the wars which are now rending France is without doubt the one which supports the ancient faith and government of the country. I detest drastic change in no matter what guise—having seen the enormous evils it has produced.

While the change that has hung over us these many years is not strictly responsible for all our misery and ruin, it must nevertheless receive the blame for setting them on foot, even if accidentally and against its own intentions. Men who shake the foundations of a state are naturally the first to be engulfed in its fall. The fruits of the disturbance are seldom reaped by its instigators. They trouble the waters for others to fish in.

By dissolving the unity and loosening the fabric of our monarchy, innovation opened the way for new and further evils. But if the instigators do the greater mischief, their imitators on the conservative side are still more vicious in following the examples of which they themselves have felt the horror. And the honors, if there be any in evildoing, must go to the original troublemakers who had the glory and courage of making the initial move.

If a part of our government becomes rotten, it is well to repair it. But to try to change the foundations is to reform particular defects by a universal confusion, to open the way to injustice and tyranny, and to cure the disease by killing the patient.

Moreover, men who propose to cure things by eliminating them are only at the beginning of their task. One evil may be succeeded by another, and worse. Cæsar brought the Republic to such a pass that his supporters all had reason to repent of their meddling. This has happened again and again, even down to our own times. My contemporaries among the French could tell quite a tale on this score.

Seeing, however, the miseries which have overwhelmed us (and for what we have not done!), I do not forthwith conclude that we are at the last gasp. The endurance of a state is apt to surpass our understanding. It is a puissant and mighty thing, and it often persists despite tyranny, unjust laws, corrupt rulers, and the licence and sedition of its inhabitants. Our government is very sick indeed, but others have been more so, without dying. For my part, I do not despair.

Meanwhile let us follow that great teacher Epaminondas, and boldly declare that there are some things not allowed, even in fighting an enemy; that the public interest does not require all things of all men; that all things are not permissible to a man of honor because he happens to be in the service of his king, his country, and the laws.

This doctrine is fitting for our times. We have no need to harden our hearts with steel armor: enough if our shoulders are hardened. It will do to dip our pens in ink, without dipping them in blood.

I abominate those mad exhortations of that lawless spirit, Julius Cæsar:

> 'When the swords flash, let no idea of love, piety, or even
> the face of your fathers move you. If they oppose you, let
> the blood of your own fathers flow from your blade.'
>
> [Lucan]

Let us deprive wicked, bloodthirsty, and treacherous men of this pretext of reason—let us cast out this atrocious and insane justice, and cling to more humane examples. To judge an action honorable and excellent because it is useful is a pitiful argument. Righteousness must be made to prevail over duty.

CHAPTER XXIX

Why I Travel

LOVE CHANGE and moving about. To be more pleased with foreign things than our own is a common trait, and I have my share of it. Those who are of the contrary mind, who like their own things best, who think that nothing can be more beautiful than the world before their doorway, are really happier, even if they are not so knowing. I do not envy their wisdom, but their luck.

This lust for new things and the unknown contributes toward my desire for travel, but many other circumstances lend a hand to it.

I am glad to drop the cares of governing my house and my estate. There is, I confess, a pleasure in ruling something, if only a barn, and in being obeyed under your own roof. But it is a monotonous pleasure, and it is spoiled by a multitude of vexations: now the poverty and oppressive conditions of your tenants, now the quarrelling between your neighbors, and again their encroachments on your rights. 'Or hail smites the vines, or rain guts the trees, or the sun burns the crops, or dearth and winter bring their afflictions' [Horace]. All in all, God scarcely sends a spell once in six months when your bailiff can't complain, or when a good grape harvest doesn't mean the ruin of your grain.

Besides these vexations, there is the new and good-looking shoe such as belonged to that man of olden days, and which pinches your foot.[1] Taking one thing with another, no outsider can know what it costs you to maintain that show of order which is seen in your family, and which perhaps you buy too dear.

At any event, the damage occasioned by my absence is not such, as long as I can stand it, to warrant my refusing any opportunity to slip away. Something is always going wrong—useless worries, or sometimes useless, but always a worry. The pettiest pierce deepest: just as small print tires the eyes most, small details are the quickest to wear us out.

I am no philosopher. Evils hit me according to their force, and their force depends as much upon their shape as their substance, if not more.

When I look at my affairs from a distance and in the large, I find—perhaps because my memory is so poor—that they are flourishing beyond my expectation. I reckon my revenue greater than it is, and its prosperity betrays me. But when I am in the thick of my affairs, with an eye to every detail, a thousand things start my fears.

It is easy for me to abandon the whole business, but to attend to it without worry is hard. It is misery to be in a place where everything occupies and bothers you. I seem to enjoy more freely the pleasures of another man's house than my own. Diogenes was asked what wine he liked best; and he answered as I would have done when he said, 'Somebody else's.'

When absent from my house I strip myself of all these thoughts and would be less concerned at the collapse of a tower than, when present, at the fall of a tile. My mind is easily calmed by distance, but on the scene I am as touchy as a vine-dresser: a bit of harness askew or a strap end flapping against my leg will

---

1. Plutarch relates that when Paulus Emilius was rebuked for divorcing his wife, he pointed to his shoe and said, 'It looks well made to you, but I alone know where it pinches.'

ruffle me for a day on end. I can raise my heart above these annoyances, but not my eyes.

When I travel, however, I have nothing to think about but myself and the spending of my money. The latter is governed by a single principle: amassing money is a complicated business of which I understand nothing; of spending it I understand a little and how to make some show for my outlay—which is its main use. But I throw myself too one-sidedly into it, which spoils it in both directions. When spending makes a splash and serves the turn, I let it roll incontinently on, and just as incontinently play the niggard when it does not shine or please me.

Travelling harms me only by the expense, which is large and beyond my normal means. For I am accustomed to travel not only in the requisite, but even in a handsome style. This compels me to cut the number and length of my journeys. I can spend on them only the froth of my income, and I have to wait until it accumulates. I do not want the pleasure of going abroad to spoil my pleasure of sitting at home.

The man who takes charge of my purse when I am on the road has full and free control of it. He could cheat me prettily when it comes to reckoning up the accounts; but, unless he is a devil, I compel him to be honest by my complete trust in him. The commonest precaution I take with my servants is to remain ignorant of what they do. I had rather be told at the end of two months that I had spent four hundred crowns, than have three or five or seven crowns dinned in my ears every night.

In this way I am as little robbed as the next man. You ought to leave a certain leeway for the unscrupulousness or impudence of your servant. If you have enough, in gross, left over for your own purpose, let the surplus of Fortune run a little at Fortune's mercy—the gleaner's portion. After all, I do not value so much the honesty of my people as I scorn the harm they could inflict on me.

Another circumstance which lures me on these travels is the sad state of our public affairs. I could easily reconcile myself to this corruption so far as the public interest is concerned, but so far as it concerns my own—no.

By the long licence of the civil wars, my neighborhood has grown so old in riot that it is a wonder the social fabric holds together. I see not one action, or three, or a hundred, but common and general behavior so ferocious, above all in inhumanity and treachery, that I have not the heart to think of it without blenching in horror.

I marvel at these villainies almost as much as I detest them. They give proof of a mentality as vigorous as it is anarchic and misdirected. Necessity unites men and organizes them. This blind union is afterwards consecrated in laws. For there have been laws as savage as human imagination can conceive which have nevertheless held the body politic together in as long and robust span of life as the perfections a Plato or Aristotle could invent.

I sometimes try to fortify myself against the situation by indifference and evasion: they too can bring us to a state of resolution. I wrap and shroud myself in the storm. Thieves and robbers have, by their nature, no particular grudge against me; nor I against them, or I would have my hands too full.

In fact I do not hate enmity which is open and above board as I do concealed and treacherous—a foe in armour so much as in a magistrate's gown. Cruelty, disloyalty, and rapine are more vicious and secure when hidden under the color of the laws. Our present fever has attacked a body that is hardly the worse for it. The fire was already raging within: it has merely broken into visible flame. The alarm is greater, the evil scarcely so.

When people ask me why I travel, I usually answer: 'I do not know what I am looking for abroad, but I know well enough what I am escaping from at home.' If they tell me that foreign lands are liable to be in as sick a plight as our own, I reply, first, that this is hard to believe, and secondly, that it is always a gain to exchange known for uncertain evils—besides, the ills of other countries are not likely to weigh upon us so heavily as our own.

Yet I must not omit that however much I rebel against France, I can never cease to look on Paris with a loving eye. From earliest youth my heart has been hers. And the more I see of other beautiful cities, the more her beauty gains upon my love. I love her for herself, and more for her native graces than for her foreign embellishments. I love her tenderly, even to her stains and warts. It is this great city alone which makes me French: great in her people, great in her fair site, but above all great and incomparable for the variety she has to offer—the glory of France and one of the noblest ornaments of the world! May God keep our civil strife from her gates! And while she endures I shall never lack for a retreat where I may stand at bay.

Fortune has greatly vexed me by interrupting the construction of the beautiful Pont Neuf in our great city, and deprived me of the hope of seeing it in use before I die.

Not because Socrates said so, but because it is my own opinion—and one I hold perhaps too warmly—I look upon all mankind as my fellow countrymen. I embrace a Pole as I do a Frenchman, and I prefer the common bond of humanity above all national ties.

I am not wedded to the sweetness of my native air. New acquaintances and those of my own choosing seem to be worth at least as much as those forged with our neighbors by necessity and chance. The friends we choose ourselves are generally truer than those made for us by blood or climate. I think I shall never become so senile and so narrowly habituated to my own country as to let it take my life—as Socrates did—rather than go into exile. That was a peculiar notion for a man who thought the whole world was his city. But, then, he despised travel and hardly set foot outside of Attica.

Besides these reasons, travel is, I think, a very profitable business. I do not know, as I have often said, a better school in life than to expose yourself to other ways of living and give yourself a relish for the endless diversity of human nature.

It leaves the body neither idle nor overworked: continuous but not undue exertion keeps it in trim. I can stick to my saddle, despite the torments of the stone, eight or ten hours at a go, without dismounting or tiring. No weather annoys me, except the scorching of a hot sun (umbrellas, I find, tire a man's arm more than protect his head). I love rain and mud like any duck. Changes of air and clime never affect me: all skies are alike.

But I hate every means of getting about except horseback—whether in town or country. I cannot endure a coach, litter, or boat for very long; and when I was young, still less. I can stand a coach somewhat better than a litter, and for a similar reason, rough seas better than calm. At the gentle nudge of the oars stealing the water from under us, I find somehow both my head and stomach upset—and by the same token, I can't teeter in a chair. When towed, or carried steadily along by sail or current, I am not bothered; it is an interrupted motion, especially when very slow, that catches me. As a remedy, doctors have ordered me to gird myself tightly with a towel around the lower part of the belly. But I have never tried it, for I am wont to wrestle with my infirmities and overcome them by myself.

I think I read in Plutarch that it is fear which causes seasickness. Though I am very subject to it, I know this cannot be the reason. I was never afraid at sea, nor indeed in any other peril—and I have seen danger enough to suffice me, if death be one. All the dangers I have been in, I have faced without blinking. A man must, in truth, have courage to fear. I do not find myself strong enough to bear the force and sweep of this emotion. If I were once conquered by it, I should never rise whole again. I have no second wind. Whenever the floods break my banks, I lie open on all sides and drown without remedy. But God has given me winter according to my wool, and emotions according to my power to withstand them. Since I am weak, Nature has made me stolid, or if you will, dull.

I am troubled only by inner perturbations which I breed in myself, and I am less liable to them when I travel. I am hard to get going, but once I am on the road I can hold out as well as the best.

I take as much pains preparing for a brief jaunt to a neighbor as launching on the longest journey. I have learned to travel in the Spanish fashion: a long day's ride at one stretch. In extremely hot weather I ride from sunset to sunrise. The other method—repairing by the way and gobbling your dinner in haste—is most inconvenient, especially when the days are short. Horses do better following my way: never a horse broke under me that was able to hold through the first day. I water them everywhere I can, provided enough of the road lies ahead to settle their drink.

My laziness in getting up mornings allows my companions time to eat at their ease before we start. As for myself, I can't eat too late. Appetite only comes to me when I begin to eat; I am never hungry until I am at table.

Some of my friends pass remarks at my continuing this love of travel now that I am married and along in years. But they are wrong. The best time to leave your house is when you have put it in such shape that it does very well without you.

As to the obligations of marital affection, some people think they are weakened by these absences; but I am of a different opinion. Marriage is a relation that easily cools by too frequent and assiduous companionship: every strange woman begins to appear charming. These interruptions fill me with fresh love toward my family and make my house more delightful to me. I know that friendship has arms long enough to reach from one end of the world to the other, and especially the friendship of marriage, in which the perpetual interplay of duties arouses the sense of gratitude and memory.

When I am off in Rome I still govern my house and keep the comforts I have left behind me. I see my walls rise, my trees grow, and my revenue mount or fall within two finger-breadths of when I am at home. If we are to enjoy nothing but what we can touch, then farewell to our money when it is locked in our strongbox, and farewell to our sons when they have gone to the hunt.

We do not promise in marriage to be tied to one another's tails; and a wife ought not to have her eyes so greedily set upon her husband's front that she can't bear to see him turn his back, if needs be. An insatiable hunger for bodily presence implies a little weakness in the enjoyment we take of our minds.

'But at your age you will never return from such a long journey!' What of it? I do not set out in order to come back. My business is merely to keep myself moving as long as movement pleases me. I travel for travel's sake. My itinerary can be cut at any point: each day brings its own end to it. And the journey of my life is conducted in the same manner. In earnest, the only displeasure I find in my travels comes from my inability to plant myself where I like—I must always think of returning home and settling down in the common rut.

If I feared to die except in the place where I was born, if I thought I should die less at ease away from my family, I'd be frightened to step outside of my parish; for I feel that death is forever at my throat—or, rather, my loins. But I am not built that way; death is all one wherever it overtakes me.

Yet if I had my choice, I think I would rather die in the saddle than in bed—away from my house and far from my own people. In taking leave of friends there is more of heartbreak than comfort. It is the only unpleasant gesture in friendship, and I should gladly forego that great and eternal farewell.

Let us live and be merry among our friends, but let us go languish and die among strangers. A man will always find someone whom he can pay to shift his pillows and rub his feet.

Besides, those who anticipate a long-drawn end to their days ought not, perhaps, lay the whole burden of their infirmities on their family. To whom do they not at length become tedious? My family has grown so used to hear the groans of my stone, they no longer heed them. Though we might enjoy their talk, isn't it too much to abuse their patience years on end? The more I would see them force themselves, out of the goodness of their hearts, to be of service to me, the more I would pity them. Decrepitude is in its nature solitary, and I should gladly recommend Venice for this broken age of life.

'But in these travels, you will fall sick in some wretched hole where you will lack for everything.' As to that, I carry all necessary supplies with me; and, besides, if Fortune has laid a trap for you, there is no escape.

I have no extraordinary needs when I am sick. What nature cannot do, I'll ask of no pill. And I have still less need of a lawyer than a physician. What I have not done while I was on my feet, let no one expect me to do when I am flat on my back.

I confess that I seldom reach my inn without considering whether I could fall sick and die there at my ease. I always select my apartments in some retired part of the house, away from noise, smells, and smoke. I would like my death to share in the comforts of my life.

As for my lodgings in general, I ask for no pomp or amplitude—in fact I hate it. I want, rather, a certain clean simplicity, which is usually found where Art is less apparent and where Nature bestows a grace altogether her own.

For that matter, great discomfort will be found only by those who must traverse the Grisons in midwinter. I who travel for pleasure order my route a little better than that. If the left-hand road is bad, I take the right; if I feel myself indisposed for the saddle, I remain where I am. In this way I meet with nothing, truly, that is not as pleasant and comfortable as my own home. To be sure, I have always found superfluity superfluous, and notice there are drawbacks even to abundance and luxury.

If I have left something unseen behind, I retrace my steps. It still lies on my road, for I follow no fixed route, winding or straight. When I do not find what I have been led to expect in a place—most accounts, I discover, are false—I don't complain at losing my labor; for at least I have learned that something or other was not true.

I have tastes and a constitution as flexible as any man living. The customs of foreign countries affect me with nothing but pleasure at their variety: every custom, I find, is right in its own way. Whether I am served on pewter, wooden, or earthenware dishes; whether my meat is boiled or roasted, hot or cold; whether I am given butter or oil, nuts or olives—it is all one. In fact, I am so catholic that, in my old age at least, I wish I were otherwise—so I could be finicky enough to curb my appetite and thus perhaps benefit my digestion.

When I am out of France, and people have asked me as a matter of courtesy if I wished to be served in the French manner, I have laughed at them and always placed myself at the table most filled by foreigners.

I am ashamed to see my countrymen obsessed with the absurd notion that they must, in duty, quarrel with every custom different from their own. They seem to be out of their element as soon as they are out of their village. Wherever they go, they stick to their own ways and wail at everything foreign.

They meet a fellow Frenchman in Hungary? What marvellous luck! They link arms, become bosom friends, and spend their time damning whatever they see about them. This or that, isn't it barbarous since it isn't French? The cleverest among them are those who can find most to sneer at. The majority of them go abroad only for the purpose of returning home. And while they are on the road they hold themselves silent and aloof, preciously guarding themselves from the contagion of an unknown air.

I, on the contrary, travel as one who has his fill of the French. I don't go looking for Gascons in Sicily—I see enough of them at home. I find few foreign customs that are not as good as our own. But, then, I've not been very far—hardly out of sight of my own weathervane.

As for the rest, most of the compatriots you fall in with while travelling are more of a nuisance than a delight. Either you have to put up with them, or they with you—both a bother, although the latter is, I think, the greater. So I keep clear of them, especially now that my advancing age somewhat excuses me from observing the common civilities.

It is rare luck to find a man of good sense and congenial manners who will delight in accompanying you. How I have missed such a man on my travels! Pleasure has no savor for me unless I can communicate it. Not so much as a quip can pass through my mind without annoying me if I must spend it on myself.

Yet it is better to be alone than among bores. Aristippus used to live as a stranger everywhere. I should choose to pass my life in the saddle.

'But haven't you pleasanter diversions at home? Where can you hope to live without some annoyance? If a man like you cannot be happy at home—who can, and where? Don't you see that all of your troubles lie in yourself, and wherever you go your self will tag along and forever complain? You must reform yourself—that alone is in your power!'

Very true, this advice, and I quite agree with it. But it could have been put in one word: 'Be wise!' Such a state of mind is the work and fruit of wisdom. Thus a doctor, instead of crying at his patient, 'Be cheerful!' might as well order him, 'Be well.'

I am only a man of the common sort. It is fine advice, 'Be content with what you have,' but I can no more follow it than the wisest man in the world. I know well enough that, literally taken, my pleasure in travel is evidence of inquietude and irresolution and that, in truth, these are our ruling and predominant traits. Yet I can see nothing, not even in my dreams and wishes, by which I would be willing to abide. Variety alone satisfies me—if, indeed, anything can.

I hate the morsels Necessity carves and sets on my plate. Any comfort, no matter what, if I had to depend on it alone, would gag me. No one cord can bind me.

You will say, there is vanity in such diversion as travel. And where is there not? All these good precepts, and wisdom too, are vanity. These exquisite subtleties are only fit for sermons—to send us, baggage packed, into the other world.

But life means physical and material motion—in its essence unreasonable and imperfect. And I make it my business to serve life on its own terms.

CHAPTER XXX

In Germany and Italy

N THE TWENTY-SECOND of June, 1580, I set out on my journey to Germany and Italy. ¶On the way I took part in the siege of La Fére, where, on the sixth of August, my good friend, M. le Comte de Grammont, died of a musket wound he had received four days before.

If you ask a man, 'What brings you to this siege?' he will say, 'The force of example and common obedience to our prince. I expect no profit from it, and as for glory I know how little it can light on a plain man like myself. I have neither passion nor quarrel in this affair.' Yet the next day you will see him quite another man—flushed and boiling with fury, pressing to his place in the thick of battle. It is the flash of steel, the fire and roll of our cannon and drums, which have infused this hate and energy into his veins. A silly reason, you tell me. A reason? We need no reason to inflame our mind: an idle fancy without body or significance is enough.

Among several other friends I conveyed the body of M. de Grammont to Soissons. Every place we passed through, I observed that the mere solemnity of our cortège aroused the spectators to lamentation and tears, for not so much as the name of the deceased was known to them.

At Beaumont, M. d'Estissac joined our party. He was accompanied by another gentleman, a valet, a sumptermule, and on foot a muleteer and two lackeys, amounting to the same number in all as our own group—which included my brother, M. de Mattecoulon. They were to pay their share of the expenses.

We set out, September fifth, from Beaumont and went on, without stopping, to sup at Meaux, a pretty town lying on the Marne. From Bar-le-Duc the leagues are measured as in Gascony, and become longer and longer as they approach Germany, until they are treble what they are here.[1]

From the sixteenth to the twenty-seventh of September we stayed at Plombières, on the borders of Lorraine and Germany. I drank the waters every morning, and bathed five times. We lodged at the Angel, which is the best inn, as it is convenient to both the baths. Our suite of apartments, though we had several rooms, cost only a few sous a day, with wood thrown into the bargain. Hereabouts the hostesses are first-rate cooks, but the wine and bread are bad. The people are a good sort: frank, sensible, and attentive.

At the request of my hostess—it is the custom of the country—I presented her, upon leaving, with a copy of my coat-of-arms, which a painter in the town executed on wood for a crown. She had it carefully affixed to the wall of her house, on the outside.

In my travels I have seen almost all the famous baths of Christendom, and have for some years made use of them. The bathing itself is, I think, wholesome; for we suffer by not taking a daily bath, as men used to do in times gone by.

As to the mineral waters, luckily I can get them down without repugnance; and they are natural and simple remedies which are harmless, even if they do no good. I have never, however, seen an extraordinary or miraculous cure, and investigation has always shown me that the reports of such were ill grounded and false.

---

1. See Rabelais, book II, chapter 23, for an explanation of these elongated leagues.

The pleasure of the company a man meets in these resorts, and the walks and exercise will, moreover, lose much of their effect if the visitor does not maintain a cheerful disposition. For this reason I have chosen to go to the baths which have the pleasantest situation and offer most in the way of lodging, food, and companionship: such as Plombières, Bagnères in France, Baden in Switzerland, and Lucca and Della Villa in Italy—which I have frequented at various seasons.

Leaving Plombières, we passed through a mountainous stretch which resounded under the hoofs of our horses as though it were hollow ground, and made a noise like the roll of drums.

We supped at Remiremont, where we found good accommodations at the Unicorn—indeed all the towns of Lorraine offer better lodgings than can be found in France. The oldest sister of the famous convent here inquired after me in Plombières and kindly sent me a gift of artichokes, partridges, and a barrel of wine. M. d'Estissac and I visited the convent immediately upon our arrival. The nuns entrusted us with a proxy for their affairs in Rome.

Bussang, a filthy little village, is the last place where French is spoken. Here we put on linen smocks, lent us for the purpose, and descended into the silver mines belonging to M. de Lorraine, which extend a good two thousand paces into the bowels of a mountain.

BASEL IS A HANDSOME TOWN, about the size of Blois, and the Rhine is crossed here by a wide wooden bridge. The municipality did M. d'Estissac and myself the honor of sending us wine by one of its officials. He made a long address while we were at table, to which I replied likewise at considerable length: and we both remained uncovered in the presence of several Germans and Frenchmen who were staying at our inn. The host served as interpreter. The wines of this district are very good.

We saw here a number of learned men, such as Gryneus, and the author of the *Theatrum,* and Francis Hotman, and Felix Platerus, the physician—whose house was the most elaborately decorated I have ever seen. The latter two gentlemen came to sup with us the day after our arrival. From what they said, I fancy the people of this region are not very well agreed among themselves as to their religion—some calling themselves Zwinglians, others Calvinists, and others Lutherans, and many were still Roman Catholics at heart. The form of administering the sacrament is the common topic of conversation, and everyone lends his tongue to it that will. We visited a very fine public library, situated on the banks of the river.

In all this part of the country, from Épinal onward, even the smallest cottages have glass windows: in the larger houses the frames are elaborately carved, and altogether they provide comfort and adornment. They have plenty of materials and good craftsmen to enable them to do this, and therein have greatly the advantage over us.

Moreover, in every church, no matter how small, they have a handsome clock and sundial. They are likewise skilled in the manufacture of tiles: their houses are covered by them, soldered with lead, in a variety of designs, and the rooms are floored with the same material.

Nothing can be cleaner than their stoves, which are of pottery. In woodwork they use chiefly pine, and their carpenters are exceedingly skilled. Even their casks are more or less carved, and usually painted and varnished.

The public dining rooms are large and well furnished. You often meet with five or six tables in a room, each surrounded by benches, at which all the inmates and guests dine together. The smallest inns have two or three such rooms, nicely equipped and lighted by windows. But they have no defence against damp and wind but the glass panes, and the windows are seldom opened at night.

Their fashions at table are quite different from ours. They never mix water with their wine; and they are right, for the wines are so thin that we thought them weaker than our Gascon vintages diluted, yet they have a very agreeable flavor. The servants dine at the same table with the masters, or at an adjoining table at the same time. For one servant is enough to wait on a large table, inasmuch as every guest has his silver goblet or cup placed at his right, and the attendant has only to fill it as soon as it is empty, without removing it. The wine is served from a pewter or wooden vessel with a long beak.

As to the eatables, they serve up only two or three dishes for each course. They are excellent cooks, especially of fish. They mix together several varieties of meat in a savory stew, but differing from ours. Radishes as well as baked pears are introduced with the meat. Crawfish are held in particular esteem, and a dish of them is always placed on the table with a cover over it as a special mark of honor; and to give it further distinction, the guests pass it to one another, a thing they seldom do with other dishes.

The dishes are sometimes served one above the other on iron stands with long legs and several shelves. This saves the servant from passing the dishes around, rather a task because of the large size of the tables. When one course is over, the stand is removed and another brought in: the process is repeated six or seven times.

Before the dessert is brought, a large basket of wickerwork or painted wood is placed in the center of the room. And as soon as the last dish is taken away, the guests throw their plates into this basket—the person of highest rank present throwing his plate first, and the others in due order. The servant then brings the dessert, usually in two dishes.

Water is not handed you to wash with, either before or after meals. But everyone, at his pleasure, uses a small washstand that is always to be found in a corner of the room, as in our monasteries. Most of the utensils are made of wood, polished to the last degree of smoothness and cleanliness. Some inns place pewter plates on the wooden ones till the dessert is served, and then only the wooden remain.

As they are cunning workmen in iron, most of their spits turn on springs or by means of weights, as in clockwork. However, some are driven by a sort of wooden sails, large and light, which are placed in the flue and worked by the draught. The meats are roasted long and gently, and indeed become somewhat overdry.

The least meals occupy three or four hours: for they eat more slowly and in a more wholesome manner than we. Provisions abound and cover the tables. The prices are about the same as around Paris. Horses are supplied with more oats than they can eat.

It would seem, however, that they pay more attention to their food than anything else; for the bedrooms are most indifferent. There are curtains to the beds, which come three or four to a room, standing side by side. But there are no fireplaces, and you can warm yourself only at the public stove. You hear of no heating arrangement elsewhere, and it is considered most impolite to go into the kitchen.

What we consider bedroom necessities are ill provided everywhere. He is a lucky man who can get hold of a white sheet. And what sheets there are, never reach to cover the bolster. Indeed, the usual covering is a sort of thin featherbed, and that dirty enough. But all their furniture and the ceilings and floors are polished and spotless. The beds are so high you generally have to climb into them by steps.

Their streets are wider and more airy than ours, their squares larger, and their windows richly glazed. Almost everywhere the houses are painted on the outside and covered with coats-of-arms and other devices, which have a pleasing effect. Further, there is no town without a number of large ornamented fountains, prominently setting off the cross streets. Altogether these circumstances make their towns much prettier than those of France.

IN SWITZERLAND the ordinary dress of the women appeared to me as neat and becoming as that of our own—even the headdress, which consists of a bonnet turned up before and behind, and decorated with tufts of silk or fur edging. Their hair hangs down the back in large plaits. If you take off their bonnet in sport, they are not angry, though it reveals all the forepart of their head quite bare. No great distinction exists between the dress of the various classes. The mode of salutation to the womenfolk is to kiss your hand to them, and offer to touch theirs. Bows and raising of the hat evoke no response. The women are generally tall and handsome, with fair complexions. They are a kindhearted people, especially to those who conform to their ways.

The only inconveniences I suffered from following their customs arose from the small size of their napkins: six inches square and not even unfolded at dinner—though they serve a great variety of soups and sauces. However, they always provide the guests with silver-handled wooden spoons; and no Swiss is without a knife for taking up his food, so they seldom put their fingers to the plates.

We soon grew used to the heat of their stoves. At all events, you do not burn your face and boots, and you are free from the smoke that chokes you in France. At home, when we enter a house, we must put on furred dressing gowns; whereas here, on the contrary, people take off their cloaks and go bareheaded indoors.

One great drawback is that however much you exert yourself, you can't extract from the natives any information as to what is worth seeing in a place—unless you light on someone with a head better furnished than usual. For instance, we were five days in Baden and made every possible inquiry, yet we did not hear a word of what we ourselves saw the moment we left the town: a stone about the height of a man, abutting the highway and bearing a Latin inscription. I could decipher nothing of it, except that it was dedicated to the emperors Nerva and Trajan.

AROUND LINDAU, in South Germany, they grow a great abundance of cabbage, which is chopped up very small and salted in tubs; and of this they make a dish all through the winter. Here I tried out covering myself with a featherbed, and found it both warm and light. Indeed there is nothing to complain of in this region but, perhaps, the beds. However, by bringing your own mattress—an article unknown here—and bed curtains, this objection would be removed.

As to eating and drinking, they give you a host of things, and diversify their courses with soups, meats, sauces, and salads far beyond what we do in France. One soup made with rice and sometimes other things, which all the guests help themselves to in common, was of such exquisite flavor in the better inns, we doubted whether the kitchens of the French nobility could furnish its equal. We never tasted meat so tender, and it is served with stewed prunes and with pear and apple tarts. Their bread is flavored with fennel, cummin, or other hot and sharp-tasting seeds. After dinner, glasses filled with three or four sorts of drinks are set on the table, so each guest may quench his thirst as pleases him best.

Only three things annoyed me in my travels: first, that I had not brought along a cook to learn the different ways of preparing food and thus, when we returned home, prove to my friends the excellence of the Germans in this respect; secondly, that I had not engaged at the outset a German valet or procured the companionship of a German gentleman—for I found it an amazing nuisance to live at the mercy of some blockhead of a guide; and, finally, that I had not read, before I left home, such books as would have told the best things to be seen, or had not brought along with me a Munster's *Cosmography*.

True, my judgment may be biased somewhat by my bitter contempt for my own country—arising from other causes—but it is certain I preferred what I found in Germany far above what I left in France. Indeed, I so far conformed to the habits of the land that I drank my wine straight—although never in larger amounts than usual.

Things are dearer in South Germany than in France. But there is one good point: they tell you at once what the charge is, neither more nor less, and you seldom get anything by haggling. The people are vain, choleric, and given to drink; but they are neither traitors nor thieves.

The first novelty we noticed in Augsburg, which is considered the finest city in Germany, showed the cleanliness of the people. On our arrival, we found the staircase of our inn covered with linen for us to walk on, so we should not dirty the steps, which had just been washed and scoured—as is done every Saturday.

We never saw dirt or cobwebs in a single house we entered. Some have curtains to draw before the windows. You seldom find tables in their bedrooms, except a collapsible one attached to the bed by hinges. In many places they hang linen curtains against the wall by the bedside, in order to prevent people from soiling the wall by spitting. What makes their windows so bright is that the sashes are removable, so they can be forever cleaning and polishing the panes. They dust their glassware with a fine hair brush fixed to the end of a stick.

On a Sunday I visited several churches in Augsburg; and in the Catholic churches, which were numerous, I found the services admirably conducted. There are six Lutheran churches, with sixteen ministers.

We did not see one pretty woman here. Their dress differs greatly. But among the men it was hard to distinguish the nobility, for all classes wear velvet caps and carry a sword at their side.

We were lodged at an inn called the Linden—the name of a tree. It adjoined the palace of the Fuggers, which is roofed with copper. A member of this family who died a few years ago left his heirs two millions in French crowns. In general, the houses are larger, higher, and handsomer than those of any French town, and the streets are wider.

After dinner we went to see the fencing. They have a great public hall for the purpose. You pay upon entering, as you do in a theater, and you must pay for a seat besides. They were practicing with the dagger, two-handed sword, quarter-staff, and braquemart. After this we went to see some matches at crossbow and longbow in a magnificent public ground.

The authorities of the city did us the honor of sending us, while we were at supper, fourteen large vessels of wine. They were brought by seven sergeants dressed in civic uniform, under the command of a superior officer. We invited him to join us at supper, as is the custom, and gave the sergeants a crown.

The officer, who supped with us, told me there were three of them in the city whose duty it was to pay this compliment to visitors of some distinction. To this end they always took pains to learn the qualities of those who came to the place, in order to provide the proper ceremonies: some received more wine than others. When a duke appears, one of the burgomasters presents the wine in person. They took us for knights and barons.

For reasons of my own I had not wished my people to tell who we were, or mention our rank. I had walked alone and unattended all day through the town; for I thought that this itself would bring us more honor. This compliment, I might say, was paid us in all the towns of Germany.

At the inn where we lodged is a machine made of iron plates, which descends to the bottom of a deep well. Worked by a boy, it moves up and down and forces the water up into a lead pipe, which conveys into the kitchen or wherever it is needed. They hire a man to do nothing but keep their walls whitewashed and clean. I left a copy of my arms over the door of the room I occupied—it was well done and cost me two crowns for the painter and twenty sous for the man who made the frame.

While in Augsburg, a German greatly amused me by arguing against our open fireplaces with the same reasons we decry their stoves. Hearing me praise the comforts and beauties of his city, he began to pity my departure chiefly because of the loggy head our fireplaces give us. Yet the smothery heat and thick smell of their stoves are just as bad for any head not used to them. All heat that comes directly from a fire makes me dull. Why don't we imitate Roman architecture? For the ancients, it is said, built their fires outside the house and conducted the heat through the walls by a network of pipes.

CROSSING THE ALPS our only discomfort came from the thick clouds of dust. The roads in all directions are perfectly safe, being constantly frequented by merchants, coaches, and wagons. Instead of the cold we had been taught to expect, we found an almost unbearable heat.

All my life I have been chary about taking other people's judgment on foreign lands. But in the Alps I truly wondered at the obstinate imbecility and narrow-mindedness of travelers who can see nothing if it is not what they are used to in their own parish. After all the tales of the dangers and discomforts of these mountains, I discovered, thank God, that the climate was mild: we had only three days of chilly weather and a half hour of rain. And in all other respects I could entrust my daughter, girl though she is, on these roads as readily as in my garden.

We now travelled by the Italian mile, five of which make a German mile. The day is reckoned by counting up to twenty-four hours. At Rovereto we found ourselves back among the fashions of our own country, and greatly missed not only the German cleanliness and their delightful windows, but also the stoves. At Trent we were pleased to find plenty of oranges, lemons, and olives—but regretted the loss of the featherbeds.

Had I been alone with my own people, I would rather have gone to Cracow or towards Greece overland, than directly to Italy. But the pleasure I took in wandering through countries new to me—a pleasure which made me forget my years and my ailments—I could not instill into my companions, who were anxious to go straight ahead in order the sooner to be home.

When, after passing a restless night, I recalled I was about to visit a town I had never laid eyes on, I would leap from bed as gay as a lark. I never complained less of pain or fatigue. On every possible occasion I conversed with strangers, and I have no doubt this diversion relieved my malady. When my friends complained of my leading them a dance to out-of-the-way places, often returning almost to where we set out, or otherwise changing our plans, I would tell them: 'For my part, this particular spot was where I had been heading for all along. I can't possibly be off my route, for my only route is to go where I have never been. As for Rome, about which you seem so eager, I am less so than about anywhere else, because almost everyone has seen it; and as for Ferrara or Florence, there is hardly a valet who can't tell you all about them.'

I seemed like a person who is hearing a pleasant story or reading a fine book, and fears lest he is getting toward the end of it. I took such delight in travelling that I hated the very approach to the place I planned to stay in, and I formed several schemes for travelling by myself and at my own will and ease.

THE CURIOSITIES OF VENICE are so well known I need say nothing about them. But I found the city different from what I expected, and was somewhat disappointed. The system of its government, the situation of the place, the arsenal, the square of St. Mark, and the concourse of foreigners seemed to me its most remarkable features.

I did not think the Venetian women by any means so beautiful as I had heard tell, yet I saw several of the most celebrated of those ladies who traffic in their beauty. As much as anything else I was struck with the style in which some hundred and fifty of the principal courtesans live: their houses, dress, and retinue could vie with kings' daughters. Yet their sole revenue came from their profession.

In Ferrara, M. d'Estissac and I went to pay our respects to the Duke. He received us standing at a table and awaiting our arrival. He raised his cap as we entered and remained uncovered all the while I spoke with him. He first asked me if I understood Italian; and when I said I did, we conversed on various topics. We also saw the state barge which the Duke had built for his wife—who is a very pretty woman and much too young for him.

Florence, a smaller town than Ferrara, is surrounded by richly cultivated hills. We looked through the church of S. Lorenzo, where the flags are still hanging which we lost under Marshal Strozzi. In this church are several excellent pictures, and some very beautiful statues by Michelangelo.

I have never been in a country where there are so few pretty women as in Italy. The inns are far less comfortable than in France or Germany; and the food is not so plentiful as in Germany, nor so well prepared. The larger windows have no panes—only shutters, which keep out the light. The bedrooms are mere cabins, the beds wretched pallets, and heaven help the man who can't sleep hard!

M. d'Estissac and I dined with the Grand Duke—a prince

much interested in the mechanical arts and, above all, architecture. His wife [Bianca Capello] occupied the post of honor, and the Duke sat at her right. She is a beautiful woman after the Italian taste, with a countenance at once pleasing and dignified, of generous build and with opulent breasts. It was easy to see how she managed to cajole the Duke into complete subjection, and would hold him in leash for a long while to come.

The Duke is a dark stout man, about my height, with large limbs, and a kindly air. He always doffs his hat when among his people—which I think a pleasant trait. He looks like a healthy man of about forty. On either side were his two brothers, the Cardinal de Medici and a youth of about eighteen.

On a Saturday, the Grand Duke's palace was thrown open to all comers, and crowded with peasants, who fell to dancing. As I watched them, it seemed to me like an image of a people's lost liberty—extinguished save for a single gleam flickering up once a year, amid the show of a saint's day.

ITALY IS AN ADMIRABLE COUNTRY for lazy folk, for they rise very late. But at Ronciglione we were up three hours before dawn, so eager I was to get my feet on the pavements of Rome.

The city did not make much of an appearance as we approached it from this direction. Far to the left rose the Apennines, and the country immediately about us was open, barren, quite without trees, and almost without houses. We reached the Porto del Popolo at about noon, the thirtieth of November.

My coffers were opened at the gate by the customs officials, and every article, down to the minutest trifle, tumbled over and rummaged—whereas in other Italian cities, the officers quietly wait while you yourself show what you have. They seized all the books I carried, for the purpose of examining them. And they took so long about it that if a traveller had business on foot, he might better give them up for lost. Our prayer book, because it was printed in Paris and not in Rome, was eyed with suspicion, as well as several German books written *against* the heretics— for the excellent reason that in order to combat these errors, the authors had to mention what the errors were!

We put up for two days at the Bear, and then hired apartments at the house of a Spaniard, opposite the church of Santa Lucia della Tinta. We were provided with three handsome bedrooms, a dining room, closet, stable, and kitchen, for twenty crowns a month—for which sum the landlord included fuel for the kitchen and a cook. The apartments in Rome are generally better furnished than in Paris; the higher class of rooms are as a rule lined with gilt leather.

I was annoyed finding so many Frenchmen here—hardly a person on the street but greeted me in my native tongue.

On Christmas Day we went to hear Mass performed by the pope in the church of St. Peter. I secured a place where I could see all the ceremonies at my ease. The pope administered the sacrament to a number of persons: they use a certain device, on this occasion, to drink from the chalice in order to avoid the risk of being poisoned.

I was surprised to remark that the pope, cardinals, and other prelates were seated during nearly the entire Mass, their heads covered, and chatting together. Altogether there was more magnificence than devotion. And I observed no particular beauty among the women—at least such as to justify the fame which all the world gives them. After all, here as in Paris, the greatest beauty is to be found among the women who put it up for sale.

A few days later, M. d'Abain, our ambassador at Rome and my old and intimate friend, proposed that we kiss the pope's feet. The pope [Gregory XIII] speaks Italian, but everything he says smacks of his Bolognese origin—and the Bolognese use the worst jargon in Italy. Besides, he has an impediment in his speech. But he is a very fine old man, with majestic countenance and long white beard. He was more than eighty, but looked as hale and strong as a man could wish at that age—without gout, indigestion, or stone. He is charitable even to excess.

I amused myself daily going about and studying every nook of Rome. At first I had a guide, but one day he went off in a huff; and thereafter I bought maps and books, read them the night before I went to visit something, and I soon could have guided my guide.

Little is to be seen of ancient Rome but the sky under which it rose and stood, and the outline of its form. In many places the modern Romans walk above the houses of their ancestors; and those who say that at least the ruins can be viewed, say more than they are warranted. Nothing remains of Rome but its sepulchre. The buildings of this modern bastard Rome, though they may well enough excite our admiration, seem to me like the nests which rooks and swallows have built in our dilapidated French churches laid waste by the Huguenots.

On the thirtieth of January I witnessed the most ancient religious ceremony that still survives—a circumcision among the Jews. I had previously attended their synagogue one Saturday morning. Their service, which resembles the Calvinist, consists of singing in Hebrew at the top of their lungs. They pay no more attention to their devotions than we do to ours, talking among themselves of indifferent matters.

The carnival this year was, by papal permission, more unrestrained than it has been for a long while; yet it did not appear to us anything to make a fuss over. The platform which I had erected for our party cost three crowns, but it was situated in one of the best parts of the Corso.

On this occasion you have an excellent chance to observe the beautiful women of Rome at your leisure, for they wear no masks. Rare and perfect beauty is not to be seen any more than in France, but the general run are pleasing, and you do not remark so many homely ones as at home. Their expressions are, for the most part, softer and gentler, and yet more majestic than with us. As for their dress, every article is resplendent with pearls and gems, and in this our women can't compare with them.

I should say that the bulk of the people here are less religious than in the large towns of France, but the forms of religion are better observed. I am writing in all liberty of conscience, and will give you two examples of what I mean. A friend of mine was in bed with a wench and exercising her in her profession, when the bell rang to *Ave Maria*. Whereupon the girl sprang from the bed and fell to her knees in prayer. On another occasion, the same friend was with a girl when suddenly the mamma (for most of these girls live with an old woman whom they call mamma or aunty) came thundering at the door, and rushed up to the girl in a perfect fury, and tore from her neck a small Madonna which hung by a ribbon. The girl acted extremely penitent at having forgotten to follow her usual custom and remove it before going to work.

On the eighteenth of March, the Master of the Sacro Palazzo returned me my *Essays* marked with the passages to be expurgated, as suggested by the judgment of the learned friars. The *maestro* had no means of forming his own opinion, for he did not understand a word of our language, but relied on the report of a French monk.

He was so well satisfied with my explanations, however, that he left it to my conscience to correct what I should, upon consideration, deem was in bad taste.

I begged him to take the opinion of the man he had appointed to read the book, rather than leave the matter to me. For I told him that the points objected to—the use of the word Fortune, the citations from heretical poets, the apology for the Emperor Julian, my opinion that all capital punishment beyond simple death is cruelty, and the belief that children should be inured to everything—all represented my firm opinion; and when I wrote them I did not regard them as errors, nor did I now. As to several other points, I denied that the censor had understood my meaning.

The *maestro*, who was a clever man, entered very much into my views, and gave me to understand that he by no means insisted upon the emendations. He even came to the defence of my opinions against an Italian who was present and who supported the opinions of the censor. But they kept back my copy of the *History of the Swiss* because the translator was a heretic.

The city is nothing but court and nobility: everyone in it shares in the general ecclesiastical idleness. No business streets are to be seen—or less than in a small town. There is no Rue de la Harpe or Rue St. Denis. I was reminded of nothing at Paris but its Rue de Seine or Quai des Augustins.

Workdays and holidays are much alike here—there is always a show or festival on foot. Going toward Ostia I met a number of peasants making their way from Savoy and the Grisons: they told me they were coming to work as gardeners and vintagers in Rome.

I heard a preacher jestingly say that the Romans turned their coaches into observatories. In point of fact, the prevalent occupation of the natives, high or low, seems to be lounging through the streets, either in coaches, on horseback, or afoot.

As to my own taste, I confess that my main enjoyment at this pastime was to look at the ladies in the windows on either side of the street—especially the courtesans, who show themselves from behind the shutters with such skilful generalship that it is impossible not to be attracted.

You get the best view on horseback, but this is adopted only by poor devils like myself, or young gallants anxious to show off their steeds. The upper classes generally ride in coaches, and many of the gayer bloods among the men have little windows in the roofs of their coaches in order to get a good look.

Yet when I alighted from my horse, as I often did, and obtained admission to my charmers, I was amazed to discover how much more beautiful they had made themselves appear than they really were. I was sometimes put out by finding they charge as much for their conversation (which was what I mostly wanted, for I liked to hear their tongues at work) as for their other favor, and are more chary of it.

Besides chatting with these fair ones, there are always sermons to be heard, sights to be seen, and beautiful spots to be visited. So Rome is by no means an unpleasant place to live in. Though I only know it as an obscure stranger in a general and passing way, the longer I stayed in the city the more I became charmed with it. And I never breathed an air more temperate and better suited to my constitution.

LORETTO IS A SMALL TOWN fortified against the incursions of the Turks. Its inhabitants are mostly engaged in the devotions attendant on the Santa Casa, or as innkeepers, or as dealers in candles, images, beads, *Agnus Dei, Salvators,* and the like— while I was there I got rid of fifty good crowns on these commodities.

Most of the shrine is covered with magnificent *exvotos.* With much difficulty and as a great favor, I secured a vacant place large enough to receive a small frame in which were set four silver figures: that of Our Lady, myself, my wife, and my daughter. As you pass through the door into the chapel, you will see my offering on the left hand, nailed against the wall.

The interior of the church is hung with paintings of every description. There are many rich ornaments, but no such number as the fame and age of the shrine would lead you to expect. I am inclined to believe that many of the older ones were melted down and put to other uses. There are more of the externals of religion here than in any other place I ever was at.

THE VILLA BATHS ABOVE LUCCA lie in a mountainous country, and consist of thirty or forty houses well adapted to their purpose. My landlord, Captain Paulini, was an actual army officer. He rented me a parlor, three bedrooms, kitchen, and servants' quarters, and agreed to supply me with salt, clean napkins every day, a fresh tablecloth every third day, cooking utensils, and candlesticks, for eleven crowns a fortnight. Dishes and so forth we had to buy. From my chamber I could hear the gentle murmur of the river below.

One morning, as I was writing to a friend, my thoughts reverted to M. de la Boétie; and the mood lingered so long without my being able to dispel it, that I sank into a painful dejection.

They have a machine here called a *doccia* which directs showers of water against any particular part of the body. I take the waters to be of very mild internal effect, and therefore safe enough for persons of a delicate turn. They are praised for removing eruptions and blemishes of the skin, and I made a memorandum of this for an amiable lady, a friend of mine, in France.

The peasants here all dress like gentlefolk. Every woman among them wears white shoes, fine thread stockings, and a colored silk apron. They are fond of dancing and perform their steps in a fetching manner.

As is the custom, I gave a ball and distributed a number of prizes, and I was glad to pay them this compliment. The prizes were hung on a hoop where everyone could see them. We began dancing on the green; but, as it was rather hot, we retired to the great hall of the Buonvisi palace, which was well suited for a ballroom.

When evening drew on, around seven o'clock, I asked the most distinguished ladies present to take charge of awarding the prizes. It all passed off nicely, except that one girl declined the prize offered her and begged me to give it to another girl whom she pointed out. But this I would not do, as I did not at all admire her friend's looks.

I then invited everyone to supper, which in Italy is a very slight affair; and I got off with a joint or two of veal and a few pair of fowl.

I gave a seat at my table to a poor peasant woman, named Divizia, who lives two miles from the baths and who, as well as her husband, works for a living. She was very homely, thirty-seven years of age, had a goitre, and could not read or write. But in her childhood she often heard her uncle recite Ariosto; and her mind became so alive to the spirit of poetry that she not only composes verses extemporaneously, but introduces into them the ancient fables and myths, the names of countries, sciences, and illustrious men, as readily as any graduate of the schools. She composed a number of verses for me on the spot; and though hardly more than rhymes, they were done in an easy and graceful style.

There were more than a hundred women at my ball; and as this was the harvest season for mulberry and everyone is engaged in the work, I was singularly favored. The people here are wretchedly poor: so much so, I have seen them eat green mulberries, which they picked as they gathered the leaves for the silkworms.

ON THE MORNING OF SEPTEMBER SEVENTH I received, by way of Rome, a letter from M. Tausin, dated Bordeaux, August second, in which he informed me that, on the preceding day, I was unanimously elected mayor of Bordeaux. He urged me to accept the office for the love of my country.

I returned to Rome and found a letter from the *jurats* of Bordeaux, reminding me in very courteous terms of my election, and earnestly requesting me to come without delay. On the fifteenth of October I quitted Rome, shortly after sunrise, leaving my brother behind to perfect himself in the practice of arms.

On Thursday, St. Andrew's Day, the thirtieth of November, 1581, I once more reached my own bed at Montaigne, which I had left seventeen months and eight days before, on my way to La Fère—or, a year to the day after I had first arrived at Rome.

CHAPTER XXXI

I Am Mayor of Bordeaux

N THE 26TH of November, 1581, the King wrote me from Paris that he was pleased to learn the city of Bordeaux had elected me its mayor; and, thinking I was still at Rome, he commanded me to go to my post. ¶The Parliament of Bordeaux had chosen me, not only when I was far from France, but farther still from any thought of such office. I had begged to be excused; but my friends told me I was wrong in this, especially since the King had interposed his command in the affair.

The office might be considered the more handsome because it has no salary or other profit attached to it, save the bare honor of its conduct. The term is two years, but may be renewed by a second election, which rarely happens. It happened to me—in the year 1583 I was reelected—and only twice before. Some years ago M. de Lanssac was reelected, and recently M. de Biron, Marshal of France, who preceded me. My successor was M. de Matignon, likewise a marshal of France; and I was proud to be of such a line.

Upon my arrival in Bordeaux, I faithfully described myself as I feel I am—a man without memory, vigilance, experience, or vigor; but also without hatred, ambition, greed, or violence. Thus they were informed of my qualities and knew what to expect from my service.

The knowledge they had of my father and the honor they paid

his memory were the only motives they had to bestow this honor on me. So I frankly added that I would be sorry indeed if anything proved as great a burden to me as their affairs and the concerns of the city had been to him while he conducted its government.

He had believed that a man should forget himself for his neighbor, that private interests must give way to public. Most of the rules and precepts of the world tend in this direction—to drive us out of ourselves and into the public square for the benefit of society. They think they are achieving great things by so diverting us, by assuming we are too much attached to our own person. It is nothing new for a sage to preach things as they serve, and not as they are.

Yet when I am put in charge of other men's affairs, I promise to take them in my hand, but not in my lungs and liver; to take them upon me, but not into me; to take pains, yes—but to become impassioned, decidedly no. I will watch after them, but I'll not sit and brood upon them. I have enough to do to govern the throng of affairs I have in my own veins and bowels.

But men let themselves out to hire: it is their tenants that occupy them, not themselves. This common inclination does not please me. We should be thrifty with the freedom of our souls, and not lend it out except upon proper occasions—which, if we judge rightly, are very few.

Such men, however, thrust themselves into wherever business is on foot. They are not alive when they are not in a tumult and bustle. It is not so much that they want to forge ahead as that they cannot stand still—like a falling stone that can't stop till it hits bottom. Their minds seek ease in agitation, as babies do by being rocked in a cradle. No one distributes his money abroad, but everyone distributes his time and his life—to be thrifty of which were both laudable and useful.

In the offices men assume, I would not like to see them refuse the attention, pains, eloquence, sweat, and even blood, that are necessary. But it is only a loan, and by chance: their minds should remain poised and sound—active, but unruffled and dispassionate.

I have been able to carry on public business without quitting my own concerns by a nail's breadth, and give to others without forsaking myself. How many soldiers fling themselves into the thick of a battle, the loss of which will not break their next night's sleep! A sharp and engrossing passion hinders more than it helps the business we have on hand. It makes us impatient at a slow or contrary course of events, and hot and suspicious towards those with whom we deal. We cannot be master of a business if the business is mastering us.

If, instead of passion and intensity, a man uses only judgment and skill, he advances with better cheer. When occasion demands, he will be quick to feint, yield, and defer at his ease. His attempts fail without worry or affliction, leaving him ready and whole for a new effort. He always walks bridle in hand. Tomorrow is another day.

Most of our business is theatre. We must act our part properly, but nevertheless as the part of an assumed character. We should not make the mask our essence, or a strange personality our own. We cannot distinguish the skin from the shirt, and it is enough to chalk up our face without chalking our breast.

I see some people transform themselves into as many new and strange beings as they undertake new employments. They pontify to their very liver and bowels, and carry their office with them even to the privy. I can't get them to learn the difference between the salutations made to themselves and the bows made to their rank, their retinue, or their mule. They puff their minds and their speech up to the height of their desk.

But the Mayor of Bordeaux and Montaigne were always two distinct persons. Because a man is a lawyer or a banker, he must not shut his eyes to the knavery inherent in these occupations. A decent man is not responsible for the vice or absurdity of his profession; and he ought not, on that account, refuse to pursue it: it is the custom of the country, there is money to be got by it, a man must live in the world and make the best of it, such as it is. Yet the judgment of an emperor should be superior to his empire, and see it as an external trapping. He ought to know how to enjoy himself apart from it, and be plain Tom or Dick to himself at least.

I cannot engage myself so wholly or deeply. When my will carries me into an enterprise, it is not so violently that my good sense is wrecked by it. Some wise men, I know, have taken another course, and have not feared to throw themselves, grappling, full upon their subject. But such as these are confident of their own strength.

Let us not, however, attempt these examples. We shall never come up to them. Cato gave up the noblest life that ever was on this account. We meaner spirits must flee from the storm as we can, and dodge the shock we cannot parry.

Whoever will desire the good of his country, as I do, without fretting or wearing himself out, will be troubled to see it threatening its own ruin; but he will not swoon away. Poor vessel, that wave, wind, and pilot veer to such contrary poles!

Without too much ado I stop the first sally of my emotions, and leave a matter when it begins to be troublesome—before it makes off with me. He who does not stop the start will never stop the career. He who cannot keep troubles out will never dislodge them once they are in. I am quick to hear the breezes rise and murmur within me—heralds of the oncoming storm.

Yet I do not mean to say that my prudence has relieved me from all difficulty. Often enough I've had to wrestle with my passions and struggle against their sudden and vigorous onset.

Some say that in my municipal office (I am willing to say a

word or two about it, not because it is in itself worth mention, but to describe my manner in such things) I bore myself as a man not deeply touched and altogether too listless. And there is some color in what they say.

I tried to keep my mind and thoughts in repose; and if they sometimes lashed out under a rude and penetrating shock, it was, in truth, against my better counsel. Yet from this natural stolidity of mine, men ought not to conclude that I was totally unable—for carelessness and insensitivity are two different things. Still less ought they to impute to me any coldness or ingratitude toward the people of Bordeaux, who employed every means in their power to oblige me, both before they knew me and after. And they did much more for me in choosing me a second time than in first conferring the honor upon me.

I wish them every imaginable good; and, assuredly, had the occasion required it, I would have spared nothing in their behalf. I did for them as I would have done for myself. They are a fine, militant, and noble people, and can be put to worthy use if properly guided.

Critics also say that my administration passed without leaving mark or trace. Good! This is to accuse me of inactivity at a time when almost everybody else was convicted of doing too much.

I, too, am impatient to be up and doing when my will spurs me on; but this in itself is an enemy to perseverance. When vigor and freedom of action are required, when a direct, brief, and, moreover, dangerous enterprise is afoot, I may do something. But if it is to be long, subtle, laborious, and intricate, somebody else had better be drafted.

Yet important offices are not necessarily difficult. I came prepared to do rougher work if need be—for it lies in my power to do more than I am used or like to do.

I did not, to my knowledge, neglect any action that duty really demanded of me. But I readily omitted everything which ambition confuses with duty, and decks out under its name. Those are, in general, the actions which strike the eyes and ears of men, and satisfy them most. Not the thing, but its appearance, contents them. If they hear nothing, they think you sleep.

But my nature is no friend to noise. I have appeased commotion without tumult, and chastised disorder without myself becoming disorderly. If I stand in need of anger and heat, I borrow them. And I do not condemn a governor who sleeps, provided the people under his charge likewise sleep. In that case, the laws sleep too.

Nowadays our people are so used to bustle and show that good-naturedness, moderation, equanimity, and similar quiet and modest qualities are no longer appreciated. Rough bodies make themselves felt; smooth ones slip through the hand unregarded.

But it is acting up for your personal reputation and profit, and not for the general good, to stage on the public square what can be done as nicely in the council chamber, to postpone till high noon what might have been transacted the night before, to be jealous to do yourself what your colleague could do as well. Such governors imagine that no one will hear of a good ordinance unless it is blared through a trumpet.

When these miniscule souls—mere soul-lets—become infatuated with themselves and go about blowing their horn because they have rendered a tolerable decision or maintained the guard of a town gate, the more they think they have exalted their heads, the more they have shown their backsides. This trivial efficiency has neither substance nor life: it vanishes in the first telling, and lasts no farther than from one street corner to another. Boast of it, if you must, to your son or your servant, like that old fellow who, having no one else to listen to his virtues or applaud them, used to play the hero to his chambermaid and exclaim, 'O Perette, what a clever man you have for a master!'

At the worst, talk of it to yourself, like a magistrate of my acquaintance. Once, after disgorging a whole cargo of law learning, as irrelevant as it was labored, and retiring to the courthouse urinal, he was overheard devoutly mumbling between his teeth: *"Non nobis, Domine*—not unto us, O Lord, but unto Thy name the glory!' If you can't get it out of another's pocket, pay it out of your own.

Fame, however, does not prostitute herself at such bargain prices. Rare and notable deeds, which she demands as her due, would not tolerate being seen with this throng of pitiful routine. Marble will exalt your titles, as much as you please, for having patched a yard of wall or cleansed a street gutter; but not men who possess an ounce of common sense. Renown shuns good deeds if they are not novel or difficult. The Stoics would not even thank a man who, out of temperance, abstained from a toothless hag.

The louder a good action resounds, the more I question its goodness, and the shrewder I suspect it was done for the sake of the noise: exposed in the market, it is already half sold. Those works have greater grace that slip from the hand of the workman nonchalantly and in silence, and that some honest soul later discovers and brings into the light for its own merits.

My task was to conserve and continue things as I found them—a noiseless and imperceptible work. Innovation makes a splendid show, but it is not to be thought of in our day when it is precisely our task, and hard enough, to defend ourselves against novelty.

To forbear doing is often as noble as to do. But it shines less, and what little good I have in me is of this nature. In short, my opportunities as mayor were in keeping with my character, and I was grateful for them. Who would want to be sick merely to see his doctor go to work? Or what physician would not deserve to be whipped who prayed for a plague in order to practice up his art?

I was never of that wicked turn—and rather common—to wish troubles and disorders in my city in order to magnify and honor my administration. Indeed, I heartily put my shoulder to relieving and lightening them. The man who will not thank me for the order, the gentle and silent calm, which graced my term of office, cannot nevertheless deprive me of my share in bringing it about—thanks to my good luck.

For I am the kind of man who would as soon be lucky as wise, and rather owe my success to the favor of God than my own endeavor.

I have already elaborated enough on my unfitness for public office. But I have something in me worse than my incapacity: I don't even regret it and do little to overcome it, in view of the course of life I have proposed for myself.

So, too, I was not satisfied with my administration, but I nearly achieved what I expected to do and far surpassed what I promised. For I am apt to promise less than what I am able or hope to perform. I feel assured I have left behind me occasion for neither offence nor hatred. As to leaving regret or desire for me, I know well how little I aspired to that.

We have pleasures cut to our cloth: let us not usurp those of grandeur. Our own are more natural, and by the same token as solid and sure as they are humble. For ambition's sake at least, let us reject ambition. To beg renown of all sorts of people and at any price—such honor is dishonor. Let our greed for glory be measured by our capacity for it.

I have as much to wish for as another, and give my desires free rein. Yet it never befell me to wish for empire or crown. I do not aim that way: I love myself too well. I should prefer to be second or third in Périgueux than first in Paris—or at least, not to lie, third in Paris rather than first.

CHAPTER XXXII

Assailed by the Plague

ISE HISTORIANS skip over calm periods as so much stagnant water, and occupy themselves with wars and rebellions, which they know are more acceptable to their readers. I question whether I can decently confess with how small a sacrifice of ease and tranquility I passed more than half of my life amid the ruin of my country.

Here, then, is still another evil which befell me on the tail of the rest. Both without my doors and within I was assailed by the plague, of surpassing violence [1585]. For the air of our country-side is remarkably healthy, and no contagion—however close it approached us—ever took hold within the memory of man. And as sound bodies are subject to the gravest maladies, for only such can gain footing in them, so our air, once it was infected, produced the direst results. 'Old and young were buried in tumbled heaps' [Horace].

I had to face this happy state of affairs, that the sight of my house became terrible to me. All it contained lay unguarded and at the mercy of anyone who coveted it.

I myself, who am so hospitable, was hard put to beg a refuge for my family—a poor wandering family, a horror both to itself and its friends, and filling with terror every place where it sought to settle. It had to take to the road again as soon as any one of us felt so much as a pain in the tip of his finger. For, in such times, every ailment is considered to be the plague, and no one waits to identify the trouble.

And the neatest stroke is that, according to medical rules, whenever you near a dangerous district, for forty days of quarantine you are shut up with the fear of the disease. Meanwhile, your imagination goes to work as only it knows how, and inflames your very health into a fever.

All this would have affected me less if I had not been forced to bear with the suffering of others, and guide my caravan for six miserable months. For I carry my own antidotes within me—which are resolution and patience. I suffer little from fears, which are above all to be dreaded in this disease. And if I had been alone and wished to flee, it would have been a more cheerful flight and into distant regions indeed! It is not, I think, the worst of deaths. Generally it is quick, stupefying, painless, and eased by the multitude who share it—without fuss, mourning, or bedside throng.

People are mistaken in saying that a man is afraid of death when they mean he thinks of it and foresees it. To consider and ponder it is in some sort the reverse of being moved by it. This served me better than any other help in ordering and regulating my retreat; so, while it might not have been altogether fearless, at least it was without panic.

But as to the people about us, not one in a hundred could be saved. 'You have seen the fields a desert, and everywhere forsaken groves' [Virgil]. In these parts, the better portion of my revenue depends on hand labor; and the land a hundred men cultivated for me long lay idle.

Yet what an example of fortitude we saw in this people! Almost to a man, they ceased to care about life: the grapes remained hanging on the vines, which is the staple of the country. One and all, they coolly prepared for and awaited death, tonight or tomorrow, with face and voice so unshaken you would have thought they had made terms with this necessity, and that it was an inevitable and universal sentence.

Death, to be sure, is always such. But upon what slender thread hangs the resolution to die! A matter of distance, a few hours sooner or later, or the mere consideration of having company changes our fear of it. Do but look at these people: because they die all in the same month, babes, youth, and old men, they are no longer terrified, they lament no more.

I saw some who were afraid to remain behind as though in a dreadful solitude: but, in general, I saw none of them concerned about anything save their burial. They were grieved to see the bodies of the dead scattered about the fields, at the mercy of the wild beasts which quickly overran the country.

Some who were yet in health dug their own graves betimes. Others lay down in them while still alive. One of my laborers drew the earth upon him with his hands and feet as he lay dying. Was not this to pull the covers about him that he might better sleep at his ease?—a gesture almost to the height those Roman soldiers reached, who after the battle of Cannæ were found with their heads thrust into holes, which they had dug and filled with their own hands while they smothered.

In sum, a whole people were willy-nilly, by the force of common action, driven to a course which yields nothing in hardihood to the most studied and premeditated resolution.

CHAPTER XXXIII

I Begin to Steal Away

 SHALL SOON HAVE PASSED my fifty-sixth year, which in some countries was considered, not unreasonably, such a natural term of life that no one was allowed to exceed it. Yet I do have occasional, though brief and fickle, flurries of youthfulness, so bright they almost recapture the health and freedom from pain of my younger days.

But I have made up my mind that I can run no longer. It is enough if I crawl. And I no more complain of the natural decay which slows my pace than I regret that my life is not as sound and long as an oak.

This mute and dead portrait I draw not only falls short of the living model, but it bears no resemblance to my prime. Much of my former vigor and cheerfulness has faded and withered. I am nearing the bottom of the cask, which begins to taste of sediment and lees.

Lately I had a tooth fall out, painlessly and of its own accord. It had reached its age and now it, as several other parts of my being, is dead; and more are half dead. Thus I melt and steal away from myself.

This, to be sure, is but a single step backward, and hardly perceptible. But I shall be retiring another step, and from the second to a third, and thence to a fourth, and all with such gentle gradation that perhaps I shall be stone blind before I perceive my sight is failing. So artfully the Fates unwind the thread of our life! And I begin to wonder if my hearing is growing dull; and you will see that when it is half gone, I shall still be blaming those who talk to me. You must press the soul to make it feel how it ebbs away.

Death mixes and confounds itself with all of our life; decay anticipates its hour and slips itself even into our growth. I have portraits of myself when I was twenty-five and thirty-five. I compare them with a recent one; and in how many ways are they no longer myself! And by how much more will my looks change before the end is reached? It is an abuse of Nature to tease her along so far that she is forced to quit us, and leave our teeth, eyes, limbs, and upkeep to the mercy of an aid we must beg from others—to resign us into the hands of art because we have tired her out.

We must suffer patiently the laws of our being. We are made to grow old, feeble, and sick—despite all medicine. It is madness in an old man to pray for full and buoyant health; to pray, in other words, for his lost youth. Gout, gravel, indigestion are the signs of long years, as heat, rains, and winds betoken a long journey.

My good friend, your business is done. No one can restore you. At best they can but patch and prop you a little, and so prolong your misery for an hour or two.

Since it is the privilege of the mind to rescue itself from old age, as far as I can I urge mine to it. Let it put forth leaf and flower as long as it is able, like mistletoe on a dead tree. But I suspect it is a traitor. It has picked up such a close friendship with my body that, when the body calls, it deserts me at every turn. I wheedle and deal with it apart, but in vain. I try to woo it from this fellowship; I offer it Seneca and Catullus, and beautiful women and royal balls: but somehow if its comrade comes down with a fit of colic, down it comes too.

Our desires and pursuits should sometimes show they are

aware of our age; but, with one foot in the grave, we still give birth to appetites. 'When death is at hand, you order marble to be quarried, and forgetful of the tomb, build yourself a house' [Horace]. However, the longest of my desires looks not more than a year ahead. Indeed, the only comfort I derive from old age is its deadening of desires and cares: care how the world goes, care for riches, knowledge, health, or myself. There are men learning how to speak when they should be learning eternal silence.

I am no longer in a condition to make any notable change in myself or put me on a new course, even to enhance me. I should complain of any outward fortune or inward gain befalling me, now that it is too late for me to enjoy it. It is almost better never to become a decent man than so tardily, and fit to live when so little life is left. I who am about to make my exit would gladly consign to any newcomer all the wisdom I am gaining for getting on in the world. Mustard after dinner!

I need no blessings I cannot use, and what good is knowledge to a man who no longer has a head? Guide me no more; I can go no further. We need no art to fall: the bottom is reached of itself. My world is done, my form expired. I am wholly of the past, and bound to give it authority and conform my departure to it. In short, I am finishing this man, not remaking another one out of him.

I have little regret for anything over and done, no matter what. I rarely repent: my conscience is satisfied with itself, not because it is the conscience of an angel or a horse, but as the conscience of a man. I content myself with believing that things happen as they must: they are part of the march of the universe, a link in the chain of cause. Neither your notions nor your wishes can budge them, unless the whole order were to be reversed and the past become the future.

And I abominate the accidental repentance brought on by old

age. The ancient who said that he thanked the years for weaning him from pleasure was of a different opinion than I. I can never feel grateful for being impotent or for the good it does me. Our appetites are rare in old age, and a profound satiety overcomes us after we satisfy them; but I can see nothing in this for my conscience to brag about.

We must not let our decrepitude impose upon our judgment. When I was young, I had sense enough to see the vice that lies in pleasure; and now, despite the dulling of my palate, I can still see the pleasure that lies in vice.

If anyone should restore to me the desires of my youth, I fancy I would have less power to resist them now than then. For my reason was freer in its palmy days, and had a harder time to overcome pain than pleasure. I see best under a clear sky: health admonishes me more cheerfully and to better purpose than sickness.

I did all I could to chasten and regulate my pleasures when I was young enough to relish them. And I would be ashamed if the miseries of my old age should win me more credit than my good and sprightly years, and that men should esteem me not for what I have been, but by what I have ceased to be. A sad remedy this, to owe your health to your disease!

I think that in old age our souls are more subject to maladies and defects than in our youth. I said the same when I was young and snubbed because I had no beard. And I still say it, now that my grey hairs give me some authority. The fact that we are difficult to please and take no joy in the passing moment, we call wisdom.

But, in truth, we do not so much forsake our vices as change them—and for worse. Besides a foolish and decrepit pride, a wearisome garrulity, an unsocial and snapping temper, and superstition, and idiotic pother over money, even when the power to use it is gone—to all this I find added a greater measure of envy, injustice, and malice. Age puts more wrinkles on our soul than on our brow.

Only rarely do we see a man grow old without reeking of the sour and musty. For it is the man entire who marches either toward his prime or his decline. Age is a powerful malady; and, despite all my resistance, I feel it growing on me. I hold out as best I can; but I do not know to what it will, in the end, reduce even me. Whatever happens, at least the world will know from what height I have fallen.

Every minute I feel myself slipping away. I am always repeating to myself the refrain, 'Whatever can be done tomorrow, can be done today.' For anything I had to do before I die, the longest leisure would be too short—even if it were only an hour's business I had on hand.

One day a friend was turning over my notebook and found in it a notation concerning something I wished attended to after my death. And I told him that, as a matter of fact, I was hardly a league's distance from my house and in excellent health and spirits when the thing came into my head; and I immediately jotted it down, feeling I could never be certain I would reach home alive.

The only way to become acquainted with death is to approach it. During the second or third spell of our civil wars (I forget which), I set out to take a bit of air about a league from my house. Thinking I was quite safe, I felt I did not need a particularly good mount, and I took a horse that was easy riding, but none too sturdy.

On my way back, one of my men, a tall lusty fellow, mounted on a powerful cob with a hard mouth, wanted to show off his dash and outstrip his companions. He lanced his steed at full tilt across my path and came down like a Colossus on the little man and the little horse, with such weight and force that he turned us both over, heels in the air.

My mount lay stunned with the fall, and I ten or twelve paces away, stretched at full length with my face all bleeding and torn, my sword flung from my hand, my belt in shreds, and with no more movement or feeling in me than in a log.

It was the first time in my life I had ever fainted. My companions tried every means to revive me; and, concluding I was dead, took me up in their arms and with great difficulty carried me to my house, about a half league away.

After being given up for dead above two long hours, as I was carried along I began to move and breathe, and threw up buckets of blood. But I recovered life so gradually that my first feelings were more of death. At the beginning I could distinguish nothing but the light of day. And my mind recovered as slowly as my senses.

I saw myself all bloody, and my immediate thought was that I had been shot in the head. My life seemed to hang on my lips, and I shut my eyes to help—so it seemed—thrust it from me; and I took pleasure in lying back and letting it depart. The sensation floated only on the surface of my mind, as fragile and evanescent as the rest; but there was no pain in it, only a mingled sweetness that comes when we fall asleep.

As I was brought near to my house—where the alarm of my fall had preceded me—and my family came running to meet me with the outcries natural to such occasions, I not only answered some of the questions they put to me, but—so they tell me—I was sufficiently collected to order a horse fetched for my wife, whom I saw struggling and tiring herself as she panted up the steep and rugged road.

This bit of attention must have come from some part of my mind that was still functioning—but as for me, I was not. I did not know where I came from or why, nor could I grasp anything that was said to me. Yet I felt quiet and at ease, without concern for myself or others.

I saw my house, but I did not recognize it. When they put me to bed, I found an inexpressible sweetness in repose; for I had been terribly shaken by the poor fellows who had taken the pains to carry me in their arms the long and rough road. In doing this they had exhausted themselves, one after the other, again and again.

When I came to myself two or three hours later, I felt suddenly plunged into an intolerable pain, and for two or three nights I thought I was dying again.

I must not omit that the hardest thing I could make my people beat into my head was the recollection of how the accident happened. But the next day, when my memory returned, I suddenly saw the man coming full drive upon me; and it seemed like a flash of lightning piercing my soul, and that I had returned from the other world.

This long account of so trivial an accident has no significance save for myself. I had been given a very real image and idea of death. And, in earnest, it would have been a happy one: I was gliding off so gently and peacefully, nothing could have been less troublesome.

There are brave and fortunate deaths. I have seen death cut the thread of a certain person[1] with so glorious an end that, in my opinion, his noble designs had nothing in them so high as their interruption. He arrived, without finishing his course, at the goal of his ambition with greater glory than he could have hoped or desired. In judging another man's life, I have always observed how he carried himself at his death. As for my own, I am mostly concerned that I die well—that is, patiently and tranquilly.

But summon yourself together, and you will find in your own breast natural resources against death: it is this that makes a peasant and whole nations die as bravely as a philosopher. Would

---

1. La Boétie

I die less cheerfully if I had not read the *Tusculans* of Cicero? I believe not. When I am at my best I find my tongue is strengthened, but scarcely my heart. That remains as Nature fashioned it, and uses only its native armour.

To see the trouble and sweat Seneca put himself to, in order to face the end, would have lessened his stature for me if he had not, when the time came, showed himself a valiant man. Why go about arming ourselves with all the apparatus of philosophy?

Let us look, instead, upon the humble folk who fill the earth, their heads bent over their toil, and who know nothing of Cato, of precept or example. Yet not a day passes but Nature evokes from them strokes of endurance and patience more manly than any we may study in our books.

How often I see them contemptuous of poverty—how many of them I see who embrace death, or yield to it without fret or fear! The man who is digging in my garden, this very morning he lost his father or his son. Even the names they give diseases sweeten and soften their sting. For them phthisis is a cough, dysentery but a looseness, and pleurisy a stitch. And as they name them, so they endure them—gently. They never keep to their bed except to die.

If you don't know how to die, never mind. When the time comes, Nature will furnish you complete instructions; she will even do the business for you.

I never saw a peasant in our neighborhood puzzle over what face and air he should assume in his last hour. Nature teaches him not to think of death until he is dying. And then he does it with better grace than Aristotle, upon whom death presses with a double weight—its own and its long premeditation.

But you say that the souls of the common run of men are grosser and therefore less easily afflicted? If this be so, in God's name teach us nothing but ignorance. Knowledge can never lead us with a kinder hand.

As a man who is continually mulling over his own thoughts, I am at all hours as well prepared as I am ever likely to be. As nearly as we can, we should always be booted and spurred, and ready to go. Above all, we should see to it that, when the moment comes, we have business with none but ourselves; for that will give us enough to do.

I have seen men troubled by their conscience who have tried to make amends for their life in the will they left after their death. But it would have been as good to do nothing as to postpone business of this import for such a length of time, or seek to right a wrong at so little cost to themselves. For my part, I shall take care, if possible, that my death reveal nothing my life has not already disclosed.

One man complains less at death itself than at dying before he has educated his child or married off his daughter; another that he must lose the companionship of his wife or son. Thanks be to God I am ready to dislodge whenever it pleases Him, with no regret whatever. Never was anyone better prepared to bid an unreserved farewell to all the ties of this world. I have said good-bye to everyone but myself. The deadest deaths are the best.

I would always have a man active to the last. But let Death take me while I am planting my cabbages, indifferent to him and still more indifferent to my unfinished garden.

A mask may cover the rest of our life, if our fine philosophy is assumed. But in this last scene between death and us, there is room no more for pretence. We must speak plain French and show what we have at the bottom of the pot—'the mask falls, the man remains' [Lucretius].

CHAPTER XXXIV

My Philosophy of Life

UMAN FELICITY, in my opinion, consists in living happily rather than in dying happily—as Antisthenes would have it. I have not made it my business to tie the tail of a philosopher to the head and body of a libertine; and I should not want this wretched stump to give the lie to the fairest, soundest, and fullest part of my life.

If I were to live over again, I would live as I have lived. I neither regret the past nor fear the future. And if I am not mistaken, my inner and outer life were nearly one.

I am deeply indebted to Fortune that my body has taken the seasons in their due stride. I have seen it in the leaf, the flower, and the fruit; and now I see it in the withered fall—and happily because naturally. I look more kindly on my present infirmities because they have come in their proper hour; and in doing so, leave less pang in my memories of the long happiness that once was mine.

I have simply and implicitly embraced this ancient rule: 'We cannot fail in following Nature.' Conforming ourself to her ways is our sovereign device. Unlike Socrates, I have not corrected my innate character by the manipulations of reason, or disturbed my natural bent by means of art. I have let myself go as I came. I contend not: my body and mind live in peace of their own accord. But my nurse's milk, thank God, was tolerably wholesome and good.

May I add this by the way? I observe the idea of a scholastic virtue held in greater esteem than it is worth—I see we are slaves to precepts and chained by hopes and fears. Laws and religion should not make our virtue, but perfect and sanction it. But I would have it a virtue born from the seed of universal reason which Nature plants in every man. It is this which rendered Socrates courageous in death—not because his soul was immortal, but because he himself was not. Ingenious and subtle, yes, but much more harmful and altogether dangerous to society is the doctrine which persuades people that religious belief—without conduct—is enough to satisfy divine justice.

No means are neglected that can lead us to knowledge; and when reason fails, we use experience. But like reason, experience has such varied forms, the conclusions we derive from it are bound to remain open to question. The commonest trait in the world of things is diversity. Neither Perrozet nor any other card-maker can so polish and blench the back of his cards that a clever player can't distinguish them merely by seeing them dealt. Nevertheless, truth counts so much for us that we must not disdain any method for discovering it.

The universe is but a perennial seesaw. In it all things are ceaselessly rocking: the earth, the Caucasian peaks, the pyramids of Egypt—each with the general motion and its own. Fixity itself is nothing but a slower rocking. If my mind could find a foothold, I should no longer experiment: I would conclude. But it is bound to apprenticeship and forever stands on trial.

The fruit we derive from the experience of others will little instruct us if we make no better use of it than we generally do of our own. As for me, I study myself more than any other subject: it is my physics and metaphysics.

In this university I allow myself to be governed by the universal law of things. I recognize its force well enough when I feel it. My learning cannot alter it, and it will not bend in my behalf.

The goodness and capability of the Governor ought to discharge me from all care of the government: the inquiries and meditations of philosophy serve no other use but to feed our curiosity.

With great reason philosophers send us back to the rules of Nature, although they falsify her and paint her face with over-sophisticated colors, which is why their portraits of her vary so widely.

But as Nature has given us feet to walk with, so she has given us prudence enough to guide our steps through life. Not the clever and pompous prudence which philosophers have invented, but ready, unlabored, and sound—a prudence sufficient to do what our philosophic substitutes only promise to do. But only if a man has the good fortune to know how to use it simply and regularly—that is to say, naturally. To give yourself over to Nature with the utmost simplicity is to do so with the utmost wisdom. Oh, what a soft and downy pillow, and wholesome, is ignorance and incuriosity—for the rightly formed head!

I had rather understand myself well in myself than in Cicero. In my experience with myself I have enough to make me wise, if I were only a good student of it. The life of Cæsar contains no better examples for us than our own. Every man carries within him the whole fortune of humanity.

Let us hearken to our own experience. The man who will call to mind his own fits of anger will see their evil better than looking for it in Aristotle, and cultivate a truer hatred for it. Whoever will remember how often his judgment was mistaken, is he not a mighty fool if he does not ever after suspect it?

When I find myself convicted of an error, I not only learn of a new mistake; but, more than that, I learn the weakness and treachery of my understanding as a whole. In all my other blunderings I do the same, and it has proved of great utility. I pay little attention to the particular stone I stumble over, but I learn to suspect my gait throughout, and try to steady myself. To learn that you have said or done a foolish thing is nothing. You must learn that you are nothing but a fool—a much more comprehensive and valuable lesson.

The false steps my memory has made, even when it is most cocksure, are not idly disregarded. By now it may swear to me as solemnly as it pleases, but I will shake my ears and refuse to trust it. If everyone will pry into the circumstances and results of the passions he is most liable to, he will foresee their approach and somewhat break the force of their career. They do not always seize us by the collar at the first jump.

Look a little into our experience: there is not a man, if he listens to himself, who will not discover within him a form altogether his own, a master form which resists both education and harmful passions. For my part, I seldom find myself dislodged by their shock. I am always in my place, like a heavy and unwieldy body. Or if I am not at home, I am close by.

My judgment sits in a magistrate's bench, or tries to. If it cannot reform my passions, at least it does not allow itself to be corrupted by them. It plays its own game apart.

'Know thyself' is indeed a weighty admonition. But in this, as in any science, the difficulties are discovered only by those who set their hand to it. We must push against a door to find out whether it is bolted or not. And a certain amount of intelligence is required—especially to learn that you do not know. As to knowing oneself, the fact that everyone thinks he does and is satisfied with what he has learned proves that no one knows anything about the matter.

I, who profess no other knowledge, find such infinite depths and variety in myself that all I have reaped from my learning merely goes to show me how much more I have to learn. It is to this I owe my bent toward modesty, toward obedience to the faith prescribed me, toward detachment and moderation in my opinions, and toward hatred of that wrangling self-satisfied arrogance which is the capital enemy of truth.

Dogmatism and assertiveness are the express signs of stupidity. A man of that cast will bump his nose against the ground a hundred times a day, and still he will be riding his high horse as headstrong as before. The incorrigible blockhead no doubt thinks that he takes on a new brain every time he takes up a new dispute.

It is by my own experience that I accuse mankind of ignorance: and this, I believe, is the most fertile lesson to be learned in the school of the world.

So, too, we must learn to endure what we cannot evade. Our life, like the harmony of the world, consists of contrary things—of diverse tones, sweet and harsh, sharp and flat, gay and solemn. If a musician should use but one of them, it would be meaningless. He must know how to employ them all and mingle them together. We likewise must learn to blend the goods and evils which are part and parcel of our life—we cannot exist without them. To try to kick against natural necessity is to repeat the folly of Ctesiphon, who undertook to outkick his mule.

With the tenderness of a mother, Nature has provided that our necessary actions should be pleasant. She invites us to them not only by reason but also by appetite, and it is ingratitude to break her laws. When I see Cæsar and Alexander, in the thick of their mighty business, enjoy to the full all the bodily pleasures—which are as necessary and proper as they are natural—I do not hold that they have demeaned their souls. No, they have exalted them by subjecting their high powers to the ordinary usages of life.

We are big fools. 'Today,' we say, 'I have done nothing.' What! Have you not lived? That is the most illustrious thing you have to do. 'Ah, if I had been put at the head of a great enterprise, then you would have seen something!' But if you have known how to plan and manage your own life, you have already achieved the greatest enterprise of all. For a man to show what he is and use what he has, he needs no signal fortune. Nature plays the same part on any stage—behind the scenes as well as in front of the curtain.

But it is an exacting life which maintains order in itself. Everyone may play an honest part on the stage; but within us, in our own breast, where nothing is forbidden and everything is hid, to be honest there—that's the rub! The nearest thing to it is to be so in your own house, in its daily conduct for which you need answer to no one, and where pose and makeup are absent.

The man who makes it his business to please the multitude is never done. Let us follow reason, and the public follow us if it will. Said the sailor of olden days: 'O Neptune, you may save me or destroy me as you will; but, meanwhile, I will hold my rudder true!' I have seen a thousand men, shrewder, more adaptable, and in public opinion more worldly wise than I, dash against the rocks where I have saved myself.

If you have known how to compose your life, you have accomplished a great deal more than the man who knows how to compose a book. Have you been able to take your stride? You have done more than the man who has taken cities and empires.

The great and glorious masterpiece of man is to live to the point. All other things—to reign, to hoard, to build—are, at most, but inconsiderate props and appendages.

I delight to see the general of an army, on the eve of assaulting a breach, give himself over to dinner, talk, and merriment with his friends; to see Brutus, when heaven and earth conspired against Roman liberty and himself, steal some hours of the night from his rounds, in order to read and abridge Polybius at his ease.

The truly wise man must be as intelligent and expert in the use of natural pleasures as in all the other functions of life. So the sages lived, gently yielding to the laws of our human lot, to Venus and to Bacchus. Relaxation and versatility, it seems to me, go best with a strong and noble mind, and do it singular honor. There is nothing more notable in Socrates than that he found time, when he was an old man, to learn music and dancing, and thought it time well spent.

Grandeur of soul lies not so much in mounting high and pressing forward, as in knowing how to govern and circumscribe itself. It esteems everything great that is sufficient, and shows itself to better advantage in moderate than in eminent things. There is nothing so handsome as to play the man properly and well. Of all our diseases, the worst is to despise our own being.

I have a vocabulary of my own. I 'pass away my time' when it goes badly with me. When it is good I do not 'pass' it—I taste it over and over again and hold it fast. The common way of speaking about 'pastimes' and 'passing the time away' is mostly in the mouths of those cautious creatures who think the best use of life is to let it slip through their fingers, to shun it as something troublesome and despicable.

But I know it to be otherwise. I find it worth clinging to, even at its tag end where I now hold it. I enjoy it twice as much as others do, for the measure of its enjoyment depends largely on our application to it. Now that I perceive mine to be so short, I try to increase its force: I slacken the speed of its flight by the speed of my grasp. As living grows briefer, I must make it grow deeper.

Others enjoy pleasures as they do sleep—without knowing it. But we should study, savor, and ruminate it, to render worthy thanks to Him who grants it to us. In order that sleep itself should not slip so stupidly from me, I used to have mine broken, the better to relish it.

Does a pleasure caress me? I do not allow it to dally with my senses alone. I bring in my mind to share it—not to lose but to find itself in it, not to entangle but to enjoy itself. I bid it look on itself in this happy frame, and appreciate and magnify it.

I present to my mind, in a thousand aspects, the men whom Fortune or their own error torments or overwhelms; or those who receive their happiness negligently and heedlessly. It is such men who indeed pass away their time, in order to give themselves over to vain hopes and shadows—who hasten their flight the more they are pursued.

I love life, then, and cultivate it such as God has been pleased to bestow it on us. I do not want it shorn of the necessity of eating and drinking, and I should hold it pardonable to wish that necessity doubled—'the wise man thirsts for the bounty of Nature' [Seneca]. I would not want us to beget children absentmindedly with our fingers and heels, but, speaking reverently, that fingers and heels might do it with conscious pleasure.

I do not wish the body to be without desires and titillations: that would be wicked and ungrateful. I accept kindly and with gratitude whatever Nature has provided me, and I am pleased and proud that I do. A man wrongs the omnipotent Giver of all things to refuse, annul, or disfigure His gifts.

Of philosophical opinions I preferably embrace those which are most solid—that is to say, most human and our own. My theories, in keeping with my practice, are low and humble. I never knew what my theories of life were, till it was nearly over and done. I am of a new school—an unpremeditated philosopher.

To my mind, philosophy plays the child when it mounts its high horse and preaches to us that it is barbarous to wed the divine with the earthly; that pleasure is a brutish quality unworthy to be relished by a wise man; that the only pleasure such a man must take from a beautiful young wife is the conscientious pleasure of having done a thing in its proper order—much as to put on your boots before going outdoors. May the disciples of such a philosophy have no more right or nerve or sap in getting their wives' maidenheads than in getting its lessons!

This is not what Socrates taught, who is the master both of

philosophy and us. He values, as he ought, bodily pleasure; but he prefers the pleasures of the mind, as having greater power, constancy, variety, and dignity. The mind comes first, but it by no means goes alone.

Is it not a mistake to believe an action less worthy because it is necessary? No one can beat it out of my head that the marriage of pleasure and necessity is not a happy one. Let us, on the contrary, give it our blessing. Let the mind rouse the weight of the body, and the body curb the flightiness of the mind.

Ask the man, some day or other, to tell you what ideas he got into his head which made him desert a good dinner and regret the time he spends at eating. You will find nothing so insipid on his table as this wise meditation of his. Indeed, we might often better sleep the day through than wake up to the use we put it to. And suppose it were the ecstasies of Archimedes himself—what then?

I do not, of course, speak of those venerable souls elevated by the ardor of religion. But, between ourselves, I have always observed a singular accord between supercelestial ideas and subterranean behavior.

Those who would flee from themselves and escape from being men engage in folly. Instead of transforming themselves into angels, they turn themselves into beasts. These transcendental humors frighten me, like high and inaccessible cliffs. Nothing is hard for me to digest in the life of Socrates, except his ecstasies and his communion with demons. There is, I think, nothing so human in Plato as the things which won him the title of Divine. Of our sciences, those seem most earthy and low which are highest mounted. I see nothing so mortal in the life of Alexander as his notions about his immortalization.

My views chime with the pretty inscription the Athenians used for welcoming Pompey to their city:

By that much you are a god
As you confess yourself a man.

It is an absolute and, as it were, divine perfection for a man to know how to enjoy loyally his own existence. We seek other lives because we do not understand how to use our own. We go out of ourselves because we are ignorant of what lies within. But even when mounted on stilts, we walk with our own legs. And perched on the loftiest throne in the world, we are still sitting on our own behind.

The most beautiful lives, in my opinion, are those which conform to the common and human stature—orderly, but without miracle or extravagance.

Old age, to be sure, needs somewhat gentler treatment. Let us recommend it to that god of health and of wisdom—but a cheerful and sociable wisdom:

Grant me, Apollo, I pray you,
That I enjoy the little I have,
Sound in body and mind,
Nor lead a miserable old age,
Nor the lyre drop from my hand.
[Horace]

The Death of Montaigne

 ONSIEUR DE MONTAIGNE IS DEAD. This is a blow that will pierce your heart as it has mine—and how deeply it pains me to be the herald of such tidings! ¶But why should you not share the bitterness of his death, you who shared in the sweetness of his life?

Yet I do wrong to speak of his death as bitter, for it came upon him gently. The bitterness of it is ours, but the sweetness of it was his, who had lived so happily and died no less—at an age when he could look forward to more pain than pleasure, for he suffered grievously from the stone.

He did me the honor to mention me in his last words, which doubles my sorrow that no one was at his side to whom he could unfold his parting thoughts. He had always wished to be like a lamp which, before it goes out, lights up in one final flare.

I know this from an experience I had. Once when we were together in Paris some years ago, the doctors despaired of his life; and I saw him repulse the fear of death, even as it stared him in the face, with a disdainful gesture and what brave and beautiful words!

Now he has gained his port, while we are left floundering in a sea of tempests. I am prostrate.

—PIERRE DE BRACH *writing to*
Justus Lipsius, February 4, 1593.

THE LATE MONSIEUR de Montaigne, upon feeling the approach of his last days, arose from his bed, put on his dressing gown, opened his room, and had all his servants and other legatees called into his presence. Then and there he paid them their legacies, as provided for in his will, in order to avoid the difficulties which he foresaw his heirs would raise.

—BERNARD AUTHOMNE *in his*
Commentaire sur . . . Bordeaux

FOR THE REST, do not think that his life was different from his writings.

He died at his home in Montaigne [September 13, 1592]. The last three days he lost the power of speech, although his mind remained in its full vigor. Consequently he was compelled to write out all his wishes.

As he felt the end draw near, he took a little sheet of paper and asked his wife to summon a number of gentlemen, his neighbors, in order to bid them farewell.

When they arrived, he asked that a Mass be said in his room. As the priest was elevating the Host, the poor man leaped forward as well as he was able on his bed, with his hands clasped; and in this last act he gave up his soul to God—a gesture which finely mirrored his spirit.

He left two daughters: the one born of his marriage, and heir to all his goods: the other his adopted daughter, the demoiselle de Jars, who inherited his works.

I cannot close without a word or two on this second young woman. She comes from one of the best families in Paris, and early resolved to have no mate in life but her honor enriched by good books—above all, the *Essays* of the lord of Montaigne.

In 1588 she made a long sojourn in Paris in order to meet the author face to face. Then she and her mother entertained him at their home in Gournay—where, in the course of two or three visits, he remained three months.

Finally, this noble young woman, upon learning of his death, crossed almost all of France (aided by passports) as much by her own desire as the entreaties of the widow and daughter who urged her to come and mingle her copious tears with theirs.

The incident is memorable indeed, and the life of this gentleman could not be closed by a fairer epilogue.

—ETIENNE PASQUIER,
writing to Claude de Pelgé.

THE END

Index

The Editor and Translator

Born in 1890 in Bradford, Pennsylvania (a town he always held close to his heart and for which he had only the fondest memories), Marvin Lowenthal was a scholar equally at home with Jewish history, Zionist politics, American literature, and French culture. His major literary accomplishment was a translation from the German of Theodor Herzl's diaries, but his life represented a full integration of thought and action. After graduating from the University of Wisconsin and with a Master's Degree from Harvard University, he travelled to the West Coast to further the Zionist movement. In 1919, he returned East to New York City where from 1921 to 1930 he worked as an editor of *The Menorah Journal*, certainly the finest of the American Jewish periodicals. In the 1950's he was appointed editor of *The American Zionist* and in 1956 was appointed Director of Special Studies at Brandeis University.

The present volume, a sympathetic distillation and arrangement of the life and thought of Montaigne, displays his broad humanism and self-deprecating humor at its best. It is no wonder that Lowenthal chose Montaigne as his model, for both men were possessed by a deep sense of history, a pervasive and pervading humanism, and profound respect for scholarship. And both took their work (but not themselves) seriously.

The Design and Typefaces

The Autobiography of Michel de Montaigne was designed and composed by Scott-Martin Kosofsky at the Philidor Company in Cambridge, Massachusetts. The text was set in Montaigne Sabon, a typeface created by Mr. Kosofsky specifically for this book (though it has appeared in many titles before the publication of this one). It is based on the work of Jan Tschichold, inspired by—though not copied from— the sketches for a never-produced foundry version of his well-known Sabon types.

Sabon was a joint commission of the the Monotype and Linotype companies during the last days of metal typsetting machines and, as such, was designed to fit the particular limitations of those systems. Most severe were the mechanical requirements of metal Linotype machines that did not permit any part of a character to overhang the space of an adjacent character. ("Kern" was the term, now having a different meaning in the world of computer typesetting.) Sabon also had to fit onto duplex matrices, which meant the the italic had to occupy the same widths as the roman. Still and all, Sabon still shined as an eminently readable typeface. Mr. Kosofsky has updated it and created an 'improved' 11–12 point version, its weight adjusted for offset printing. Other modifications include a new set of lower case characters for the italic, changed vertical proportions (a reduced x-height), new overhanging characters, and completely reconsidered spacing.

The titles were set in Duc de Berry, a *lettre bâtarde* made for Linotype. The ornaments and initials are from various sixteenth century sources.

Eclipse Fever by Walter Abish
352 PAGES; *036-5; $15.95

The American Boy's Handy Book by Daniel C. Beard
448 PAGES; 449-0; $12.95

The American Girl's Handy Book
by Lina and Adelia Beard
504 PAGES; 666-3; $12.95

Borstal Boy by Brendan Behan
384 PAGES; 415-6; $14.95

La Bonne Table by Ludwig Bemelmans
446 PAGES; 808-9; $14.95

The Decline and Fall of Practically Everybody
by Will Cuppy
256 PAGES; 514-4; $14.95

The Geography of the Imagination by Guy Davenport
400 PAGES; *080-2; $18.95

The Franchiser by Stanley Elkin
360 PAGES; 323-0; $10.95

Searches and Seizures by Stanley Elkin
320 PAGES; 253-6; $10.95

The Kitchen Book / The Cook Book by Nicolas Freeling
352 PAGES; 862-3; $16.95

**In the Heart of the Heart of the Country
& Other Stories** by William H. Gass
240 PAGES; 374-5; $12.95

On Being Blue by William H. Gass
96 PAGES; 237-4; $11.95

The World Within the Word by William H. Gass
352 PAGES; 298-6; $11.95

Bright Stars, Dark Trees, Clear Water by Wayne Grady
334 PAGES; *019-5; $16.95

String Too Short to Be Saved by Donald Hall
176 PAGES; 282-X; $14.95

In the Springtime of the Year by Susan Hill
192 PAGES; 852-6; $10.95

Strange Meeting by Susan Hill
192 PAGES; 830-5; $10.95

A Distant Trumpet by Paul Horgan
656 PAGES; 863-1; $18.95

The Gardener's Essential Gertrude Jekyll
by Gertrude Jekyll
288 PAGES; 599-3; $13.95

Dance Me Outside by W. P. Kinsella
160 PAGES; 982-4; $12.95

The Moccasin Telegraph by W. P. Kinsella
188 PAGES; 981-6; $12.95

Aubrey's Brief Lives by Oliver Lawson Dick (ed.)
560 PAGES; *063-2; $20.95

The Old Man at the Railroad Crossing
by William Maxwell
192 PAGES; 676-0; $10.95

Over by the River by William Maxwell
256 PAGES; 541-1; $10.95

Court of Memory by James McConkey
288 PAGES; 983-2; $13.95

The Autobiography of Michel de Montaigne
408 PAGES; *098-5; $17.95

Collected Stories, 1948-1986 by Wright Morris
288 PAGES; 752-X; $10.95

Disappearances by Howard Frank Mosher
272 PAGES; 524-1; $14.95

Images and Shadows by Iris Origo
288 PAGES; *103-5; $15.95

War in Val d'Orcia by Iris Origo
256 PAGES; 476-8; $14.95

Dr. Bowdler's Legacy by Noel Perrin
320 PAGES; 861-5; $14.95

Giving Up the Gun by Noel Perrin
136 PAGES; 773-2; $10.95

Hamlet's Mill
by Giorgio de Santillana & Hertha von Dechend
512 PAGES; 215-3; $20.95

The Maine Reader by Charles & Samuella Shain (eds.)
576 PAGES; *078-0; $19.95

Fading Feast by Raymond Sokolov
320 PAGES; *037-3; $16.95

Cocteau by Francis Steegmuller
608 PAGES; 606-X; $17.95

The Philosopher's Diet by Richard Watson
128 PAGES; *084-5; $14.95

NB: *The* ISBN *prefix for titles with an asterisk is 1-56792. The prefix for all others is 0-87923.*